Friendly Fallout 1953

Friendly Fallout 1953

ANN RONALD

UNIVERSITY OF NEVADA PRESS   RENO • LAS VEGAS

University of Nevada Press, Reno, Nevada 89557 USA
Copyright © 2010 by Ann Ronald
Manufactured in the United States of America
Design by Kathleen Szawiola

LIBRARY OF CONGRESS CATALOGING-IN-PUBLICATION DATA

Ronald, Ann, 1939–
Friendly fallout 1953 / Ann Ronald.
p. cm.
Includes bibliographical references.
ISBN 978-0-87417-825-8 (alk. paper)
1. Nuclear weapons—Fiction.
2. Nevada Test Site (Nev.)—Fiction.
I. Title.
PS3568.O56583F75 2010
813'.54—dc22
2010014699

The paper used in this book is a recycled stock made from 30 percent post-
consumer waste materials, certified by FSC, and meets the requirements
of American National Standard for Information Sciences—Permanence
of Paper for Printed Library Materials, ANSI/NISO Z39.48-1992 (R2002).
Binding materials were selected for strength and durability.

FIRST PRINTING

19   18   17   16   15   14   13   12   11   10

5   4   3   2   1

For Eve and Suzanne,
who keep me on my toes!

Contents

Preface

I've always been fascinated by atomic testing. When I was a little girl, I was thrilled when my dad's best friend, a fisheries expert, flew off to Bikini to participate in that 1946 explosion. We drove him to Seattle's Boeing Field—surely the first time I'd ever been to an airport—where we waved good-bye as he boarded a bulky Army transport. Upon his return, we went to the airport again. "Uncle Enos" brought me tiny white shells from the atoll and wondrous stories of what he had seen. Hanging on every word and fingering my new treasures, I heard enormous excitement in his voice. And I was thrilled. When he died of cancer a dozen years later, I never connected the dots.

As an adult, I moved to Nevada, home of so much stateside experimentation. Even though I never saw a nuclear explosion, I heard many locals describe the phenomena in the sky. Their intrigue matched my own. I wanted to see more. Once the 1993 Comprehensive Test Ban Treaty put atomic testing on hold, the Nevada Test Site became more accessible and I was able to visit the place in person. I toured with a group of officials imagining ways to combine the government's research agenda with the state university's. I signed on as a gofer with a U.S. Geological Survey team, spending the better part of a week prowling the area and picking up rocks. I took the public bus tour, more than once, viewing a post-apocalypse version of Doom Town and standing on the edge of the immense Sedan Crater. I even wrote about the place in an earlier book, *Earthtones,* calling the Nevada Test Site a rare treasure of incomparable worth.

Places off the beaten track, like Tippipah Springs and Rainier Mesa and the slickrock formations in between, are incredibly beautiful. The rich Paiute and Shoshone heritage overlays magnificent geology. Leaving aside the two pockmarked desert playas that felt the brunt of the detonations—which of course are intriguing in their own special ways—the rest of the scenery could belong in a national park. Because the area hasn't been grazed since World War II, it actually resembles pre-pioneer Nevada more than any other part of the Silver State. In a way, *Friendly Fallout 1953* is a recognition of and an accolade to that unexpected charm.

This book also reflects a hobby of mine. I not only love to read about contemporary politics on the Internet, but I even enjoy the cable pundits who talk to death each day's machinations. Between 2001 and 2008 while researching the years of atomic testing, prowling the Internet, and then ending each writing day with cable news, I began to see a pattern repeating itself in the twenty-first century. In the face of an unknown and unknowable enemy, a complicated combination of heightened patriotism and governmental obfuscation takes hold. Just as we're frightened by anonymous terrorists, so Americans in the 1950s were scared to death of Russia's Red Menace. Just as we're cognizant of battles in Iraq and Afghanistan, so our predecessors worried about the horrors of Korea. Just as we may be told that any dissent is un-American, so an earlier generation of citizens watched the McCarthy debacle unfold. Just as the naked truth about unrestrained wiretapping or torture was initially covered up, so the Truman and Eisenhower administrations kept silent about harmful effects of atomic testing. And just as today's brave troops occasionally face the horror of "friendly fire" from their own side, so yesterday's patriots innocently confronted what ironically might be called "friendly fallout."

So I'm telling a story of 1953 while I'm fully cognizant of the years following 9/11/2001. I hope my readers are, too.

That story is neither fact nor fiction. I'm tempted to call *Friendly Fallout 1953* a series of linked short stories, but the vignettes aren't short stories in the conventional sense of the term. They're arguments, more than narratives. Or I could call *Friendly Fallout 1953* nonfiction, like all the other books I've written, but that wouldn't be quite true, either. Even though most of the details are based on fact, none of my characters actually existed. Rather, they're composites—imaginary men, women, and children affected, I think, by the federal government's aboveground atomic testing program in that fateful year. So *Friendly Fallout 1953* is what happened, what might have happened, what probably happened, what could have happened. I've pasted these possibilities into a collection of snapshots, like an old photograph album of bygone faces and places and poses, caught all together by the camera of time.

Friendly Fallout 1953

Ten! Nine! Eight! Seven! Six! Five! Four! Three! Two! One! Happy New Year!! An explosion of sound bombards the midnight desert air. Whistles, shouts, laughter, sirens, bells, car horns and party horns, firecrackers, and even an echoed gunshot or two. Outside the Desert Inn casino, a conga line snakes from the front door and winds around an oval fountain that shoots water sixty feet in the air. Tight sheath dresses and starched white shirts, black pumps and polished cowboy boots, cashmere and leather, martini glasses clanging, confetti everywhere. Onstage at the newly opened Sands, Frank Sinatra croons a soft rendition of "Auld Lang Syne" while the audience sways in their seats, and sighs. Meanwhile, inside the Sahara the jangle of slot machines and the whirr of shuffling cards scarcely pause. Some revelers choose to dance, but most stay intent upon their games. A croupier calls out a roll of the dice; a blackjack dealer flops an ace on his king; a roulette wheel spins a die onto black thirteen. Las Vegas, every night and every day, bringing the American Dream to life. No one loses here.

Jack

Smoke from a dozen cigarettes filters down the narrow aisle. Jack clears his throat, lights a Marlboro, draws a deep breath, and then blows smoke rings that twine together in the stale morning air. Rather like a mushroom cloud, Jack imagines, as he stretches his legs on the empty seat beside him. With any luck, the seat will stay vacant. Checking his watch, he turns to peer through sand-pocked window glass at a parking lot filled with similar yellow boxes on wheels. Clark County School District, ready to transport an array of reporters and civic dignitaries to the Nevada Proving Ground eighty miles away. A long drive, in a rattletrap bus, to see the Doom Town setup, soon to be demolished by an explosion that will start the 1953 atomic testing series with a bang.

Hoping he can protect his space, Jack almost immediately realizes he's made a mistake. He should have kept his legs sprawled sideways and his eyes front and center.

"Excuse me, sir." A stubby young man, earnestly polite, stares down at Jack. "Excuse me, sir," he wheezes, dipping his head and tipping his porkpie hat. "All the other seats seem to be taken."

Jack sighs, as he swivels into a more upright position and makes room. A blend of Old Spice and cheap pomade cuts through the smoke, and settles beside him for the long ride. When the young man's briefcase brushes Jack's knee, the nasal voice repeats itself. "Excuse me, sir. I'm Sammy Cerillo. From Las Vegas. On the mayor's staff." He pats his briefcase. "Anything you want to ask me, go ahead. I can tell you anything about Doom Town you want to know." Thrusting his hand toward Jack, he smiles with sudden self-assurance.

Jack wavers. He wants to snub the guy, and he especially wants to be rid of the sweet scents emanating from the guy's pompadour. On the other hand, he might pry some newsworthy information out of the mayor's man. By riding next to him, all the way to Mercury, Jack might scoop the competition. So he nods, holds out his own right hand, and acknowledges that he's Jack Windsor from Seattle, a *Post-Intelligencer* staff writer whose column, "Windsor Wind-Up," circulates throughout the West.

"Delighted to meet you, sir, delighted," the mayor's man responds. And so the long, monotonous ride begins. For miles, nothing but creosote bushes, tumbleweeds, and blowing sand. Or so it seems to someone born and raised in emerald moisture, a Pacific Northwest of ferns and fir. Staring out the bus window, Jack yawns and nods his head just often enough to encourage Sammy Cerillo, who natters nonstop about the day ahead.

More than six hundred observers—newspapermen like Jack, civil servants like Sammy, career politicians like the men in the seat just ahead—are caravanning together to look at what soon will be ground zero. Once they reach the Nevada Proving Ground, they'll tour the Civil Defense setup and learn more facts and figures about the impending action. They'll see buildings, underground shelters, cars, manikins, food, furniture, everyday household appliances, all set out near a tower where a bomb euphemistically called a "device" and whimsically named Annie, is ready to fall.

Sammy doesn't say much that Jack hasn't already heard. Yesterday a half dozen Sammy look-alikes spent hours droning on about the Doom Town design and about the atomic explosion that will occur on St. Patrick's Day. At the outset Sammy's boss, Las Vegas mayor C. D. Baker, had welcomed the reporters to Las Vegas. A no-nonsense, ex-military, stiff-backed politician, Baker is a ramrod Las Vegas booster. That means he's a Nevada Proving Ground booster, too, with grand plans to bring more and more tourists to his own atomic city. First Helldorado Days; now atomic Annie. At the day-long briefing a reporter from Reno sitting next to Jack had leaned over and whispered, "This is nothing. You ought to hear His-oner when he's really on."

When Jack asked for more material, the Reno man gave him an earful. It seems that Exalted Ruler Baker, at a recent Las Vegas Elks Club meeting, had pranced around with a pair of antlers on his head, whooping it up for his personal pet tourist project, Helldorado Days. "No telling what he might wear as an atomic Annie," the Renoite chortled, making fun of the fledging Nevada city to the south.

After that tidbit, the seminar went downhill, with repetitive recitations about Doom Town, the Proving Ground, and the patriotic support of all Las Vegas residents. "Trying to project a good image," whispered the Reno reporter. "Lots of gossip about the mob influence down here, buying into the local casinos and building new ones. Lots of innuendos." Jack waited to hear more, but the fellow suddenly stared across the room and pursed his lips. A minute later he excused himself, never looking back.

Now Jack wonders about Sammy Cerillo, who matches the mobster stereotype to a T. Not likely, Jack decides about a guy so full of booster buoyancy and glib generalizations. Besides, the Seattle reporter isn't in Las Vegas to write mob exposés. He's supposed to focus on Tuesday's atomic test. Annie alone is enough to fill one man's imagination.

Indifferent to the monotonous scenery and increasingly uncomfortable in his narrow school bus seat, Jack whiles away the miles largely by ignoring Sammy and by making up headlines. "The Nevada Desert Blooms in the Morning Sky." Too trite; they used that one last year. How about "Atomic Bomb Atomizes All." Not quite true—just the up-close places get really fried. "Fantastic Fireball of Flame." Too flowery and alliterative. "Bombs Away." Boring. Besides, the public relations people never use the word "bomb." Too graphic, too violent, and too reminiscent of Hiroshima and Nagasaki. The upcoming event is supposed to be different, a demonstration to show off civil defense procedures and possibilities to the public. Plus some Army maneuvers, of course. But the emphasis is supposed to be on defense, rather than offense, or so they've been told. So how about something like "Manikins Melt in March Magic." More alliteration, and misleadingly oversimplified. The whole detonation thing in the desert is far more complicated.

No matter, headlines aren't his job anyway. He never makes up banners, he writes stories. Jack draws his salary from the *Seattle P-I* but earns extra pay as a stringer for a syndicated Sunday supplement, so he pens paragraphs, not one-liners. His job is to make a day's events sound sexy, winding each story up in an engaging package—The Windsor Wind-Up. A national audience might be unfamiliar with his byline, but West Coast readers trust his point of view. Jack looks forward to describing for them the desert oasis called Doom Town and then the atomic explosion day after tomorrow that will blast the pseudo-city into particles of dust. Right now, though, he wishes this interminable drive would end. Soon.

Mid-reverie, almost mesmerized by a road that's roller-coastering over an uneven desert floor, Jack is startled by a military Jeep, going flat-out fast, speeding past and rocking the bus in its wake. A couple of miles farther on, a deuce and a half hogs its full share of the two-lane highway, causing the bus driver to let out a curse and tap his brakes. The military truck hardly pauses. Jack jumps inadvertently, and even Sammy straightens up with a start. Then the mayor's man grins, and gleefully announces, "They call this road the widow-maker. Can't see anybody 'til they're right on top of us. The military, they act like they own the center of the road." He pauses. "A couple more years, and they will. Big plans ahead, to make the highway four lanes wide. Need more space to move equipment, like atomic cannons."

In response, Jack makes a notation in his spiral notebook. Atomic cannons—he'll need to remember that. End of conversation, though, because Sammy is off on a tangent, dredging up gory details of multiple deaths, every month, along the killer country road that can hardly handle the current stream of traffic. Jack leans back toward the window, easing his weight from one hip to the other. Sammy continues. "Too narrow, too many ups and downs with obscured distances, and, at night, too many beer-bedraggled drivers." While he describes the latest mayhem, a head-on smash-up just three days ago, Jack loses interest. No wife, so no potential widow waits at home in his tiny Queen Anne Hill apartment. No one with a life like his could sustain a family. Phone calls from his editor, often in the middle of the night, or on weekends. Go here, go there, get this story now. Out of town more often than not, weekly deadlines, sometimes daily. No time for anything or anyone except his job, and the tap of the typewriter at midnight. But he loves his work, and he's anxious to get to their destination.

The bus slows briefly where the road widens a bit, but they're not at the Proving Ground yet. Off to the side, Jack sees a sign indicating Indian Springs, which he knows is a sparsely populated Army air base. He tries to imagine being stationed there. God-awful barren and dry. Nothing seems to grow in Nevada at all. Stunted, hip-high Joshua trees are the tallest—and greenest—things around. As the bus pulls away from Indian Springs and picks up speed, Jack wonders if the Proving Ground scenery will be any different. Probably not. They're only twenty or thirty miles away. Besides, that's why the government decided to test its weaponry in the desert, where it doesn't hurt to blow everything up and where there are so few people that any fallout can't be a problem. Lighting another cigarette, Jack blows more mushroom clouds.

Beside him, Sammy is reciting all the safety precautions they'd already learned at yesterday's briefing. The newsmen, from their lookout spot on News Nob, would be totally protected. Seven miles from the blast—close enough to see the fireball, far enough to escape its effects. They'd see the famous newscasters' rocky outcropping today, in daylight, so they could scope out the view from News Nob across Yucca Flat. "The television crews will get first choice." Because he personally worked with the New York media men, Sammy looks pleased. That will be another high point of Doom Town and Annie—a real live television transmission of an atomic explosion. Hoping they'll get eighteen million viewers. A record for live TV. Silently, Jack wonders how much those eighteen million viewers will actually see? A flash in the dark. How much will they hear? A big boom. Jack is certain he can do better with words than the camera guys can capture on film.

Lurching to the right, the bus slows and loops onto an even narrower road. Ahead and to the left, Jack spots what he supposes is Camp Desert Rock, where the military men are housed. Barren and dusty, with tents so rigidly aligned they look out of place in the haphazard desert vegetation. Rows of olive-green canvas, enough to house thousands of men. Jack read somewhere that the only permanent Desert Rock facilities are the latrines. He shakes his head. On the other hand, a stateside assignment in Nevada is a distinct improvement over Korea these days or the war-torn South Pacific a decade ago. Whatever, Jack's glad he doesn't have to sleep and eat at this forsaken pile of dirt and sand. Raunchy Las Vegas, replete with greasy mobsters and buxom showgirls, sounds civilized by comparison.

The long line of cars and buses hardly moves now, inching toward the Proving Ground fence. Sammy leans his head into the aisle so he can see out the front window of their bus. "Guards and guns ahead," he announces. "We're approaching the gate."

Getting through the checkpoint takes a while. As soon as the bus stops completely, two burly guards climb aboard and meticulously begin checking badges. Usually dosimeters are individually assigned at the arrival gate, but this big crowd of sightseers was "badged" in Las Vegas the day before. That was the phrase used by the cute blonde at the City Hall desk, "Step right up and be badged." So Jack and everyone else on the bus are badged already, with yellow and green squares hanging on cords around their necks. If anyone receives a radiation overdose, the dosimeter squares supposedly change colors. "That's silly," Sammy insists. "Absolutely won't happen here. You wouldn't believe all the precautions. No way any radiation can hurt anybody."

Once past the gate, the bus moves slowly through the skimpy new community of Mercury. "Community" sounds like a euphemism for shantytown, Jack decides, as they drive past rows of Quonset huts, prefab cubicles, and cement-block barracks. The place looks slightly more substantial than Camp Desert Rock, but holds little appeal. Even though the scientists, engineers, and craftsmen who live here temporarily have better facilities than the military, the place still isn't much. Sammy points out a cafeteria and talks about a recreation center—complete with bowling alley—that's in the works. Better housing next year, or the year after, too. When Jack asks about the dorms, however, Sammy doesn't have much to say. Not part of his job, to spend a night in a place like Mercury.

Out of town, the bus laboriously climbs a steady grade. A couple of short switchbacks take them to the top of a hill where a cluster of spectator bleachers faces a vacant expanse called Frenchman Flat. On that playa scientists and military men conducted the first Nevada tests. Able, then the Ranger sequence, and last year's Tumbler-Snapper series. This year's exercises, packaged overall as "Upshot-Knothole," will mostly take place on Yucca Flat, the next alkali stretch to the north. Jack, looking with some interest at the scene from the immediate past, jots down a few more notes. But he's eager for the bus to move on, anxious to see where the "Operation Shot" St. Patrick's Day action will all take place.

As if heeding his wishes, the convoy picks up speed, spiraling down the hill and along the edge of an empty expanse. Dust spreads thickly from both sides of the vehicles, nearly obscuring the individual buses and cars. Radioactive dust? Jack assumes the road runs away from the bomb craters. They wouldn't bring this many people so close if there were any danger. Sammy reassures him, though the asthmatic Las Vegan seems to be holding his breath until they're past the blowing dirt.

A little farther on, the convoy starts up another hill, then eases over a second crest. "News Nob, ahead on your right," the bus driver chimes in. "And Yucca Flat, there in the distance." Jack's on the wrong side of the bus. He can't see much of anything at all, and the bus barely pauses before accelerating downhill again. "Later," the driver promises, and Sammy echoes his words. "We'll stop here on our way back. Plenty of time then to see the view."

At the bottom of the hill, the bus bounces heavily to the right, turning onto a dirt track that drifts straight onto a crumpled playa practically devoid of vegetation. A few Joshua trees, some more creosote, and occasional dry-brown grasses. More dust fills the air, so the passengers can hardly see outside. Jack makes out some parked cars, though, and what looks like a structure of some sort. "End of the line." As the bus jerks to a halt, the driver announces their destination. "Doom Town dead ahead. Watch your step."

Sammy jumps from his seat. "Nice to meet you," he shouts over his shoulder, as he bursts toward the door. Jack, inherently suspicious of men who smell like Old Spice, shakes his head and relaxes in his seat. Content to peer out the window until the dust settles, he waits for most of his fellow passengers to precede him off the bus. Just ahead—his own mayor from Seattle, along with another Baker look-alike who wears a nametag from San Diego. Behind, two more Sammy types, scuttling after their bosses.

Outside, a helmeted Civil Defense worker herds everyone toward the first point of interest, the closest of the endangered two-story houses. A Civil Defense official named Bennett introduces himself and then begins explaining how city mayors and government officials will study the houses post-detonation, gathering data for real-life precautions and plans. A kind of bomb-site laboratory, as it were.

Dutifully, Jack takes more notes. He hasn't yet heard the right tagline for the columns he'll write, but he'll think of something. Unless the desert sun saps all his creativity. He watches a cameraman trying to set up his tripod, a tough task with so many people in the way. Jack takes in the scene at a more leisurely pace, content to be jostled to the back of the group. He pauses, lights another cigarette, and stretches the kinks out of his back while he waits for the dust to settle. He also helps himself to a cup of coffee, nodding to a smiling gray-haired lady who offers cream and sugar. The Las Vegas Chamber of Commerce is trying damned hard to make the desert hospitable. That's apparently Sammy's job, too. The young man, porkpie hat slammed tightly back on his head, is talking fast on the other side of the table. Gesturing at the coffee and sending another woman off for more sugar.

In the distance, well beyond Sammy and the ladies, a lacy steel tower holds Annie tightly. Day after tomorrow, a 16-kiloton force will rock the tower and mostly obliterate everything nearby. A three-hundred-foot drop; then an explosion unlike anything Jack or most of the men around him have ever seen. The vertical structure looks spider-thin in the sunlight, almost too puny to hold its 2,700-pound payload. Gazing at the fragility, Jack finds the potential power hard to believe and the coming explosion almost impossible to imagine.

Taking one last puff, Jack throws his cigarette in the dirt and grinds it with the heel of his shoe. As he does so, he tries to concentrate on the Civil Defense spokesman's spiel. Houses completely furnished. Manikins placed in normal positions. Some in basement shelters. Study the effects. Develop safety measures. Future protection for families and cities. Jack decides the two buildings look odd. Hardly an accurate replication of a real town or even a neighborhood, though a nearby road sign proclaims the intersection of Main Street and Elm. The lonesome houses don't have any electricity, or any plumbing, and the inside walls aren't even painted. As usual, the government is saving money, though Bennett doesn't say so directly. Instead, the monotonous official reads from his notes, blathering on about a white exterior to help prevent fire. And aluminum venetian blinds that are supposed to deflect thermal energy.

Jack assumes the venetian-blinds people donated them for the free advertising. He wants to ask if all patriotic Americans are supposed to go out and buy venetian blinds now, but their group leader is already hurrying them on to their next stop, a string of cars arrayed across the playa. "Look at all the different makes and models," one man observes, as they stroll past a Dodge, a Ford, a Cadillac, a Nash, even a United States mail truck. Someone laughs, and calls them "rolling foxholes"—when a bomb drops, just drive like hell away. Another man points out a sign hanging off one of the vehicles. "This car will go through the Atomic Blast." More advertising, obviously. Those cars that survive intact will be driven back to Las Vegas where they'll grace the auto dealers' lots. Customer drawing cards. Local residents will come to see the survival cars and stay to buy a new Plymouth or Chevy, or so the dealers hope.

Jack thinks more about the commercial aspects of this atomic test while he playfully counts the manikin drivers, manikin passengers, manikin adults and manikin children, wearing clothes from J.C. Penney. That morning Jack had looked at a full-page Penney's ad in the *Las Vegas Review-Journal*. Dozens of faux figures clad in chic outfits that might soon be vaporized. Or might not be, depending on their exact locations and distances away from the shot tower. "White duck pants and shirt, nylon jacket with fleece lining, leather shoes." Possibly safe; possibly not. Ditto "mauve heavy rayon suit, white crepe blouse, navy nylon mesh shoes." Doesn't sound good for "chenille robe, blue felt slippers," though. Being dressed only in robe and slippers probably spells domestic doom for that gal.

As the group nears the second two-story house, the one closer to the tower, the eager-beaver cameraman bounds ahead, camera equipment ricocheting off his hips and shoulders. "Stop right there, sir," Bennett calls out. "We must stay together. No one is allowed to depart from the group." Several of the men guffaw, Jack included. Officious government guy, like Jack remembers from the war.

When the photographer rejoins the throng of onlookers, he looks more amused than chastened. Now the group clusters in front of a second house, rather like the first, only closer to the tower. Where the other one stands

7,500 feet from ground zero—roughly the equivalent of twelve city blocks—this one is poised 3,500 feet away, more like six city blocks from the detonation point. This sucker is gonna totally evaporate, Jack decides. It seems weird to walk around so cavalierly, like gawking at an open grave. He knows they're only dummies inside, but the ensemble feels sacrilegious somehow. Whatsername, in her chenille robe and blue felt slippers, snuggles alongside manikin kids clad in "pink seersucker pajamas." All poised and posed and cutesy. With Dad nearby, "cotton broadcloth pajamas, beacon robe, leather slippers." He'll be incinerated, too. Best not to think of them as human stand-ins; just dummies.

But Jack has seen too many photos of postwar Japan, the layered burns, the shriveled limbs. Broken glass, twisted girders, concrete cavities, city blocks absolutely leveled. Children forever maimed. Not a pretty sight. Not something you want here in the United States. Not something you even want to think about.

That's part of the purpose of the Annie exercise, though, to get people to think about nuclear holocausts. The Federal Civil Defense Administration, the FCDA, orchestrated the invitations. Two hundred and fifty newsmen, three hundred and sixty politicians, dozens and dozens of civil defense workers, all here at the Proving Ground for public relations purposes, not just to witness the test but to take crucial information back home. How might Seattleites survive an atomic attack? That's what Jack's supposed to write about, stressing survival in every paragraph. What materials should people use for new-home construction? Something other than homegrown Douglas fir? Would bomb shelters be helpful? Should they be built in every block? What might you do if you're in a car when a bomb explodes nearby? He remembers the joke about "rolling foxholes," and knows the answer. And what should you be wearing? Maybe not rayon and plastic, as if that would make any difference at ground zero. But the government is eternally optimistic. The Federal Civil Defense Administration is confronting the Red Menace head-on by heightening public awareness and urging local preparedness. That's what Sammy boasted about, over and over again, on the bus.

Now the tour group, still bunched together by their earnest guide, pauses near a black lead box almost buried in the sand. Jack recognizes the equipment. Rising out of the box, a series of protected periscopes aim directly at the house closest to the tower. Supposedly a sequence of photos will be shot automatically, capturing the house's expected destruction in the seconds immediately following the detonation. Twenty-four frames per second, he recalls. Some trick, not only to get the timing right but also to protect all the gear from radiation. Something for Jack to write about, for sure.

Back near the line of buses and cars—more than seventy vehicles in all—a crew of men has set up more tables and now the Chamber of Commerce women are spreading out a buffet lunch. Jack's hungry after the long drive, and more than a little tired of listening to repetitive information from Sammy-sound-alikes. While he waits for the buffet, he checks his notes. Hopefully he'll get some in-depth before-and-after comparisons. Once the radiation disperses, the Federal Civil Defense Administration plans to bring all the citizen onlookers back to the playa, showing them the damage first-hand. For the story he'll file tonight, though, just today's desert will have to do. He can foresee tomorrow morning's headlines: "Manikins in the Mesquite." And maybe after Tuesday: "Manikin Murders" or "Manikin Mayhem." Probably too evocative for the tightly wound FCDA.

After lunch, more coffee and more lecturing. Jack jots down as many details as he can, and even calls out a question or two. Why "Upshot-Knothole"? Do the names have any significance? The answer is yes. The development tests are part of a series called "Upshot," while the military effects tests belong to "Knothole." All together, they comprise the 1953 sequence of testing events. Why "Annie"? The answer is less precise, probably somebody's daughter or wife.

"Or a Las Vegas showgirl," cracks one wag in the crowd.

Finally the unwieldy group loads themselves into their vehicles. Most will head directly back to Las Vegas, but Jack's driver still plans to pause at News Nob. So does Sammy, who wedges himself onto the bus just as its doors are closing. Jack agrees, better to see the lookout by daylight than to stumble blindly in the Tuesday morning darkness. But he wishes he could see the place by himself, without the incessant monologue of his new buddy.

News Nob, though windy, turns out to be far less sandy than the playa. A black lava outcropping with several good vantage points, it also boasts rows of bleacher seats, just like the media spot on the hill overlooking the other flat. The accommodations look damned uncomfortable, though. Jack is eye-balling the wood and metal design, dreading the thought of sitting there in the morning chill and wondering how he'll ever get settled, when he hears a shout. "Hey, Jackster! What the hell are you doing out here in the middle of nowhere?"

Jack immediately recognizes an East Coast baritone he hasn't heard for years. He'd been in the South Pacific with Lou in the early '40s, both covering the news and trying to stay alive, all at the same time. They'd ducked their heads in tandem under some pretty heavy mortar rounds, played countless games of pickup baseball, and hoisted more than a few glasses side by side at night. Lou had been there in the field hospital, after the flak chewed up Jack's right side. And Jack had furnished the beer when the "Dear Lou" letter arrived from Lou's wife. They hadn't seen much of each other lately, though. After the war Lou had gone back to New Jersey, and found a job with NBC News. Television was recruiting print journalists at the time. Lou saw a way to get ahead. His career had taken off, so he's now a successful executive who produces and directs segments of the evening news.

"What do ya think of all this?" Lou's arm sweeps toward the playa. "Quite the operation."

Jack agrees that he's never seen anything quite like it. It's clear the Civil Defense officials have gone to a lot of trouble, and so has the fourth estate. In fact, he's never laid eyes on so many reporters—or so many officious bureaucrats—in one place at one time. As if on cue, the Seattle mayor and his San Diego cohort approach the two old friends. The Californian wants to hear more about the live television operations, while Jack's city official just wants to be sure he's included in the press. The men obviously crave publicity, although neither is willing to say so directly.

In response, Lou plays News Nob host, showing off his relay equipment and bragging about the upcoming St. Patrick's Day show. With ABC's Chet Huntley in the trenches close to ground zero and Walter Cronkite manning the live feed for CBS, Lou's NBC crew needs to transmit the clearest pictures. Maybe the two mayors would like to get in on the action? Say a few words on Tuesday morning after Annie drops? An enthusiastic conversation ensues, with Sammy eavesdropping so he can report the details back to C. D. Baker.

Jack listens, too, but doesn't say a word. Usually he finds it easy to fill paragraphs with political pablum, but the News Nob/Yucca Flat scenery somehow seems more monumental than that. Atomic testing isn't quite the same as Helldorado Days or, in Seattle's case, the new Seafair with its hyped-up hydroplane racing thrills. Civil defense, to Jack, doesn't equate with civic sales jobs, so the mayors' incessant need for headlines seems specious. He breaks off mid-thought. "Manikin Mayor." Now there's an appropriate headline, for sure.

Jack lights another Marlboro, and angles away from the group of talkers. He's intrigued by the famous News Nob sign leaning against a broken chunk of lava.

NEWS NOB RECEIVED ITS NAME WHEN TOM SHERROD, ONE OF THAT
FINER BREED OF MEN KNOWN AS "CONSTRUCTION STIFFS" TOOK A
WEATHER BEATEN BOARD WITH A DOOR KNOB ATTTACHED FROM AN OLD
OUTDOOR 'PRIVY,' PAINTED ACROSS IT IN YELLOW AND PLANTED IT
AT THIS POINT. THE BOARD IS GONE BUT THE MEMORY LINGERS
ON.

Jack chuckles at the irreverent words. He likes the Proving Ground esprit de corps. It reminds him of the camaraderie in the South Pacific, where the boys watched out for each other as best they could. Like he did for his buddy Lou. And vice versa. He misses such jousting and joking in his solitary Seattle life, and he finds the current cadre of Proving Ground politicians a poor substitute as well.

Smiling again at the sign's message, he's glad to see that Lou has extricated himself from the mayorality and is headed his way. "How 'bout some action tonight?" Lou raises his eyebrows, tacitly reminding Jack of their surreptitious gambling in the South Pacific.

Jack responds quickly and enthusiastically. Once he phones in today's story, and yes, he'll include the Seattle mayor's name in one of his paragraphs, he'll be raring to go. Last night he discovered the showgirls in the Painted Desert Showroom, and he's eager to compare notes with Lou. Short skimpy skirts in Las Vegas; horny hula dancers in Hawaii; which is best? The men shake hands again and grin, remembering lonely nights in the South Pacific on godforsaken islands and gleeful respites in broken-down bars.

That evening in Las Vegas turns out to be a hell of a lot of fun. Jack and Lou start out at the famous Fremont Street bar, where owner Joe Sobchick takes advantage of the local infamy. Renaming his place Atomic Liquors, he sells "atomic cocktails" that are all the rage. Jack finds the combination of gin and fruit juice overpoweringly sweet, but both he and Lou like the shapely glasses and the sexy swizzle sticks.

Sexy, too, are those girls at the Painted Desert, where they go for the late-night show. Long-legged, wearing flounces and sequined bodices, the red, white, and blue Atomic Angels give quite a performance. Jack's favorite is the brunette farthest to the right, especially when she does handstands and cartwheels on and off the two black-and-white dice stacked onstage. Lou prefers the blonde, who always looks like she's enjoying every minute, her eyes sparkling as much as her sequins. When their Wheel of Fortune routine repeats itself, he claps and claps. Most of all, though, Lou loves the live music. He's always been a big-band man, and the Desert Inn has one of the best in Las Vegas. Sweet horns and snappy brass; detonation sounds. Jack and Lou lean back in their chairs, enjoying what seems to be their fourth or fifth round of drinks,

At the table next to them, an explosion of voices erupts, competing with and almost overpowering the music. The noisy threesome is arguing about the Communists, about Annie, and about the politics of civil defense. Jack recognizes Hank Greenspun, the feisty editor of the *Las Vegas Sun*, who seems to be egging his companions on. Should we be in an arms race with the Soviet Union? "Absolutely," spouts a heavyset man, waving a Cuban cigar in the air. "Gotta win." Should we be spending so much time and money? "You bet." Was it right to bomb Japan? "Had to be done." Should the U.S. agree never to bomb anyone else again? "Always bomb our enemies," says the man on patriotic autopilot. "Kill 'em dead!" Any problems with fallout from Upshot-Knothole? "Hell, no. There's a big empty desert out there just waiting for some action."

Always intrigued by global issues and by international implications, Jack can't help listening in on the debate. He wonders if the loudmouthed fellow has ever been to war, though the man makes a good point when he talks about Hiroshima and Nagasaki. "Think of all the American fighting men whose lives Truman saved," he hammers insistently. That innocent Japanese civilians bore the brunt of the birth of the Atomic Age is meaningless to him. "Who cares about a bunch of Japs anyway?"

The out-of-towner ratchets up his voice and expands his political purview. The Japs were evil. Now the Commies are just as dangerous, perhaps fatally so. The Soviet Union proved its atomic capabilities nearly four years ago, setting off its own bomb in the Ust-Urt desert. More thermonuclear Russian tests are set for the near future. Communists control China, too, although the Chinese so far lack atomic capacities. When Greenspun muses about the recent invasion of Korea, the man cuts him short. "Not to worry!" And not to worry about America's nuclear testing program, either. It's critical to keep this country's technologies ahead of every other country's. Our Annie, she's bound to be a success. The man tosses back his vodka tonic and slams down his empty glass. "That's imperative! We have to keep our country safe!"

Jack wishes the verbal dustup would quiet down, but agrees that the dramatic pull of Annie, a siren luring all of them onto desert shoals, is irresistible. Like the rest of his colleagues in Las Vegas that week, he finds the test operations all-consuming and even awe-inspiring. Science and showmanship coming together in a practical union, a masterful form of fusion. Phrases like "American Annie" and "Patriotic Preparedness" headline in his head. He happily can dismiss disputes like the one at the next table as irrelevant compared to the St. Patrick's Day spectacle ahead.

And he has to admit he's eager to get back to News Nob and he can't wait for countdown! Lucky Lou. NBC chauffeurs its guys back in two station wagons that head north right after dinner on Monday. Jack is less fortunate. His bus leaves Las Vegas at midnight, and without the aid of an atomic cocktail the drive seems just as interminable as before. Twisting uncomfortably in his seat, he chain-smokes and even secretly admits a bit of apprehension. He's read as much as he can find about the previous detonations, and he's been assured over and over again by the Civil Defense and public relations people that at this point the tests are totally routine. But 16 kilotons sounds like a hell of a lot of energy and power. And he's never quite figured out where all the fallout goes.

Sammy said they only test on windless mornings. Or, if there's a slight breeze, it has to be out of the west. "You wouldn't want any radiation drifting toward Los Angeles," he'd lectured. "Or back to News Nob, for that matter." Jack wonders what's located to the east of the Proving Ground. He doesn't suppose anybody lives out there, but he doesn't know. He'll have to check a map.

He must have dozed off, because he doesn't notice his cigarette burning down to his fingertips. Then the sharp turn onto the Mercury road jars him awake with a start at the same moment the embers singe his thumb. Glad Sammy's not alongside to see his momentary confusion, Jack watches the armed guards board the bus again, and holds his badge out to be checked. Still the regulation yellow and green, just as Sammy had predicted. Not a dose of anything.

At the top of the second hill outside of town, several hundred onlookers already are gathered. Jack exits his bus quickly, and elbows through the crowd, people-watching while he looks for a seat. The night is chilly, if not downright cold. What a difference compared to their daytime visit on Sunday. They'd all been warned to bundle up because Nevada temperatures in March are schizophrenic—seventies, even occasional eighties in the daytime, down near freezing every night. March 17 is no exception. Jack's glad he's wearing wool pants and a wool sweater, and that he remembered his gloves. Hard to take notes, though, with his fingers encased.

Spotlights brighten the entire hillside, turning News Nob into a veritable city. No problem finding a seat in the dark—the place is as light as day. Everyone seems to be talking at once, high-pitched tones of nervous energy. Most clutch cups of coffee, trying to warm their hands and their insides at the same time. The aura is festive, a party above the playa. Men with megaphones attempt to get the congregation organized, but no one pays much attention to their voices.

Still nearly two hours until Annie explodes, so there's no real hurry. Jack doesn't plan to sit down until the last possible minute. He spots Lou hovering near the NBC outfit. The crew is busy fiddling with their transmission sets and the boss is fretting about the relay equipment and its effective range, so Jack decides not to interrupt. Instead, he walks over to a Civil Defense table and strikes up a conversation with the worker there. Handing him a blanket, a woman tells him he'll soon be warm enough. "First the blast, then the sun. Should be degrees warmer by noon."

He asks if she's seen any other tests in person.

"Most of them. My husband and I drove out to Mount Charleston a couple of times. That's the mountain west of town. You can see pretty clearly from there. Or we'd just watch from Las Vegas." Glad to have an audience, the woman rattles on. "When the tests were done on Frenchman Flat, Las Vegas would get jolted. So the AEC moved them out here. Yucca Flat's farther away. And more protected. Should keep the shock waves from rocking the casinos. As if they don't rock themselves."

Jack remembers newspaper articles about last year's tests. Tumbler-Snapper broke a lot of plate-glass windows. The woman expects more excitement today. "Up close is always better than farther away. I watched a couple of Frenchman Flat shots last year from the other media hill. They were spectacular. Wait 'til you see the colors and hear the sounds. Unlike anything you've ever experienced." She rubs her hands together in anticipation. Jack asks for more details. Sammy's eyewitness descriptions had been pretty trite. Maybe hers will be better.

"You know," she smiles ruefully, "every event is different. No two exactly alike. I know Annie will be gorgeous."

"Gorgeous." Jack can't imagine using that precise adjective to describe a bomb, a "device," or even a "gadget." But the woman is enthusiastic and eager to please. He thanks her for his blanket, and leaves her smiling at the man behind him. "Blanket, sir?"

At the next table, he finds Sammy handing out goggles. Jack frowns. The mayor's man is like a bad penny won from some weary slot machine. Jack turns away, hoping Sammy hasn't seen him, but Sammy's nasal perseverance pulls him back. "You don't want to take any chances with your eyes."

Jack opines that Annie's supposed to be perfectly safe.

"Just take these, sir. You'll be glad to have them."

Clutching the goggles in one hand and tossing the blanket over his other shoulder, Jack moves around the perimeter of the crowd, trying to overhear people's comments. Most of them are dangling goggles, too. Meanwhile, megaphones and a piercing loudspeaker are trying to bring order to chaos. "Please take your seats," the voices insist. "You need to be in your seats."

By 4:30 almost everyone settles down. Jack wedges himself between a newsman from Dallas, a fellow he had met when covering a Louisiana hurricane a couple of years ago, and another guy from the East Coast. The Boston accent and the Texas drawl make the event seem more American somehow, regional and universal all at the same time. Exchanging war stories, they make the time pass quickly. Someone farther down the row hands along a flask. Momentarily, Jack forgets his discomfort, although balancing on the rickety bleacher seat on a bad hip remains somewhat tricky.

Then the bright lights go out, cloaking the entire group in darkness. Far out on the playa, a single red light glows, marking the tip of the tower where Annie hangs high. Jack remembers being in New York City one time for the New Year's Eve celebration, where he watched the ball drop at midnight in Times Square. First the countdown, then the descending light. Will Annie's light drop like that in the distance? Or will the faint glow just disappear, replaced by one much larger? He'll soon find out.

The crowd grows increasingly quiet. Somewhere off to the left, Walter Cronkite speaks in hushed tones, building his television audience up for the spectacle ahead. Several radio men are talking, too, giving play-by-play accounts that resemble the spiels of announcers at baseball games. Glad he doesn't have to perform in public that way, Jack keeps himself amused as usual. "Darkness Before Dawn in the Desert." And "Accolades for Annie." He doesn't doubt that she'll be stunning.

At the very last moment, Jack tugs on the protective goggles. They're heavy and awkward. Despite Sammy's admonitions, he plans to pull them off as soon as the initial light flashes across the desert. He'll follow the Civil Defense orders, though, and look away at the moment of impact. Those instructions had been repeated more than a dozen times. "Don't look directly at the flash."

Shading his eyes, hands sweating a little inside his gloves, he waits while the public address system overrides the other voices. Everything else is suddenly soundless.

"Ten, nine, eight."

At zero, Jack's breath catches and his world emphatically turns upside down. Even with his eyes closed, the white light is whiter than any white he could imagine. Then comes the rumble, the long freight train sound that grows decibel by decibel. Jack can't resist. The moment the extraordinary illumination subsides, he opens his eyes and yanks off the goggles. Blackness; utter blackness. And then a bright blossoming cloud appears, simultaneously accompanied by a sharp jolt that rocks the viewers' stand and a loud noise that resounds in everyone's ears. A few seconds later, a second convulsion hits from the opposite direction, like a fist slamming into Jack's body. Then another bounce; and another. For five full minutes, the seat underneath Jack vibrates and shivers continuously.

At the same time the entire landscape before him spins horrifically into the sky. He's read a lot of descriptions of mushroom clouds, but none has prepared him for the arcing rainbow rising from the desert floor. Blinking, he tries out a palette of colors—purple, violet, eggplant, mauve. None of the shades sounds violent enough. How to write about the massive turbulence? For perhaps the first time in his whole life, Jack can't find appropriate words.

Black, brown, sepia, the entire desert floor whirls upward; 50,000 cubic feet of desert, instantly vaporized. Moment by moment, the colors transform themselves, exploding into red and orange and yellow hues. Peach-colored whorls. Rainbow is too bland, too pallid to describe what's happening. The scene on the flat is oxymoronic, an exquisite rage, a beast simultaneously beautiful and brutal. The domed cloud looks unreal, unnatural, inhuman and incomprehensible. But we did this, Jack realizes. We did this. Men like me, we did this.

And almost as if on cue, dawn starts lighting the sky, too. Those natural streaks of pink pale in comparison to the artificially vibrant red and cerise of Annie's cloud. In no way is Jack a religious man, but he momentarily feels devout, an inversion so powerful that it leaves him speechless.

"My God. Can y'all believe what we're seeing?" The Texan elbows Jack in the ribs.

Jack shakes his head, unable to take his eyes off the distant valley and the sky above it. He can't, in fact, see the valley floor at all. The seething cloud of dirt tumbles cactus and alkali and, he assumes, radioactive fallout together in a powerful, interlocking vortex. An exquisite nightmare. The chaos obscures any view he might have of Annie's tower, which he believes has vanished, and the houses, which might or might not still be standing. The lonely tower light is long forgotten. Idly, he wonders what happened to the carefully protected camera. If it's operating, he realizes, it's taking a hell of a sequence of shots.

One more amazing thing is still to come, the timing. One moment the maelstrom is boiling furiously, the next moment it's gone. In less than fifteen minutes, the whole show anticlimactically disperses to the east. The cloud breaks off from its stem, the colors dissipate, the turbulence evaporates. By the time the sun comes fully over the horizon, there's nothing much more to see. Except for the dust, of course. But Jack finds the rapidity almost unbelievable. All that energy, breaking up in hardly more time than it would take to drink a cup of coffee.

Time now to find a fresh cup. Climbing gingerly down from his bleacher seat, he limps a little as he walks away. The blanket, though welcome, hasn't helped much. Rubbing his lower back and hip, he tries to massage out the stiffness caused by sitting so long in the cold. Soon they'll all be lining up at the buses again, eager to drive down on the playa and witness the damage directly. Politicians and newsmen alike, representing every state in the union, they each want to be first. Jack doesn't need to be first, but he has to be best. Already the story is shaping itself in his head. He might as well stretch his legs, and think about the sentences he'll write that evening. The inconsequential nature of human beings in the face of such dominating force, the pettiness of politics, the gargantuan glory of an atomic rage.

At the coffee urn, he runs into Lou, who's reacting in a totally different way. He's disgusted. "Hardly worth the effort. Too much light at first. Wobbly flashes, then just a white glare on the screen. All those colors, they just looked gray. Someday soon we'll be able to broadcast in color, but right now we're helpless. Besides, we couldn't really see a damn thing. Too much dust. The TV screens looked almost blank. That's why I have time for coffee. A damned shame." With that, he clutches his paper cup and hurries back to where his crew and the two mayors are waiting.

Jack walks some more, delighted he's a better eyewitness than the camera's eye. Lou boasts that television will eventually eliminate the need for print journalism, but Jack doesn't agree at all. He'll generate lots better descriptions, compounding adjectives and verbs, finding language to balance man's mastery of the atom with the necessity to use it wisely. Finally he forces himself to head for the abominable school bus, where he joins throngs of other onlookers, including the noisy trio from Sunday night, all talking at once and all impatient to see the damage up close. The loudmouth is still pontificating at everyone in earshot, and sounding like a ghoul agog to get a good view of some horrendous accident that happened to someone else's family.

Fortunately, the loudspeaker interrupts, crackling as the announcer urges them to climb aboard their buses as quickly as possible. The newsmen, the politicians, and the bureaucrats, however, straggle back to the road very slowly. Right now, thick dust still covers Yucca Flat completely, so they know they'll have to wait a while before recovery hour is declared. No hurry. An all-clear signal isn't likely to come anytime soon.

Finally the public address system replaces the rasping with a scratchy recording of some choir, first singing "My country 'tis of thee" and then "O beautiful for spacious skies." Some of the waiting crowd hums along with the chords, and one couple even harmonizes a little.

"O beautiful for spacious skies." It's perfect.

Jack has his headline.

Annie

17 MARCH 1953 • 0520 HOURS

Three Marine hrs helicopters hover ten feet off the ground. Two wait eleven kilometers from ground zero while the third is six kilometers farther away. As protection from the atomic flash, the three helicopter copilots wear high-density goggles. The three pilots will duck their heads, hoping their visors shield their eyes. Simon drops from its tower on schedule and on target, but little else about Simon is predictable. The yield is huge, the equivalent of 43 kilotons of tnt when only 35 kilotons had been projected. The colorful cloud is gigantic, tornadoing to 44,000 feet, where the wind picks up at 48 knots. A Navy drone Skyraider aims for the top of the mushroom stem, where a pressure wave decimates its witng panels and sends it plummeting to the ground. Radiation, both visible and invisible, sails eastward, spreading quickly and closing highways. Commercial flight is banned across the intermountain West. The aec quickly sends out word, however, that there's no need for alarm. Calling Simon a "miscalculation," Commissioner Thomas Murray reiterates the quid pro quo. "Gentlemen, we must not let anything interfere with this series of tests—nothing."

Dennis

Dennis and Ted are sitting in their Jeep when Annie hits the ground. Wearing goggles, they can look directly at the flash.

Big one.

Yeah.

Whiter than white.

Good vibes, too.

The sound surrounds the dry air before the desert floor begins to shudder underneath them. Ted claps his hands over his ears. Dennis, leaning back in the passenger seat, smiles. He loves the moment of impact, that instant when night turns to day and the whole world trembles. Like an orgasm. A quiver of explosive ecstasy that lasts and lasts and lasts. He loves the rumble that grows into a windswept roar. He relishes the swirling clouds of color that soon shape themselves into characteristic mushroom and stem. Different every time. Every time the same.

He remembers a night at Camp Lejeune, a dozen years ago, when a gunnery sergeant kicked the raw recruits out of their barracks to feel a hurricane blow through. Most of the boys despised the storm, and the sergeant too. Not Dennis. He stood in the wind for hours, legs spraddled, arms akimbo, pushing his body against the omnipotence of the gale. So loud his eardrums almost burst, the gusts buffeted him from side to side. The rest of his boot camp platoon soon sought shelter. In a foxhole. Behind a tree. Dennis didn't budge.

Now the ex-marine wishes he could stand in the storm of an atomic bomb. Dead center. Feel the power. Head-on. Foolish notion, of course. The front seat of his government Jeep is as close as he'll ever get. He watches the black and purple cloud bulging in front of his eyes. A whirling dervish of a cloud, boiling red, twisting higher and higher. Pulling the dirt of the desert into the sky. Mustard yellow and chocolate brown.

A nasty one.

A real beaut.

We'll measure a lot of dust today.

The counters'll be clicking, that's for sure.

How soon should we get started?

Blake said to wait a while. Let the dust settle. Maybe half an hour. Let the big cloud start to drift.

Dennis reaches for his pipe and tamps in some fresh tobacco. Might as well relax.

Ted climbs out of the Jeep. He leans against the hood, watching the sun rise behind the mountains to the east. He thinks they're called the Spotted Range. Apt name, all khaki colored. Hardly a smidgen of green.

Still smoking his pipe, Dennis joins him. His eyes stay focused on the cloud. It's starting to break apart. Four planes fly close to the largest plume, darting just to the edge of the color and then veering away. Dennis wishes he was up there too. Close. He wonders what the pilots feel. He thinks he knows. He's jealous. He points out the planes to Ted. A C-47, two B-29s, and one B-25. Guys must be taking cloud samples, flying so neighborly.

See anything else?

No. Too much dust.

Anything of the tower?

Not likely.

What about the houses?

I thought I got a glimpse of one of 'em. Hard to tell.

I can't wait to get out there.

Me neither.

Dennis relights his pipe. Ted waters a nearby bitterbrush.

I wish we had more coffee.

Thermos empty?

Yeah.

Ted spots a trail of dust angling alongside the playa from the north. Another Jeep. Their vehicle is parked on the southwestern edge of Yucca Flat. He watches the other Jeep come toward them.

Time yet?

Maybe so.

The oncoming Jeep flashes its headlights, then turns sharply toward the empty desert.

Are we supposed to follow?

For a ways. They're going out toward the trenches. We're assigned the houses.

So they get the live ones and we get the dummies.

Something like that.

I bet the baby dolls got knocked around pretty good.

Guys in the trenches probably got jolted too.

Ever want to be out there with them?

Yeah. For sure.

The two men climb back in the Jeep. Ted folds his lanky frame behind the steering wheel. Engaging the clutch, he starts the engine. The Jeep coughs. As Dennis settles in his seat, he stares straight ahead. He thinks he might see one of the houses silhouetted in the sand.

They park where they've been told to park. Big wide-open playa, and they've been assigned a parking place. Go figure.

Nobody nearby.

They can see other Jeeps headed in different directions. Each one has a crew of two inside. Just like Dennis and Ted. One to aim the Geiger counter. One to note down the readings. Click here. Click there. Just another day at the office. Only more fun.

Dennis reaches down and snugs cloth bootees over his shoes. With a roll of duct tape, he attaches the bootees to his overalls. Behind the wheel, Ted struggles. Not enough room. Ted bangs an elbow and curses.

I'm gonna open the damn door.

Better put on your mask first.

Nah, we're not close enough yet.

Ted jerks the door handle. Dennis finishes with his bootees and pulls on his gloves. More taping. Close any gaps. Like Ted, he wishes they could leave the masks behind. The goggles, too. He feels like a Martian, or at least what he imagines a Martian might look like. If there is such a thing as a Martian.

Both men wear jumpsuits, with the words "Property USA AEC" stamped on their backs. A cloth hat perches on Dennis's head, although the redhead's hairline is still visible and an inch of freckled skin shows below. He adjusts his goggles and tugs at his mask. The breathing apparatus isn't working very well. It always clogs in the blowing dust.

About ready?

All set.

Ted reaches behind the driver's seat and pulls out his Geiger counter. He shakes it. Click. Click. Sporadic sounds. Not much action yet.

Dennis picks up his clipboard. It's awkward, holding it in his gloved hands. Writing the numbers down is awkward, too. But at least he's close to the action, even if he's all bundled up.

Let's go.

Wanta get a reading here first? A kind of baseline?

Good idea. And every twenty paces from here on in.

Okay.

Ted waves the Geiger counter at the Jeep. Not much happens.

A hundredth of a roentgen per hour.

Dennis dutifully writes 0.01 R/h.

Hardly worth a notation.

Ted scoffs. And tries to scuff up the sand by dancing a little jig.

Let's stir stuff up.

Not fair.

The dance doesn't last long. Ted's protective outfit hampers his movements. He stumbles, and nearly drops the Geiger counter.

Take care. That's government property.

Me or the clicker?

Both men laugh.

They edge stiffly forward, leaving boxy footprints in the dust. It's still early, but already they're starting to perspire. The suits from outer space are damned uncomfortable. A trickle of sweat begins to cloud Ted's goggles. He's tempted to wipe them dry.

Dennis tugs at his mask again and readjusts the filter. The hot air makes him cough.

After twenty paces, they pause. Another reading. A little higher. 0.07 R/h. Nothing special yet.

More footprints. More paces. More notes.

I feel like a Martian.

On Martian landscape.

I like being out here alone, though. Makes me feel like an explorer. You know, tracking unknown territory.

Yeah. I like it too.

Wish we didn't have to wear these silly suits.

Ditto.

Ted wipes his sleeve against his forehead. Too damned hot.

With the heat, the dust is settling. They can see the first house. The walls are seared, like a barbecue cooker got too close to the paint. Ted says something about special enamel. Dennis sneers. The government ought to know better. Fire-resistant enamel indeed.

A mail truck was parked nearby. It lies on its side now, apparently lifted and dropped by the blast.

Dennis and Ted stand beside the right rear tire. The counter clicks a little faster.

How many roentgens per hour?

More than alongside the Jeep. Nearly 0.1 R/h. Still not enough to worry about.

They step around the truck and walk closer to the house. The counter sounds like it's hiccupping.

Hot spot here.

Should we go inside?

Let's wait a while.

Can you see through the window?

Yeah. The dummies didn't fare too well. Mostly upside down.

What about the furniture?

Pretty broken up. Stuff fell off the shelves and out of the cupboards, too. Books and cans all over the floor. It's a mess.

The men walk around the house to another window.

If these had been live people?

Probably dead.

Or in pretty bad shape.

Hope real families—living Americans—never get ground-zeroed.

Dennis puts the inference out of his mind. He focuses on his clipboard, on the numbers he writes down. No reason to think about the deaths of dummies. This is just an exercise, after all.

Let's go see the other house. If it's there.

It ought to be dead ahead and slightly off to the right. I think it's gone.

Let's go see.

Better check the other vehicles first. The boss wants a radiation count for each of them.

Okay.

At every car, Ted swings the Geiger counter up one side and down the other. Dennis writes the numbers down carefully. So far, so good, though the roentgen level is climbing higher with every step. Up to 0.2 R/h by now.

They take particular care with number 49, a green Dodge with blistered paint and whitewall tires and a melted odometer. A female manikin is slumped inside, her arm smashed against the door.

Looks like Josephine didn't make it.

Josephine?

Yeah, she was my son's date.

You're crazy.

No, Steve drove her out here last week. Each kid in the Las Vegas High School drivers' ed class got to bring a car. They caravanned. The teacher supervised. Steve's manikin rode in the front seat right next to him. All dressed up in her new J.C. Penney clothes. He pretended she was his girl-friend. Named her Josephine.

Why not a sexier name?

You know the song, "Come Josephine in my flying machine."

She didn't fly this morning.

Nope. Josephine looks fairly well grounded.

Whatever her name, Annie didn't do her any favors.

Steve'll be disappointed. That's for sure.

Dennis adjusts his air filter for what seems like the hundredth time. He's tempted to rip it off. The whole damned Martian suit, in fact, is too hot and too confining.

I wonder if the guy who designed these outfits ever tried one on?

Not likely.

Ted drops his Geiger counter in the dirt and rubs at his mask. The sun is getting higher in the sky and the clouds are mostly dispersed. No shade any-where, unless they crouch beside one of the cars or kneel alongside the house that's still standing. The house is behind them, though. They need to keep moving forward, to the other house, the one that clearly isn't there anymore.

Wow!

Pancaked.

Nothing left.

Just some charred debris.

Two cars in pieces, too.

Yeah. Smashed almost flat.

Can you see if the camera's still there? In the lead box?

I think so.

Can you see any cabling?

A little bit.

Better not get too close. Those camera guys are fussy about their gear.

Don't I know it. We have strict instructions. Stay away from the periscope and don't kick up any nearby sand.

Think they got any pictures?

Hard to tell.

Another camera over there, on the ground.

Torn loose. Flipped in the air.

Pretty smashed now.

Film's prob'ly ruined.

Maybe. Maybe not.

What's the count?

Ted moves the Geiger counter closer to the burnt remains. Waving the wand left and right, he calls out the numbers.

Still pretty hot.

We'd better stand back.

No point in getting fried.

Are we getting more than our max dose?

Close call. We're okay.

Dennis checks his dosimeter. Still yellow and green, but he imagines the combination shading faintly toward blue. Last year he had to sit out the last two Tumbler-Snapper shots. His rad count was too high. Radiation Acceptable Dosage. Highfalutin words for the human reaction to the gamma and X-ray exposures they're calculating today. Added together last spring, his rad count exceeded the amount allowable in a single year. Maximum 3.9 roentgens per test cycle. His badge hit 4.3. Dennis is glad to put 1952 behind him. New year, new dosages.

While Ted circles the leveled house from a distance, Dennis stands and stares at the damage. He's seen burned ruins before, whole blocks of British houses destroyed by German bombers, but he doesn't remember anything quite so thorough. Some walls usually were left standing in London, and he'd been able to make out individual buildings. Here, not much left at all, except blackened pieces that look like giant matchsticks. He thinks about analogies. Pickup sticks, totally charred. Or a teepee campfire, toasted and fallen in on itself. Maybe a forest fire, though he's never seen one in person. And two unrecognizable cars. Maybe an Olds, maybe a Nash.

Dennis fervently wishes he'd been on the spot for the conflagration itself, in the moments just after Annie's impact. Once again he recalls the hurricane's roar. Maybe the cameras caught the fire on film. Instantaneous flame, the whole house flaring like a Roman candle. Just a second or two from blast to ruin, white-hot like white lightning. Dennis sighs. He hopes the filming was successful. Maybe he'll be able to watch vicariously, though he'd rather see the decimation in person.

Ted breaks the reverie. Announces they've hit the line.

2.5 R/h radiation intensity line.

Can't go any farther.

Okay. But look over there!

Dennis points in disbelief. Beyond the annihilated house, there on the hot desert floor, apparently undaunted by the recent firestorm, a single mottled brown lizard prances toward them. It's the only living thing, besides the two white-suited men, for miles. It's headed for the ruins, seeking shelter in the shade.

How on earth did that thing survive?

Prob'ly underground when the gadget dropped.

Like an earthquake under there.

Doesn't seem bothered by much at all.

'Til it gets a radiation overdose.

And turns red.

The two men chuckle, as the lizard reaches the edge of the fallen house. Unfazed, the lizard hoists itself up and over a shattered piece of wood and crawls down the backside. Where the desert sand has melted from atomic heat, the lizard leaves no tracks.

More wildlife coming.

Ted indicates two dusty fishtails sliding toward their own Jeep.

Looks like we have company.

Yeah. Must be the boss, and probably that AEC guy from D.C.

Better go meet them. They'll want our numbers ASAP.

Probably here to take pictures, too.

Dennis and Ted go as close to the erstwhile house as they dare, finish counting the roentgen levels, set the radiation intensity line, then walk back toward the vehicles. They take their time, still stumbling awkwardly in their bootees and protective suits, and perspiring even more heavily. Now two other Jeeps are parked next to theirs. No one has stepped onto the playa, though. Must be putting on their protective gear.

I hope they roast.

That's no way to talk about the management.

I never like those guys looking over our shoulders.

And speaking of shoulders, how come your neck is so red?

Ted reaches toward Dennis and flicks the back of his suit.

Looks like you're getting a sunburn.

That's a problem for us redheads. Plus it's hard to remember to put on suntan lotion in the middle of the night.

You might want to pull up your collar. Shouldn't have any skin showing anyway.

Regulation number one thousand five hundred and sixty-six. Or sixty-seven. I forget which.

Aw, just pull up your collar and stop whining.

Right.

Dennis and Ted step up the pace. Their guess is correct. Clyde McVeigh, a midlevel guy from Washington, D.C., accompanies their immediate supervisor, Rodney Blake. Plus a radioman. And someone to take photos.

Hi, boys. How're ya doing?

Fine, Mr. McVeigh. Just fine.

What's the count?

Variable. Hottest near the house that isn't there anymore. Set the line just beyond it. Coolest back here. Sort of midrange when we walk between the manikins' cars.

Any sign of the tower?

Nope. We didn't even try to take a count out there. Way too hot.

Been in the other house?

Waiting for you.

Look in the windows?

For sure. Those dummies are all topsy-turvy. Must have gotten a good shaking.

Let's go check 'em out.

The six men head directly to the house still standing. Ted repeats his measurements, calling out the readings as they walk. Pretty consistent. Mostly 0.2 R/h to 0.8. Well within the safe range. Dennis, pleased with the accuracy, smiles at his boss. In truth, he and Ted are the A-team. They rarely make mistakes. Otherwise they wouldn't be out here in the initial hours after the shot.

At the house, the two supervisors step in front of the other four men.

McVeigh reaches a gloved hand toward the doorknob and twists it open gently. The door swings in, and everyone steps inside. As Dennis and Ted promised, the living room is a mess. The manikins lie tumbled, with legs oddly bent. Canned goods and utensils and books litter the floor. A soft dust layers everyone and everything. The six men leave footprints in the sand.

Clementine wasn't much of a housekeeper, was she?

Clementine?

Friend of Josephine's.

The newcomers look puzzled, and wonder what on earth Ted and Dennis are joking about.

Do you think she ever vacuumed?

Doesn't look like it.

She wasn't much of a mother, either. Couldn't protect her kids.

The female manikin has been tossed sideways onto the sofa. One arm is broken, and one slipper-less foot splays to the left. Her face is dirty; her nightgown, torn. The three children playing on the floor have been flung in a heap. Their blocks are scattered beside them. The daddy figure still sits at the table, but his head is flopping awkwardly backwards. Dreadful sorry, Clementine.

The men, realizing such damage could occur in any American city, laugh nervously. The Red Menace is real. The Soviets have the bomb. This isn't a game.

What's the count in here?

Not too high.

Looks like more damage from the shock waves than from radiation.

Hard to tell. We don't know the dosage when Annie hit the ground.

The count seems to be steadily dropping, though. Not much problem any longer.

The newshounds will be glad to hear that. They're chomping at the bit—all lined up and ready to come storming in here.

Be sure to get some pictures, before all those spectators get on the scene.

Snap the mother and kids. With luck, we'll get something we can use for PR purposes. This could happen to you. A kind of Iwo Jima photo op of atomic warfare.

That's crass.

I know. But the public will eat it up.

Should we position Mom—Clementine—a little more gracefully?

Nudge her foot a little. Maybe pull her robe over her knees.

Okay.

What about the kids?

Let 'em lie there. Looks more dramatic.

While snapping the pictures and checking the radiation levels upstairs as well as downstairs, the men get to laughing.

Shall we try the food?

Probably overcooked.

McVeigh cocks his head toward the jokers. Dennis reads his mind. The AEC official is uncomfortable with the bantering, even though he's taking part. What if the bomb were real? If it blasted a city like Los Angeles? Or San Francisco? Maybe he's thinking of the Mission District—far enough away from the heart of downtown, but not quite far enough. Those old tri-toned Victorians would be filled with people like these manikins. Dummies. Doomed. Maybe he's picturing the Embarcadero, the tourists tossed helter-skelter along the pier. Not to be laughed at, not really. To the AEC, civil defense is serious business.

Good thing the masks hide facial expressions. Dennis grins, and points.

Boiled eggs.

Fried spam.

Fresh-roasted peanut butter.

Hot banana.

The bunch of bananas looks mushy and soft. The peel has blackened, and the yellow has disappeared. Ted opens the bread box and looks at the shriveled loaf. Wonder does not look wonderful.

Toast.

McVeigh and Blake lose patience.

Come on, let's go see the other house.

What's left of it.

We need to get a move on. The news boys are anxious, downright eager, and they can't do anything until we give a heads-up.

Once again Dennis and Ted lead the way, following their own footprints back to the scene of Annie's most destructive moment. McVeigh and Blake, so deep in conversation that they almost forget about the others, fall behind. Ted keeps clicking his Geiger counter, which gets noisier and noisier as they approach the disintegrated house. Still too hot. 1.0 R/h.

Call that number back, McVeigh orders the radioman. Can't let the news people come this far.

The men listen intently to the radioman's conversation. Someone isn't happy at the other end.

Says the crowd is getting antsy. Tired of sitting in their buses. All lined up and no place to go. Pulling rank. Hard to control.

Ted strides past the house, and finds an even higher count.

Better stop right there.

The data confirm their speculations. The collapsed house is way hotter than the one still standing.

We can let the public come as far as the first house. It's relatively clean.

Relatively is a relative word. Dennis notes that the radiation level actually is double the measurement taken yesterday, before Annie's detonation.

Still well within the allowable limits, though.

If the dust would settle, we wouldn't have any countable rads at all.

But tower drops always kick up a lot of playa.

Aviation devices are cleaner.

'Cause they're higher. Less direct contact with the earth.

Look at that. Still some old dust devils spinning around.

I don't suppose we ought to let the newsmen near until all those tornados-in-training have worn themselves out.

Dennis is getting bored with the inaction. He doesn't care about the newsmen, and he's tired of pacing back and forth between the houses.

How about a picture with Josephine?

He tells the other men about his son's adventure. They laugh. The bosses join the conversation. Rodney Blake has a teenage son, too, and Clyde McVeigh has a nineteen-year-old daughter. The photographer poses the men in different stances, showing the Dodge and its manikin from every angle. He even snaps photos of the white trinatite melted on top of the hood. Science guys, they'll want to see that for sure.

Meanwhile, everyone is getting hotter and hotter. The sun is high in the sky, and Dennis's neck is burning. No one wants to be the first to suggest taking off the masks and ventilators, but everyone is thinking exactly the same thought. Finally, Clyde McVeigh takes the lead. He looks toward Rod Blake, who nods back.

Safe enough?

Absolutely.

Let's take off the headgear. We can always put our filters back on if we get a higher reading.

Or if the wind comes up.

Not a problem. Let's get comfortable.

Terrific!

I feel like a stuffed pig in these clothes.

Ditto.

Good to breathe fresh air.

Gloves off, too?

Sure. I'm certain there's nothing left to worry about.

Did you see how quickly the big cloud dispersed?

Yeah. If Annie hadn't been so close to the ground, there'd be no sign of her at all.

She kicked up a lot of dust.

Still hanging in the air.

Not a problem. Annie dropped four hours ago. We're home free.

All six men strip off their gloves and push their masks around to the backs of their heads. Dennis unplugs his filter and shakes it. A fine dust falls on the playa and softly dissipates. Pulling off his goggles, Dennis is coughing. He feels better without the mask, but he has some dust caught in his throat.

You okay?

I'm fine. The damned filter is clogging up again. I'm glad to get it off.

How's the sunburn?

Dennis reaches back and touches his neck.

A little hot, but nothing serious.

Good.

McVeigh and Blake want some more car pictures. McVeigh, looking serious, leans against the front fender of a DeSoto. He makes sure the sun is shining on his face, so the photo will clearly show he's on the job. He avoids touching the blue and white scorched stain.

Blake reaches inside a Ford Victoria and puts his arm around the dummy driver. For him, levity seems more appropriate outdoors than in, perhaps because the manikins in the vehicles suffered less damage than those in the house still standing. These manikins could still laugh.

The officials soon turn to more serious thoughts, however, as they talk about rating the various Civil Defense options. Clearly the distance from ground zero is a distinct predictor of survivability. The manikins in the house closest to Annie never had a chance. Just as clearly, car passengers fare better than people indoors. These dummies may have been tossed around in their seats, but they probably would have stayed alive. Hard to tell, without living breathing guinea pigs.

Out on the playa, such guinea pigs exist. The men all know about the Navy's animal experiments, the caged rats and rabbits stationed at carefully calculated intervals. And then there are the Air Force's drone aircraft, "flown" by monkey pilots. Soon pigs will be at the Proving Ground, too, wearing clothes, no less. Scientists hope to measure how various materials withstand radiation contamination. Cotton versus wool, or nylon versus rayon. Not so great for the pigs, but important for future planning.

Dennis doesn't worry about the animals' fates. From his point of view, a monkey or a pig is as expendable as a manikin dressed in seersucker pink. Dennis never worries about the soldiers in the trenches, either. They're all volunteers, and the Army treats them well. First-row seats, in fact. Lucky bastards! Likewise, Dennis rarely thinks about the Soviets or the Chinese or the Koreans. International affairs are better left to the politicians. His job is to calculate the numbers. Let McVeigh and Blake and all the other bureaucrats consider the man in the street, the American family man, and how he and his wife and kids might best be protected from fallout.

That's all Dennis measures—fallout. He never reflects about it much. He knows radiation can be dangerous, but he assumes the government is diligent about setting up the proper procedures. The annual rad limit, for example. Too low, Dennis thinks. Probably picked out of a hat by a bureaucrat somewhere, just to be safe. No real scientific rationale. Ought to be higher, so men like Dennis can work longer at the Proving Ground. Waste of expertise, to send him home early last year. Still makes him mad, to miss the end of Tumbler-Snapper. But the government thinks it knows best. That includes setting an arbitrary rad count ceiling, no exceptions.

So Dennis follows the rules. Even though he regularly imagines himself flamboyantly confronting an atomic explosion, Dennis actually is quite careful in the field. He obeys orders. That's how he keeps his job. On the A-team.

Over here.

Huh?

You're a million miles away.

Nah, I'm just imagining this morning's countdown. Then boom! All those colors. All that noise. Stupendous!

Well, forget about it. We've got work to do.

How so?

They need us over here.

More photo opportunities. Clyde McVeigh and Rodney Blake pose near several other vehicles, though they decide not to shoot any pictures of the overturned mail truck. Too provocative.

Taking pictures inside the various protective shelters turns out to be prohibitive. Not enough light. Or else too much contrast with the sun's glare on the desert floor. Middle of the day. Time for lunch.

House over there. Plenty of food.

Fresh-roasted hot dogs.

Deep-fried potatoes.

Limited service, though. The would-be waitress and the wannabe wife, they're out of commission.

At least for now.

Dennis knows the manikins are all going back to Las Vegas, then on tour around the country to show off their Penney's clothes. At least the ones that didn't get frizzled. Like Josephine, semi-safe in her car.

Laughing, the men gravitate back across the playa.

Finally the two administrators declare a spectator cease-fire. Clyde McVeigh gestures toward the radioman.

Tell the news boys to get ready. We'll be there shortly.

Declaration of recovery hour, dead ahead.

The radioman grins.

Ted takes a final reading.

Seems cool enough.

Not perfect.

Not if a man got this dose day after day. But tonight the reporters'll all be back in Las Vegas and tomorrow they'll be headed home. Politicians, out of sight, out of mind. Shouldn't be a problem for anyone. Especially if they stay away from zero. And they will.

What about us?

How so?

Should we have left our masks on?

Nah. We're okay. Besides, it's too damn hot inside these outfits. I'd rather chance a little outside heat.

McVeigh slaps his gloves against his thigh.

See, hardly any dust at all.

Let's take a reading.

Okay.

McVeigh, gloves in hand, extends his arm.

Ted moves the Geiger counter wand in close, moving it from wrist to shoulder and from shoulder to knee.

Not much there.

Hardly a day's worth.

Nothing to worry about.

Blake laughs aloud.

Typical Nevada. We're hot all the time. Annie or no Annie.

How about you?

Ted, over here.

Ted moves the wand over to Blake's side and checks the measurement.

Same numbers, nothing more.

Let's go get those rubberneckers. Let's turn 'em loose.

Maybe let 'em go as far as the first house. The other one's still plenty hot.

The men wander toward their Jeeps. Despite the decision to let the Civil Defense observers advance a ways, they're in no hurry to let the throngs parade around the cars and into the first house. Dennis, in particular, hates to see anyone else gain access. If he had his way, he'd keep the whole place to himself. Dennis's Doom Dominion, that's what he'd name it. Dennis's Doomed Dummies, too.

Dennis is possessive about Yucca Flat. He thinks of it as his own special place, his personal responsibility. He knows he can't single-handedly keep the radiation in check, realizes that each event generates a different amount of fallout and that sometimes the fallout has a mind of its own. Might go south; might go east; might leapfrog clear across the country. But he can keep the numbers in check, here, on Yucca Flat, just as he did on Frenchman Flat last year and the year before. He can log an accurate tally. Be better, though, if he could keep all the onlookers away. Even these AEC officials. They just put a damper on the fun.

Ought to brush off before we get in the Jeeps.

Before we talk to all those people too.

Ted reaches inside the one Jeep and pulls out two brooms.

Here.

He hands one broom to the photographer and hefts the other one himself. He walks over to McVeigh, the D.C. dignitary, and begins sweeping his back.

Now, turn around. We need to do the front, too.

McVeigh swivels, balancing on one foot. Ted brushes vigorously, making sure that every trace of dust falls onto the desert floor.

Next?

Blake steps forward, then Dennis. Meanwhile, the other two men are plying the other broom, taking care to sweep each other clean. Cautiously, gently, they dust off their camera gear and radio equipment, too.

All done?

Looks okay to me.

Dennis tosses his mask and filter into the back of his Jeep. His gloves follow. He removes his cap and bangs it against the door. He reaches down and pulls off his bootees, unfastening them and wadding the protective tape in a crumpled ball. The ball and the bootees and the cap end up alongside the gloves. Finally, Dennis unzips his jumpsuit and steps out of it. He shakes the outfit once, twice, three times, knocking more dust onto the ground. Then it goes in the back of the Jeep, too. Ted follows suit, throwing his gear inside.

Before driving off, Ted picks up the broom one last time. Methodically, he sweeps down the Jeep, brushing any desert dust back onto the desert floor.

Can't be too careful, he says.

Recovery hour. Dead ahead.

Nancy

The nondescript gray-brown burro blends with her desert surroundings. Heavily pregnant, she is resting below Wiregrass Springs, on the west flank of the Sheep Range. When the dawn sky lights up, she stumbles awkwardly to her feet and braces her hooves against the ground. Nearly thirty miles away, on Yucca Flat, a crescendo of sound moves in waves away from Nancy's tower. By the time the rumbling cacophony reaches the burro, the earth is starting to quiver. She shivers in fear, and turns her head away from the roar. Overhead, the sky erupts in an array of color, turning first red and then purple and then darkly orange. Layers of white ash begin to drift from the sky. The powder covers the grasses below the spring, where the burro soon will graze, and the broken patch of dirt where she currently is poised. It also floats onto her back, until she resembles a white ghost, standing there in the early-morning light. She flicks her tail, dislodging some of the ash, and shakes her head, snorting and even coughing a little as the ash falls on her whiskers and nose. She sniffs, and listens, and now hears only a meadowlark, a killdeer, and the scream of a sharp-shinned hawk—normal everyday sounds for the hour after a desert dawn. Since the ground is no longer shaking, she's no longer uneasy. She nickers softly. Ignoring the rainbow cloud growing and glowing 35,000 feet overhead, she begins to feed on the whitened grass.

Ruthie

"Atta girl, Ruthie!"

Music to my ears. I scooped the trick across the table and squared it onto the pile in front of me. Six no-trump, bid and well made. Howard was delighted. Game, set, and match. Just like that. *Buzz, honey, you would have been proud!*

"Lucky cards," Don rationalized. He was right, of course, but I just laughed.

"Queen of Hearts, my dear." Howard enthusiastically clapped his hands and waved a pretend kiss in my direction. Then he pulled his flask out of his pocket and offered drinks all around. I took a long slow sip of Southern Comfort, sweet and strong. Because I adored it, Howard always brought Southern Comfort to share. Another sip, and then I passed the nightcap on to our opponents.

Don grimaced at what he calls Southern Swill, and said he wished he had a beer instead. When Ralph reminded him of the Coors stashed outside the window of their dormitory room, they quickly agreed. Time to call it a night. At least until they got back to their digs. Howard wasn't ready to quit. He never is. Warmed by the six no-trump victory and also by the whiskey, he was ready to play a few more hands. Thank God the others shook their heads. I was exhausted. Had to be at work before eight this morning; ditto tomorrow. I needed to be on top of that game, not this one.

Howard finally acquiesced. As usual, the trio walked me home. Home! Huh! Every time I think of that one-room dormitory cubicle, I wrinkle my nose. Some pretty poor excuse for a home. The best Mercury has to offer, though. Imagine if we had to live in tents, like the boys at Camp Desert Rock. At least constant dust and wind don't seep into our beds and blankets. But I hate the dorm. We all do, us girls stuck off by ourselves as if we had the plague. That's why I play bridge in the cafeteria. That's where the men hang out, and besides, the temperature's more inviting.

So we folded our cards away until tomorrow, pulled on our heavy coats and headed out into the chilly Nevada evening. We moved right along, almost racing the two blocks to the women's section of the infamous communal housing. When we got there, I gave Howard an extra victory hug, and then hurried indoors. I know he'd love more than a peck on the cheek. Not likely, though, not from me. *Not with your memory still so strong in my heart.*

I think the boys all know that, but they still hope. Tonight they turned away toward the men's dormitory entrance as soon as I opened my door. Too cold to be gentlemanly. I wonder if their accommodations are any better than mine. I don't know because I've never seen the men's side.

I do know that my tiny room is like a prison cell. Betty was there, as always, sprawled on her narrow cot. Fierce metal curlers filing up and down her head, she was reading a paperback with a lusty-looking cover. We share a room out of necessity. Mercury isn't exactly designed for female comfort and there are no other available places to stay. Together, Betty and I add up to twenty percent of all the women employed at the Nevada Proving Ground. The ten of us are wedged into a corner section of the largest men's dormitory, though the girls' rooms are totally separate. We share five cubicles and a single bath with two toilets, two washbasins, one shower stall. In each double room, just two beds, two lamps, two dressers. Not even extra space for a chair. We can barely move; *you wouldn't even be able to turn around!*

Betty looked up and asked if I'd won. I smiled, curling my upper lip sardonically, and told her about my six no-trump coup. Betty supposed that was good. I nodded. I've explained the game of bridge to Betty about a hundred times, or so it seems. No point in going into the details once again. Betty's no more interested in cards than I care about those torrid romances she loves. But as long as we don't have to talk too much, we get along fine. We're both tidy housekeepers; we both love our jobs. But other than that we don't have much in common. The Proving Ground's like that, odd combinations of people all crammed together in close quarters. Because everyone is pursuing the same goal, the combinations work out. Most of the time.

I hid my amusement at Betty's ignorance and agreed that six no-trump was darn good.

Hanging up my coat in the narrow two-by-four closet, I turned my back while I got ready for bed. Bright red flannel PJ's, left over from Christmas, and a chenille robe to wear down the hall. *You would have laughed at the getup.* Overnight case in hand, I scooted out of the room. I could hear someone in the shower, probably Lois. Susan was already standing in the doorway, impatiently stamping her foot; Janet was brushing her teeth. I heard another door opening, so I quickly commandeered the other basin. I know the routine. Grab a place in the bathroom while the grabbing's good.

The next morning differed little from the night before. A lineup at the shower, all of us scurrying back and forth while getting dressed. I set my alarm for 5:45 A.M., a bit early, so I could take my shower before the rush. As always, I wanted a little extra time to check out my appearance. *I promise, I never really flirt, but I do like to look nice.* Today I chose my gray corduroy skirt (tastefully hemmed just below the knee—wish I could move it up a little), a white rayon blouse (no cleavage, not here), and a red wool jacket (just right on the Queen of Hearts). Nylons and black pumps finished off the outfit. I bent toward the mirror, made sure my lipstick wasn't crooked, then fluffed my permed brown hair. If Betty had a perm, she wouldn't have to sleep every night with those god-awful curlers. But I can't convince her. I found my purse, and slipped out the door.

I like to arrive in the office before anyone else for a couple of reasons. I'd rather make the coffee myself because no one else's tastes any good. More important, I always want to be the first to check the teletype machine. I like to boast that I'm the only secretary at the Proving Ground with a Top Secret Q clearance. No other women are allowed to see what comes over the wire. Of course the men in the office have top clearances too, but they can't be bothered with the teletype mechanics. So every day I measure the coffee and then right away check for coded documents. My job usually involves just typing routine letters and reports, but first thing in the morning I'm like a general instead of a private.

Today was no different. After carefully spooning out the Maxwell House and starting the coffee perking, I went over to the teletype. Two messages, both encrypted. I set to work, operating the machine so the new tapes were decoded.

The first summarized "Atomic Cloud Fly Throughs." I learned nothing I didn't already know. In 1948, during Operation Sandstone in the South Pacific, a plane and its crew accidentally penetrated an atomic cloud. Nothing happened. "No one keeled over and no one got sick," the supervising colonel had observed. So, ever since, aviators happily have been flying into atomic clouds on purpose. Today's message simply reiterated the current guidelines for sampling atomic clouds while in the air, regulations the Air Force pilots have been following in Nevada since before the current Upshot-Knothole test series began. *Don't I wish you could be one of those boys!*

The second encrypted message was more provocative. A memo to the Chief of Army Field Service, it sketched out operative details regarding soldiers in the trenches near ground zero. Normally I would type without thinking about the words, but today I paid attention. "It is possible that inclination to panic in the face of AW [atomic warfare] and RW [radiation warfare] may prove high. It seems advisable, therefore, to increase research efforts in the scientific study of panic and its results, and to seek means for prophylaxis." Huh? In plain English, it sounded like the brass were outlining a kind of psychiatric condom for scared soldiers. Better not say that to my boss, though.

I kept on transcribing the enumerated orders: "Continue studies in psychology of panic" and "Seek techniques for reducing apprehension and for producing psychologic resistance to fear and panic, especially in presence of radiation hazard ('emotional vaccination')."

"Psychologic resistance" and "emotional vaccination"? They've got to be kidding. Mixing their medical metaphors, too. They need to go back to high school. "Spread knowledge of radiation tolerance, techniques of avoidance, and possibility of therapy through military and civilian populations and measure their acceptance."

That's more like it. The whole rest of the memo seemed more sensible to me. It went on to explain, "It is still necessary to initiate measurements of the effects of moderate doses of radiation in man." Moreover, "advantage should be taken of any opportunities for the study of biological effects of radiation particularly in man." Well, that's one big reason why we're here after all, and why my boss pays such close attention to what's happening in the field.

Remember my boss? Did you ever meet him? John Cartwright from Los Alamos. I call him Dr. C. His job at the Proving Ground is to resolve any complications that might inadvertently develop from the scientific experiments. He brought me along with him when the Atomic Energy Commission sent him to Nevada for the 1953 tests. Calls me his "right-hand man." We trust each other. Some of the fellows envy my insider status, but most of the staff treats me okay. A smile here, a wink there. I know how to make 'em all feel good. Like Howard, they call me the Queen of Hearts, too. Suits my style.

I know the limits, though. Actually, I'm thankful for the rules because an ill-chosen affair would get me flat-ass fired. *Besides, I've never found anyone to replace you, Buzz. I still dream of you all the time.* My dear Air Force husband, whose plane disappeared somewhere off Guam nine years ago. After that, I was a basket case. The other military wives helped me pick up the pieces. One of them introduced me to Dr. C, an old family friend, and urged him to hire me. I'd been a secretary in Denver before the war, so I was experienced.

Bingo! I moved all my belongings from Albuquerque to secret Los Alamos (cryptically known as the Hill) and took to my new job like a duck to water. I loved being a part of the war effort, especially the nuclear operations. When the bombs fell on Hiroshima and Nagasaki, I felt like I personally played a role in that success, *doing my special part to honor you.* Even if it's just typing memos, my job's important.

Now I'm in Mercury, Nevada, a long way from New Mexico but still serving my country. Even though I detest the cramped quarters of the dorm, I'm pretty happy at the Proving Ground. Last week, Dr. C even took me to the Control Center to watch a test in person. *Wish you could have been there, too.* I held my breath while the gigantic orange and yellow mushroom shape filled the eastern sky. *Actually, I imagined you flying high alongside the billowing atomic colors, looping your fighter plane in and out of the rainbow cloud, soaring skyward just like the atomic fly-throughs described in this morning's memorandum.* I didn't tell anybody about my fantasy, though. One more thing, like the coded messages, I'd never reveal.

Dr. C promised that pretty soon I'll get to see an atomic crater firsthand. Maybe by Jeep; maybe from the air. He didn't say. Not today. Too much work to do. After reading his messages, Dr. C called me in for some dictation. Reassurances, mostly, details about the safeguards in place all across the Proving Ground. I didn't pay much attention, just took down the words. From the soldiers in the trenches to the pilots of the planes, from the craftsmen responsible for building the towers to the technicians laying the wires, from the scientists calculating the data to civilians like me, safety first. I do respect the way Dr. C keeps his finger on every pulse, checking and double-checking whatever falls under his control.

Occasionally I've asked him about the human tests. I'm kind of intrigued by the soldiers (*maybe I just like men in uniforms*) who volunteer for the forward trenches, and I've wondered about physical dangers and psychological stresses. This morning's teletype made me especially curious. What, exactly, does "psychologic resistance to fear and panic, especially in presence of radiation hazard" mean? Is "psychologic" even a word? And what does "emotional vaccination" imply? Another kind of "prophylaxis"?

Dr. C laughed at my questions and explained that the memo was just jargon for preparing the boys for whatever happens. In case of real atomic warfare, a soldier will need to know how to react without panic or fear. He'll have to rely on pure instinct, and that comes with familiarity. Once a soldier has seen an atomic explosion firsthand, he'll not only know its power but he'll also realize that, with the proper precautions, he'll be okay. He'll be psychologically protected, so he can go on to fight, to help others, to do whatever is needed.

Whenever Dr. C switches into his lecturer mode, my eyes glaze over. I kind of smile secretly inside. This time, my boss caught my eye. He stopped talking and turned back toward his desk. Picking up a square pamphlet titled "You and Atomic Warfare," he asked me if I remembered it. I did recall typing part of the draft a year or two ago. Now every soldier carries a copy in his pocket, like a Bible. Dr. C told me to look at the last page. That's what comes after emotional vaccination.

I turned to the emphatic final paragraph on page 12. "WHEN THE BOMB GOES OFF, LET THE DEBRIS STOP FALLING. CHECK YOURSELF, THEN GET UP AND GET TO WORK—YOU'LL BE NEEDED!!" So that's the upshot of emotional vaccination: get up and get to work! As I read, I wondered about the personal dangers of radiation exposure. Page 3 said, "This blast itself won't do much damage to you." Page 8 dismissed the notion of "radioactive snow." Nothing to fret about. "The amounts of radiation involved here are far too small to hurt any of us and certainly do not present a military hazard." The pamphlet confirmed what Dr. C always has said: the biggest atomic problems are likely to be panic and fear. "If people realize that after the blast-wave passes and the debris has stopped falling, the damage from the bomb is over—there won't be any panic," the pamphlet reassured its readers. It's up to the soldiers to prevent any such chaos.

I'm not sure I believed every word I read, but I surely do trust Dr. C. No more fretting about "emotional vaccination," at least not while there's so much work to do today. I went back to my typing. Dr. C had scrawled out several memos by hand, so I needed to translate his crabbed handwriting. Almost immediately, one disquieting "Certificate" reminded me that, even if the soldiers stay safe, other Proving Ground workers might not be able to avoid atomic residue.

This is to certify that the below listed individual received the listed total dosage of gamma radiation during the period indicated, as read from a Dosimeter Film Packet, DuPont Type 502606 (high range film), Film Emulsion Number 100-1. The control film used in the reading of the final exposure is listed below.

Name: Dennis Rutherford   Radiation Specialist   Las Vegas

Total Exposure 4.37 R/r

Inclusive dates: 17 March through 19 March 1953

Control Film No. 022093 & 022094

As Dr. C's notes made clear, not everything always goes as planned. Not a faceless soldier in a trench, but a name, a real person. Dennis. Dennis Rutherford. Not a soldier at all but a civilian radiation specialist, a man who checked the air for everyone else. He must have gotten in a hot spot, quite a hot spot according to the data on the page. Nice guy. I met him last month in the cafeteria, and I saw him again a couple of days ago. He was complaining about a sunburnt neck. Driving him crazy. Wanted to borrow some lotion from one of the women. I didn't have any, but Betty did. She shared the little tube she always carries in her purse.

While I typed, I wondered if Dennis was radioactive at the time. Probably not. He'd obviously had time to shower, wash his hair, get the dust out of his clothes. Too bad. Nice guy. I hope it's nothing serious. He'll probably lose his job, though. Or at least be reassigned. You can't go back in the field after your dosage accumulates. Not until next year. I couldn't help myself. I glanced down at my own badge, now such a part of my daily costume that I hardly think about it. No color change. All was well.

I moved from my desk to the encrypting teletype machine. It works like a typewriter, so all I had to do was retype the memo on its keyboard. As I made my keystrokes, the machine simultaneously coded the tape and scrambled Dr. C's words. The process wasn't terribly complicated. I just needed to take particular care with the capitalization. Actually, the input procedure was the exact reverse of my decoding operation earlier that morning. Once I finished typing, I pushed the single green key. Within minutes, the Rutherford memorandum was sent to Los Alamos, to Las Vegas, to Washington, D.C., and to Albuquerque. Pretty soon the whole world would know Dennis's fate.

While I was waiting for the message to go on its way, I glanced at my watch. Time for lunch? The hands pointed to 8:15 on the dial. Or 0815 as they've trained me to translate. Since I'd already done what seemed like half a day's work, 8:15 wasn't likely. I shook my wrist. Nothing happened. So I looked toward the wall clock: 11:40 A.M. Almost time for a bite. Time, too, for a visit to a Las Vegas jeweler on my next trip to town. That it accidentally magnetizes nearby wristwatches is the secret aftereffect of the encoding teletype machine. Just part of doing business, but I've often wondered if this wasn't another reason why none of the men like to operate the mechanism.

The rest of the day imitated the rest of my days. More typing. Two more messages to decode. More typing. More encrypted memoranda to send across the country. A little teasing with a major who came to talk to Dr. C. As the hours passed, I quit looking at my useless wristwatch. I meant to ask Dr. C about Dennis Rutherford, but he was busy and so was I. Before I knew it, the clock showed 6:00 P.M. My workday was finished. Emptying the remains of the coffee, I cleaned up the tiny kitchen. Then I tidied my desk, squaring the typewriter cover so the insidious Nevada dust wouldn't get into the keys. Dr. C was on the telephone. I ducked inside his office door, but he motioned me away. Time enough to talk tomorrow.

At bridge that night I wished I could tell the other players about Dennis. He was on my mind, but he's classified, so I didn't dare mention his name. The radiation dosage is classified, too. *Maybe that's why I talk to you in my head.* Outwardly, I always have to keep everything to myself. It's hard, sometimes, to be so secretive, to bottle everything up. That's part of my job, though, to keep every confidence.

Because of Dennis, it was hard to concentrate on the game. Besides, I was paired with Don, who rarely pays attention and who never counts cards. He almost always loses, especially when he takes the bid. It was easy to be the dummy. I just leaned back and relaxed. Don misplayed a finesse and then lost a meager two-heart bid. Should have ruffed, but he didn't. Down by a trick. Phooey!

Howard dragged out his inevitable flask and suggested a little Southern Comfort to wash away my pain. Winners or losers, partners or not, there was always the ritual of Southern Comfort. I happily enjoyed two full swallows and then another sip before passing the flask back to Howard. Once again, Don and Ralph turned up their noses, preferring the nightcap beers waiting for them in the dorm. Howard quaffed his share of the whiskey, and perhaps a little more. There's not much recreation at Mercury except cocktail hour, cards, and after-dinner drinks. Lots of the men, especially the craftsmen, work long into the night. So do the scientists, the physicists and engineers. But us card players all have desk jobs. We work nine-hour days, six days a week, but we're almost always free in the evenings. By that time, I'm more than ready to relax.

Rumors say there'll soon be a new Mercury cafeteria, and maybe even a bowling alley. Probably after I'm long gone back to New Mexico. Somebody told me there might be better accommodations, too, but I'm not holding my breath. Even if they built separate housing for women, it's likely to be dorm-like rather than individual rooms. I sure would like a bowling alley, though. *Remember how we used to bowl regularly when you were based at Kirtland, in the league with other pilots and their wives?* After I moved to Los Alamos, I switched to cards. Counting suits and tricks keeps my mind busy, gives me something to do after work. I was mighty glad to find Howard and Ralph and Don at Mercury, lucky to hook up with three other bridge buffs. Doesn't even matter that Don isn't very sharp.

The four of us rarely discuss anything beyond the game at hand. That's the unspoken Mercury rule. You leave your work at your desk. No talking about anything connected to the actual tests. When we first arrived in Nevada, Dr. C had cautioned me. Back in New Mexico, government informers had been planted on-site and wherever the workers might gather to drink in public. He was pretty sure the Cantina, a Santa Fe grill and local watering hole, hired FBI agents as bartenders to listen in on all the conversations. Dr. C thought the same might be true of some of the cafeteria workers at Mercury. Might be FBI, too, and might be listening.

I wasn't so sure. At dinner I'd looked around for the umpteenth time. The cooks were spooning out corned beef stew with overcooked cabbage and bus-boys were slinging plates and wiping down tables and everyone was just too busy to have time to be spying on anyone. I didn't take any chances, though. I never, ever, talk about Dr. C or what I actually do from eight to six every day. That's secret, always. So I buried Dennis somewhere in the back of my mind. I didn't discuss him all evening, and I certainly won't anytime in the weeks to come. In fact, I'll try not to think about him again. Still, he seemed like such a nice guy. I hope he'll be okay.

I could see Howard watching me, wondering why I seemed so lost in thought. He even teased me a little, waved the flask under my nose and pre-tended it held smelling salts instead of booze. I grinned weakly, and said I'd be up for another hand. Good sport; good soldier. That's me. When Howard and Ralph bid five clubs successfully, Don and I lost again, but I didn't really care. I was playing pretty mechanically.

A couple of times, though, I sneaked a look around the cafeteria. It was pretty much shut down for the evening. Only one worker stayed around, not too far away from us bridge players. The young man, head cocked to one side, seemed overly interested in polishing metal trays. Remembering Dr. C's words, I distrusted him immediately. Was he listening because he'd like to play bridge, or was he something more sobering than a casual kitchen boy? I couldn't tell, but I didn't much like his crew-cut looks.

Another game, won this time by Ralph, and then our foursome headed back to the dorm. As we left the cafeteria, the workman sidled back into the kitchen. I made a mental note to look for him tomorrow night, then snugged my coat tight across my shoulders. Outside, an ugly, scowling wind. The boys laughed about wannabe spring in Nevada, and nattered on about the blowing dust. Not like other parts of the country, they said. I disagreed, but I didn't say so out loud. I actually think the Proving Ground is kind of similar to New Mexico's high plateaus. On the whole, I like it. *You'd like it, too.*

I slept badly that night, dreaming of sneaking cooks and lurking busboys and radiation clouds spreading overhead. When I woke up at 4 A.M., my neck was burning and my PJ's were soaked with sweat. Unable to go back to sleep, I finally tiptoed out for an early shower. At least I was ahead of everyone else, though Lois arrived just as I finished drying off. We grimaced at each other and at the early hour, but agreed we were glad to be first.

Back in my room, I paused while I decided what to wear that day. Maybe a shirtwaist dress, the dark blue one with the white piping. It looks good with the short white jacket, and my navy heels are the most comfortable pair I own. Sometimes I think the unspoken dress code is silly. Frankly, I'd much rather wear slacks to the office, but no one ever does. Just ten girls, and we never break the unwritten rule. Pulling on my nylons, I wondered if I'd hear any more about Dennis. Probably not. So I put him out of my mind. *Brushing my hair, I tried to think only of you.*

Back in the office an hour later, after gulping down a sweet roll and a glass of grapefruit juice and looking in vain for suspicious kitchen workers, I settled into my morning routine. For perhaps the hundredth time, I measured out the Maxwell House, then turned to the teletype machine. Nothing there this morning, so I picked up my notebook and got to work on Dr. C's memos. Sometimes he scrawls things out, sometimes he dictates his words carefully. I'd rather take dictation because his penmanship is so horrid. It's easier to type from my notes than his.

I needn't have hurried. Dr. C was late, most unlike his routine. I waited nervously, because a potential crisis suddenly was pushing everything aside.

Just after 9 A.M., a top secret memorandum arrived from the deputy test director. I worked quickly to decode the startling information. Last year, in Los Alamos, I saw some confidential messages that indicated some minor problems with fallout east of the Nevada Proving Ground, but Dr. C had assured me the occurrence was rare. He explained that by the time any radiation moved off-site, the intensity was fairly well dissipated.

Today's memo, headed "Fallout, Madison Mine," suggested there might be more of a problem this spring. "Following a nuclear detonation at Target Area 4, Yucca Flat, on 24 March 1953 at 0510 PST, a radioactive cloud passed over and partial fallout occurred on, Madison Mine, Nevada." Some twenty miles from Mercury, just outside the Proving Ground boundary but square in the center of the direction most prevailing winds would blow, a miner named LaMar Madison ran a hand-to-mouth mining operation. He'd been warned that he and his three men should evacuate on those mornings when nuclear tests were scheduled. I overheard some of Dr. C's telephone conversations with the deputy test director and also with the U.S. Public Health Service sanitary engineer who monitored the air flow to the northeast. They all wished Madison would disappear, or at least make himself scarce on shot days. Madison refused. He won't go away.

Now a real problem was unfolding. The "log of events" that I was decoding explained the situation. Apparently the deputy test director had advised the Groom Mountain rad-safe officer that "personnel there should remain indoors as much as possible the remainder of the day" because all four miners had been exposed to radiation levels that far exceeded the recommended limits. I rechecked the numbers. Less than two hours after Nancy dropped from her tower, the gamma exposures were climbing as high as three hundred and fifty. Then, just after 0700, the measurements shot up to five hundred. Six minutes later, five hundred and eighty. Wow! I could hardly believe what I was reading. Way too high. Even though the numbers were receding before noon (down to a hundred by 1140) they still seemed excessive.

I typed the final sentence of the memo. "On the basis of the above data, the equivalent total dose for the first twelve hours is approximately 1.3 roentgens and the total life dose approximately 3.4 roentgens." Too close, way too close, to the dosage Dennis received right up next to Annie's fallout. Dr. C will be horrified, although there's no firm indication that the men were personally contaminated. Just a very real likelihood. I realized that, in addition to the danger to the miners, this could be a public relations nightmare for the AEC. Where was Dr. C? We needed him.

When he arrived half an hour later, I handed him the memorandum directly. He quickly skimmed the words, uttered a single sharp curse, shook his head, and stomped into his office. The door slammed behind him. He picked up the phone almost immediately, and I could hear his voice through the flimsy prefab wall. He sounded agitated at first, then calmer as he talked with one subordinate and then another. I wondered if he'd phone Washington, D.C., or if he'd keep a lid on the problem until he personally could get it solved. Then I remembered the memo's distribution list. Too late, but maybe not too late to keep the news from the press, at least until Dr. C figured out what to do. Of course LaMar Madison might already be talking to reporters, though I doubted it. The mine, located at the northeastern end of a dry playa called Groom Lake, was pretty far away from any newspaper anywhere.

My inclination, whenever there's a crisis, is to bury myself in my work, so I picked up yesterday's typing and made my fingers fly. Only half my mind was on my business, though. The rest was rerunning those numbers, and wondering if the miners realized what had been wafting their way. Dennis knew what he was doing, knew the risks and knew that his service to his country was more important than any old excess radiation. I wasn't so sure about LaMar Madison's involuntary patriotism.

At lunchtime Dr. C reappeared, this time with a sideways smile on his face. He walked over to my desk and asked if I was busy. Should have been pretty obvious that I was working as hard and as fast as I could, but I nodded dutifully and held out a finished stack of letters to be signed. At the same time I gestured toward another pile of papers, explaining that I still had a few more pages to go. Dr. C clamped his hand down on the unfinished stack. He grinned even more broadly. A little taken aback, I looked up and asked him what was going on.

Dr. C explained. He needed to see the Madison Mine for himself, to check out the distances and directions and to do a little aerial reconnaissance. He'd arranged for a helicopter to fly him over Groom Lake that afternoon. He wanted someone to take notes. Tongue in cheek, he wondered if I'd like to come along.

Looking at my eyes, he knew the answer before I could even say yes. I tried to hide my face so Dr. C couldn't see how excited I was. Last month he

had mentioned that I might be able to fly over the Proving Ground someday before the Upshot-Knothole series was completed, but I hadn't really
believed him. Surely the security must be too tight. Why would they let a
secretary go up in the air just for fun? Now it sounded like there was a real
job to do. Dr. C needed me. In the air.

Quickly I finished the page I was typing, and filed the rest of my work
away. I hurried back to my room, kicked off my heels, and pulled my penny
loafers out of the closet. I hung up my jacket and dress carefully, then
changed into the slacks and sweater I wished I could wear every day. Zipping
my parka up tightly, I wrapped a scarf around my hair. A check in the mirror,
to make sure my lipstick hadn't smeared, and I was all set to go.

I've flown many times before, and I love the sky. *You know that. Makes me
feel closer to you, although that's another secret I never reveal.*

Dr. C, idling a military Jeep, was waiting at the curb outside the dormitory. I hopped in beside him, and we sped off for Indian Springs, where the
helicopters were housed. Because Dr. C doesn't like to call attention to himself, he never orders a helicopter to pick him up at Mercury. He'd rather make
the forty-five-minute drive. I didn't care one way or the other. I was just
eager for the adventure ahead.

Parking the Jeep outside the Indian Springs headquarters, Dr. C marched
over to a row of Army whirlybirds. *Remember how you'd laugh at me when I
called them by that slang name? "Civvie talk," you'd say. As I recall, you never liked
helicopters at all because, unlike fighter planes, choppers are too unwieldy and too
slow. Now I'll find out what you meant,* though I suspect I'll like a slow whirly-
bird just fine.

Our particular flying machine was a Bell 47D-1, recently retired from service in Korea. Dr. C said that there's a new version (the G model, just recently
christened an H-13 Sioux) specially designed for medevac operations, so the
old Ds were available for use around the Proving Ground. This one resembled
a goldfish bowl. Its molded canopy gave a 360-degree view to its passengers
and crew. The red tail boom looked skimpy, much like latticework or metal
lace. The blue rotors appeared flimsy, too. I wasn't scared, though. I'm pretty
cocky about aircraft (*I learned from you, my number one pilot*), so I was raring
to go.

Mounting a narrow ladder, I climbed into the metal machine. A sergeant
gave me a hand, then held out a parachute. He ordered me to put it on, and
was more than a little surprised to see that I knew which end was which. I

shrugged into the harness, knowing full well that the whole apparatus would be of little use at the low elevations we'd be flying that afternoon. Military regulations, though. Safety first.

Settling into a seat alongside Dr. C, I surreptitiously glanced down at the chopper's floor. Both the sergeant and Dr. C caught me looking at dark purplish spots just beyond my feet, but neither said a word. Might be leftover bloodstains from the Korean conflict, might be something else. The men tacitly let my imagination work overtime. They both knew this helicopter had seen a lot of recent action. Perhaps the gory details were best left unsaid.

I buckled myself in, and peered out the 3-D windows at the Nevada desert. Having never been in a helicopter before, I didn't quite know what to expect. The sounds of the rotors drummed loudly in my ears, and the lurch upward was a total surprise. *I remember how you always talked about flying as if you and your crew were sailing softly on clouds. No noise, no sudden bumps and jerks, no pitfalls in the bottom of a passenger's stomach.* My plane rides have always been relatively smooth, too. This flight was different, beginning with a liftoff that not only bounced me from side to side but pulled me upright as if I was on some sort of carnival ride. Any momentary uneasiness vanished, though, as soon as I saw the ground spreading out below.

The helicopter gained altitude quickly, leveling off as it swung up the Indian Springs valley. Due south I could see snowcapped Mount Charleston and the ridge below it, Angel's Landing, where civilians gather to watch the nuclear explosions. To the west, there was the highway between Las Vegas and Mercury. I wished we'd fly over Mercury itself, but instead the chopper was traveling north before it turned west toward Frenchman. Moments later, after we slid past a low, unshapely conglomerate of brown rocks and green juniper that Dr. C called the Ranger Mountains, we were over Frenchman Flat. From the sky, the desiccated terrain looked spotted and scarred, as if the alkali flat had a bad case of acne. None of the craters was particularly huge, but each one was clearly visible. Dr. C tolled their names. Able, Baker, Easy, Fox.

Dropping down a little, the helicopter hovered over the sand and stirred dust devils in the air. Dr. C pointed out the obvious, that when the chopper flew too low it stirred up so much dirt that it was difficult to see what was on the ground. I wondered if the dirt was radioactive, but I didn't ask. Soon we lifted higher, and the dirt dissipated. Now we were flying sharply toward Yucca Flat, where we should see the remains of Annie and Nancy. We

passed French Peak and then News Nob and suddenly scuttled down toward
another expanse of nondescript alkali playa.

I immediately spotted the Doom Town house, the one wooden frame
still standing. It appeared somewhat isolated because the surrounding
cars had been taken back to Las Vegas. The dummies were gone, too. Like
the cars, they also were being displayed around the country by the Civil
Defense Agency and various contributing commercial interests. I sighed,
and remarked about how lonely the deserted village appeared, like a ghost
town after most of it has decayed into dust.

Dr. C asked the pilot to parallel the soldiers' trenches, back and forth, so
he could see how the reinforced dirt walls had withstood the latest blast.
Because I always have my eye on my job, I wondered if I should be taking
notes, but Dr. C shouted that it wasn't necessary. For one thing, it was really
too loud inside the helicopter to conduct any extended conversation. And
besides, we weren't inspecting Yucca Flat in any official capacity, just trying
to get a bird's-eye view. Our real goal today was Groom Lake and the ill-fated
Madison Mine.

The helicopter looped onto a northeast trajectory that took us over a
series of high buttes. The sergeant called the landmarks by name. Survey, Oak
Spring, Slanted Buttes, the Rhyolite Hills. I loved the scenery. Junipers, colorful rocks, flat-topped mesas alternating with bone-white playas. As colorful as New Mexico, sometimes like the red-layered browns just west of Albuquerque, sometimes like the dark folded cliffs of the Sandia Mountains to
the east. *Remember how you used to tell me about the flights over White Sands?*
The Nevada Proving Ground, from the air, was sort of like that. Starkly beautiful. Different, khaki-colored instead of silver-white, but nakedly gorgeous
in its own special way. It almost felt like home. The best kind of home. Not
the ugly Mercury dormitory kind.

Just as I was relaxing (and dreaming a little), the helicopter lurched, gy-
rating like a bucking bronco at a rodeo. I clutched my hands together, then
realized the pilot was playing in the wind, tracking a widespread herd of
antelope along a ridgeline and making them run from the unfamiliar sound
of the rotor. I adored the creatures' wildness, their white rumps pivoting
south to north. The Texas-born pilot grinned. One of his favorite sidelines,
he drawled, was herding Nevada antelope from the sky.

Another few minutes of flying time, and the helicopter slowed and began
circling over Groom Lake. The dry lake bed was undistinguished, just another

flat spot in the corrugated terrain, but without any atomic scars. The mining operation sat slightly north of the playa (funny, that all that aridity is called a lake), but it was difficult to see either the shaft or any excavation tucked into the jagged edges of the Groom Range. Buried on a north-to-south parallel, the adit itself was nearly invisible. Finally the sergeant located a ramshackle building with a couple of old trucks parked just outside. Apparently the miners were still working underground.

As the pilot hovered the aircraft, Dr. C and the sergeant examined what little they could see of the lead and silver operation. About a dozen cabins and outbuildings. That was all. Their sheet-metal sides lay in tatters, stripped and twisted off by some violent force, undoubtedly atomic. It appeared as though most of the windows had been broken, too. Meanwhile, I tried to recall the details about Nancy's atomic cloud. The fallout, with all those high roentgen numbers, had swirled directly over the mine, contaminating at least briefly all the immediate surroundings. Three hundred? Five hundred? An up and down circular carousel of high-level radiation. Dr. C interrupted my train of thought by pointing to another pair of buildings not far away, where a research group from UCLA, working with rabbits, housed their experiments. Unlike the miners, that group had heeded advance warnings, evacuating immediately once the cloud began traveling in their direction. The miners chose not to leave, and now the miners were upset.

Even as Nancy's atomic cloud began its mushroom ascent, press releases had been issued to reassure the public, insisting that every safety precaution was being taken and that there was never any need for concern. I knew there often was a discrepancy between what the AEC said publicly and what its coded messages revealed, but like all the other good citizens at the Proving Ground, I always shrugged off the variance. A little radiation in the middle of nowhere seemed to me a small price to pay for the knowledge gained. I glanced proudly toward Dr. C, knowing he would surely agree.

His mind was on the geography stretched out beneath us. Dr. C wanted to know how far we were from Nancy's ground zero, as the crow flies. The answer was precise. Thirty-five klicks. Too close for cloud comfort. I asked about aftershocks. The memo said nothing about aftershocks, but the miners may have felt the effects underground. Dr. C volunteered that yes, the miners were complaining about the shocks, too, and angry about the dirt and rocks that had fallen inside the shaft. Dr. C dismissed their concerns, though, as the cost of doing business.

Then he asked the pilot to widen our range, to fly farther east so he could see for himself the scant population. He checked his map. Some ranches beyond Groom Lake. A couple of little towns, Alamo and Hiko. A trio of bigger ones farther to the east, Pioche, Panaca, and Caliente. None of them with more than a few hundred residents, or maybe a thousand. Dr. C would never use the word "expendable," but if he compared an Alamo or a Caliente with a New York or a San Francisco, he and all the others easily justified the value of atomic testing in the desert. The AEC would take precautions, but no matter what complications might arise, the testing would continue without fail.

Our helicopter dipped over a series of green pastures that looked out of place in the dry desert surroundings. To the south, I saw what looked like a shallow lake, with actual water splashing against shores lined with cottonwoods. Before I could ask about it, the pilot pointed down and called out an old Indian name. Pahranagat, a wildlife refuge with good birding. Supposed to be a nice place to go camping, if anyone had the time or inclination. *Can you imagine me sleeping anywhere in a tent?* And surely not way out here. My idea of a night away from Mercury involves a steak dinner and a private room at Las Vegas's Desert Inn.

Picking up both speed and altitude, the helicopter lifted over another rocky ridge and dropped along a broader valley of green, pausing to hover over each of the three little communities that line up south to north, the middle one smaller than the other two. I was aghast at the isolation. I wondered how on earth they make a living in such a godforsaken place. Dr. C shouted that people do earn livelihoods in what's called the Meadow Valley. Mining to the north and ranching to the south, all pretty much subsistence level these days. He didn't believe anyone was getting rich anywhere nearby.

He soon decided he'd seen enough, and ordered the pilot to turn back toward the Proving Ground. With that, the helicopter bent in a U-shaped half-circle, rotoring speedily to the south and west. I was sorry. I wished we could fly on forever. I moved my eyes from the ground to the sky, and dreamed again of you. *Today would have been too tame for you, but I could feel your presence anyway. I missed you, Buzz, as always.*

Pale cumulus clouds glided past the helicopter. I smiled my secret smile.

When we reached Yucca Flat again, Dr. C asked the pilot to fly over the tower where the third shot will be detonated the day after tomorrow. I loved the fact that the next test is named Ruth. I knew the choice had nothing whatsoever to do with me (the Livermore boys chose it, not the Los Alamos crew), but I liked to imagine otherwise. I hoped it would be a sensational shot, though I realize Dr. C doesn't have much faith in the Livermore scientists. If he had his way, the entire Upshot-Knothole series would be Los Alamos driven.

The helicopter hovered above the tower that will hold the gadget called Ruth. I could see technicians and craftsmen at almost every level of the steel structure. The entire scene resembled an anthill, the tiny figures scurrying about their business.

Mercury looked like an anthill, too. When we flew over it, the pilot hung the chopper in the sky, and gave me time to pick out the cafeteria and then my dorm on Trinity Avenue. I was delighted. Wait 'til I tell the boys about my bird's-eye view. I felt almost euphoric. How long until I can work up my nerve and ask Dr. C for another flight?

I wouldn't wish for another bad luck memo, though. First I was fretting about Dennis Rutherford; now I'm worried about foolish LaMar Madison and the other miners. Even though Dr. C reassured me that the chief will check on them again in a few days and that they'll be fine, I couldn't forget the radiation numbers that were too high for "they'll be fine." I'd never question Dr. C's judgment, though. And tomorrow I'll probably type the memorandum to the AEC that explains the incident away. The wind was gusting, the actual time sequence was rapid, the men stayed deep underground inside the mine. Nothing to worry about. I could almost dictate the memo myself.

Nothing to worry about. I put everything out of my mind except the glorious helicopter ride and my first view of the Proving Ground from the air. I couldn't be happier.

That night I told my partners every detail I could remember about Frenchman and Yucca Flats. I pictured the Ruth tower for them, and compared its surroundings with the pitted places where previous tests occurred. Another three days, and that part of Yucca Flat will be bomb-scalloped, too. I described News Nob, where the reporters and their cameramen congregate in the early-morning hours before each blast. By day and by air, it's nondescript, a rocky knoll hardly worth mentioning. Mercury, though—I could have hovered over Mercury all day. The Queen of Hearts loved looking down from on high. Now I was lording it over my friends. I can't wait to fly again.

What I didn't describe was the remainder of the flight, the inspection of Groom Lake and the Madison Mine. Not allowed to explain why we flew to that particular spot, I just didn't mention it at all. I didn't tell the boys about the rural communities, either. It sounded harsh to characterize them as insignificant, too isolated, too Mormon, too small. Better to keep that part of the helicopter ride to myself, just as I never said Dennis's name out loud, just as I mustn't comment on "psychologic resistance" or on "emotional vaccination." Some words are best left unsaid. *I didn't tell them I dreamed of you, either. I never do.*

The Queen of Hearts found words for other things that night, though. My luck held in every way. I bid and made four hearts, bid and made four spades, bid and made another baby slam. Howard passed the Southern Comfort to toast my many successes. Even Don and Ralph succumbed, taking tiny sips while they saluted my almost-perfect day.

"Atta girl, Ruthie!" they shouted in unison. "Atta girl!"

Ruth

Ruth is a bust, as atomic tests go. She thuds onto Yucca Flat from a 300-foot tower and yields only 0.2 kiloton, far less energy than expected. The top of her mushroom cloud barely clears 13,600 feet. The on-site fallout turns out to be minimal. One observer notes that there seem to be more planes in the sky than such a piss-poor experiment should warrant. Twenty-two aircraft, to be exact. A P2V circles the radiation area in a cloverleaf pattern, starting at 6,000 feet above the desert and climbing in 500-foot increments. A C-47 flies in a holding pattern at 10,000 feet south of ground zero until the blast occurs. For the next fifteen minutes, onboard personnel photograph the mini–mushroom cloud's development and dispersal. A B-29, nicknamed "Catnip," spends a total of 132 minutes sampling the radiation cloud. An F-84G, called "Snooper," precedes Catnip to ensure that the nine-man Catnip crew will all be safe. After the flights land at Indian Springs, the pilots and crew members are monitored and their flight suits decontaminated as necessary. Shirt-sleeved privates and corporals then hose down the aircraft, while helicopters hover nearby.

Hal

From Newton, Massachusetts, to Cactus Springs, Nevada. Via Normandy. And Baltimore. And Dallas. A real pathway to success. Zigzagging. Ending, for now, in the empty desert, tending bar. Hal draws two more pitchers of beer for the flyboys, pours a scotch and soda plus a Jim Beam with water back for the pair of majors, shakes two martinis for the men in suits. Not much action tonight, although Sally is doing her best. Short black skirt, tight white sweater, hose and spiked heels, she sways from table to table. The men like to watch her work, tend to order more booze when she's around. Filling the beer drinkers' mugs, she leans over each pilot, flirts a little, brushes her hand across the back of a lieutenant's neck, pats another one's shoulder. Smiling, Hal sets up another round.

The door swings open, and half a dozen more customers enter the smoky room, followed by a blast of frigid night air. Maybe business will pick up after all. It should, the night after Nancy's detonation, in a bar halfway between the Indian Springs Air Force Base and the Mercury entrance to the Nevada Proving Ground. No other place to drink. Not for fifty miles. The six men commandeer the largest remaining table, settle into their chairs, take off their coats, shout to the bartender to hurry up. Sally's still busy with the Air Force, so Hal takes orders from the new clientele. More pitchers of beer. Coors this time, instead of Schlitz. Only two kinds on tap, here in the middle of nowhere. Lucky to have two choices.

One of the newcomers walks over to the jukebox, drops in a quarter, and punches all the Kay Starr numbers he can find. "Wheel of Fortune" spins through the smoke. Hal draws a pitcher, gathers six frosty mugs from the icebox, and heads back to the table. The men smile as he pours the frothy brew. One fellow, who seems to be in charge, lifts his glass to make a toast. The others follow suit. With a towel, Hal wipes a corner of the table where a little beer sloshed over. He listens.

"Here's to Jackson."

"Mr. Fix-It."

"What a great idea. Paving the desert."

"Tamped down all the dust."

"What'd you put in the slurry?"

"A combo of desert dirt and good old-fashioned cement."

"And don't forget the alkali water. Gotta have the alkali water."

"Made a cement mat two inches thick."

"And sprayed with sodium silicate. More salt, like the desert."

"Sure did work."

"Yeah. And Nancy was a dusty one. Most desert stirred up so far."

"Now we can go ahead and lay down more cement. ASAP."

"Yeah. Jackson says we'll need 700,000 square yards by the time that atomic cannon's ready to fire."

"In . . . credible!"

"Jackson plans to use vacuum cleaners, too."

"Huh? I didn't hear about that."

"After we got the pavement laid, we used a power vac every six hours or so. Do that for the cannon, and we'll keep the dust to a minimum."

"The plastic bags helped, too."

"Clean lenses until almost the last minute."

"When did you finally pull off the covers?"

"Two and a half hours before shot time."

"Short window."

"You bet. We hopped in there, stripped off the plastic, loaded the film, and came back to the trailer as fast as we could."

"Any exposure worries?"

"Nah, I think that's a dead horse."

"How so?"

"Each gadget generates a whole range of light intensity. So some film's bound to be overexposed, some under, and some just right. The trick is to line up a bunch of cameras and set 'em all differently. Sure to end up with some beauties that way."

"When'll you know for sure?"

"Just a day or two. Cessna flew out to L.A. at noon today. Carrying two hundred pounds of film."

"And there's more going out tonight."

"Right. Mike and I spent the whole afternoon unloading camera after camera."

"Is that why your eyes are gleaming?"

"Funny!"

"Seriously, do you ever worry about the radiation?"

"Nope. Never. We wear coveralls and bootees and caps on our heads. And we don't stay out there very long at all. I think we're safer than you guys, in fact."

"Why?"

"'Cause after we get all our remote-controlled cameras set up, we watch the shots from inside the trailer. You're outside, in the open, taking moving pictures."

"We're far away from ground zero, though. Never even get close."

"How far?"

"About four miles. Give or take. And they always put us upwind."

"As long as the wind stays in the same direction."

"Hasn't shifted so far. Besides, the Army is looking after us. Our badges tell us so."

"The way we look after our cameras?"

"That was a fluke."

"What was a fluke?"

"The camera that did a back flip in the air during Annie. Blast tore it right off its casing."

"Did you see the results?"

"Yeah! Terrific photos of flying desert dirt. Horizon tilting in the background. Then boom! No more pictures! Lucky the film wasn't totally ruined."

"Had to send the camera back to Lookout Mountain. Needed some serious cleaning and recalibration."

"Better watch what you're saying, Mike."

"How so?"

"Lookout Mountain. Not supposed to say the words."

"Ah, nobody's listening. And if they are, they won't know what we're talking about anyway."

By now Hal has turned his back on the photographers' table and is checking to see how the two martinis are doing. They need another round. So do the photographers. One stands up as Hal walks back toward the bar. The Lookout Mountain employee waggles a finger, then two. Hal nods, smiling to himself as he pulls out two clean pitchers and begins to draw the Coors. Not much head. Just a little. The way these boys like it. Lookout Mountain, indeed. Top secret base in the Hollywood Hills, where all the Upshot-Knothole photography is developed. Very hush-hush. No one's supposed to know about it. But everybody does.

As he fills the pitchers, Hal keeps an eye on a lone man sitting at the bar.

The fellow has been here several nights recently. Looks like a prospector, and not a prosperous one. Says he's hunting for gold in what's called the Specter Range. Southeast of the Proving Ground. Odd, to come this far for booze, though there's really nothing closer. Always orders a single beer, then waits for someone else to buy another round. Gregarious guy, likes to talk. Doesn't say much about himself, though. Won't say exactly where his claim lies or why he's here in Cactus Springs. Hal'd like to know more. Last Wednesday he saw the prospector talking to another customer, someone from Mercury, though Hal couldn't pin down the man's job there. Not military, no uniform. Maybe a scientist. Or an engineer. Whatever, the conversation went on for a long time, with lots of gestures. The men kept their voices down, though, so Hal couldn't hear what they were saying. Odd. Very odd.

Sally interrupts his train of thought, tells him the two suits are asking for their martinis. And the photographers want their beer. Better keep an eye on the paying customers, instead of the deadbeat at the bar. Hal pushes the full pitchers Sally's way. Let her pick up the photographers' tips. They're always generous. Then Hal mixes the martinis, carefully. He'll deliver those himself. Hand the tips over to her later. Hal likes Sally. She loosens everybody up. But she hasn't had any luck with the prospector. Doesn't trust him. Thinks he has shifty eyes. Says he don't smell right either. Clean, when he ought to be musty. Worse yet, according to Sally, he never tips. Not at all. Deadbeat. That's what she calls him. Deadbeat.

Hal nods at the man as he picks up the martinis. The fellow lifts his half-empty beer mug, sips a little, doesn't make eye contact. As Hal moves toward his customers, the tall photographer goes back to the jukebox. Punches in another quarter's worth of songs. More Kay Starr. The prospector joins him. They chat a little, then the photographer gestures toward his table. The prospector nods, pulls up a vacant chair. Holds his mug out. Someone tops it off. Deadbeat. Hal turns to the two suits, makes change for a five-dollar bill. Wipes their table with his towel. Listens. Nothing there. Just two salesmen on the road. Taking a break. Heading for Las Vegas. Got bored with the drive.

Hal pockets the tip for Sally, walks slowly back across the room, pauses at the big table, asks the cameramen if they'd like another round. Not just yet. Later, for sure. They're busy with Sally right now, telling her more than she wants to know about apertures and focus. The prospector is engaged in conversation, too, asking questions about camera precautions. Mike and Phil are happy to answer.

"Shield 'em in lead boxes."

"Inside concrete bunkers."

"Turn 'em backwards, too."

"How does that work?"

"Mirrors. Mounted at the tops of the boxes, then screwed at a forty-five-degree angle."

"Wire trips the mirrors. We send the signal from our trailer, and bingo. The wire breaks and a counterweight drops."

"Sets everything in the right position. At the right degree, and ready to go."

"I don't think I understand."

"Here. I'll draw you a picture."

Hal watches the garrulous photographer, Mike, apparently, reach for a napkin and then for a stub of pencil in his pocket. He diagrams the setup, showing exactly how the thick lead glass plate operates, how the mirrored image comes out right side up and correctly realigned. The prospector, fascinated, asks more questions about the camera work. Before long, the conversation turns to blast line photography. Mike calls it Project 1.2. His buddies got edgy when Mike blurted out the words "Lookout Mountain." Now they don't seem to care that he's sketching out a classified mechanism and explaining a top secret operation. Maybe it's the beer.

"Blast line photography. That's when you take pictures of the shock wave."

"Right after a device explodes."

"How's that work?"

"Well, you need a smoke line and a rocket line. Set 'em off just before a countdown hits zero."

"That gives you a triple point."

"What's that?"

"Intersection of the incident, plus reflected and Mach shock waves."

"You get other blast phenomena, too. Like the precursor."

"Boys, that's too complicated for me."

"Actually, it's really simple. The refraction of light. That's what makes it all work. And air density."

"Here. I'll draw you another diagram." Grabbing a clean napkin, Mike pencils in ground zero with a blast line going one direction and a smoke line going the other. Intersecting the smoke line is the rocket line, with half a dozen camera points lined up left to right. "People always ask about the funny lines in the pictures," he says. "The hooks and crooks. That's the shock wave bucking up against the rocket smoke. Kinda nifty, don't you think?"

"Whoever thought of that?"

"Herb Grier. He's one of the Gs in Egg."

"Egg? What's that?"

"EG&G. The company we work for. Edgerton, Germeshausen, and Grier."

"They know all there is to know about high-speed photography."

"Special camera for that?"

"Yeah. It's called a Rapatronic."

"How's it work?"

"A magneto-optical shutter. Operated by remote control. That's what we put in the cement camera banks. Six, eight, ten, as many as sixteen Rapatronics, clicking a millionth of a second apart. Like a movie. Only more so."

"Draw me another picture."

"Better not, I've already said too much."

"Sorry. Didn't mean to ask too many questions. Just curious, I guess. I don't know much about photography at all."

"What do you do, anyway?"

"Just picking around the hills. Looking for gold."

"Where? I thought everything around here was restricted."

"Oh, here and there. Nothing near the Proving Ground. More toward the south."

The prospector pushes his mug to the center of the table. Mike hoists the pitcher, now nearly empty. Another cameraman signals Hal. Time for another round. The bartender fills one more pitcher, and gets out clean icy mugs. Gotta be good to these guys. They spend a lot of time and money in Cactus Springs. Sally picks up the tray, carries it to the table. She's not surprised to see that Hal added an extra mug for the prospector. Nice guy, Hal. She wonders, as she does so often, what he's doing in a place like this. He seems like a city boy, and Cactus Springs ain't no city. In his own way, Hal's as mysterious as the prospector. Cuter, though. Sally wishes she could go to town with him someday. He's never asked. He makes the trip every other week, like clockwork. She wonders what Hal does there. This and that, he answers. Laundry. Maybe drop a few nickels in the slots. Catch a movie. Catch a show. He never stays overnight, so there must not be a girlfriend. Strange man, Hal. But Sally likes him. Appreciates the cut of his Levi's, and the way his western shirts snug over his shoulders. A handsome man, well built. He must have been in the Army, once upon a time, but he never says. A drifter now, apparently. Bartender in Cactus Springs this year. Somewhere else the next.

Sally finishes serving the photographers and saunters back to the pilots. They're getting noisier and noisier. Maybe time to cut them off. She glances toward Hal, but he's watching the camera guys instead. Seems fascinated by the conversation. Maybe he's into shutters and apertures and all that nonsense. Bores her silly, that's what it does.

Turns out Hal's just being a good employee, making the rounds, trying to take more orders, though it's getting late and most of the men are tapering off. He laughs with the boys, cleaning up the clutter, wiping spilled beer off the tables. The martini men are finished with their drinks, ready to hit the road again. Hal invites them to stop by on their way back north. They smile, and say they might. He pauses by the two majors, who immediately stop their serious discussion about something and begin to joke instead. No more booze for them tonight, either. Busy day tomorrow. They push back their chairs and put on their caps. The photographers decide to call it quits, too. They've got work to do in the morning, making sure every camera's still working, maybe setting up some new locations.

"More desert pavement coming up, Jackson?"

"Absolutely!"

"Just don't make us any more of those Monsters. They're heavy as hell."

"What's a Monster?" Inquisitive, that prospector.

"The protective housing. Have to lift up the top part to get at the cameras between shots. Feels like it weighs a ton. Monsters."

"You boys have it all figured out, don't you?"

"Well, we try to come up with something new every week. Each gadget's a new challenge."

"Ever get any time off?"

"Not much. Sometimes a quick trip to Lookout Mountain, but usually we're stuck here."

"Mike. Enough of that."

"Ah, don't worry. We're among friends."

"This Lookout Mountain place sounds pretty special."

"Nothing we can talk about, though."

"Not even a hint?"

"I s'pose it's okay to say it's where the film goes to be processed. A kind of atomic archive. And where the Egg bosses hatch new ways of doing things."

"Nearby?"

"That's something I really can't talk about. They'd have my head on a platter."

"Earlier, you said something about L.A."

"No reason to connect the dots."

"I can't resist."

"How come you're so curious?"

"I dunno. Bored, I guess. Wandering around by myself all day, nobody to talk to. Just good to have a conversation for a change."

The prospector follows the cameramen outside, climbs into a battered Chevy, and drives away. Hal watches until the pickup turns right, steers toward Mercury. Then he jostles the pilots out the door. Not too steady on their feet. Fortunately, they don't have far to drive. Once the place empties out, he and Sally tidy up. She empties ashtrays. He sweeps the floor, pushing a heavy commercial broom back and forth from one wall to the other. Then, after handing her the extra tips he collected, Hal sends Sally on her way, saying he'll take care of the trash. She's glad to get off her feet. It's been a long day.

MOST WEEKS follow a pattern at the Cactus Springs bar. Leading up to a test, not much business at all. The night right before a test, Hal generally takes off. Not much point in hanging around pouring nothing. The night after a test, though, and a few evenings after that, lots of men on the loose. Unwinding. Celebrating. Perfect weather. A yield greater than expected. A successful remote-control mechanism. Or complaining. About a camera flipping off its mooring. Or an engine overheating. Or a dust cloud obliterating everything in sight. Then everybody at Mercury, at Indian Springs, at Lookout Mountain, gets busy again, under pressure to get themselves and their equipment ready for the next shot.

After Ruth, the grousing is particularly loud. Two-tenths of a kiloton, for God's sake. Hardly worth the effort. Didn't generate enough radiation to get much data at all. All kinds of stuff gone wrong. Inaudible radio transmissions. Dust everywhere. Acrid smells. Engine failure. And the unexpectedly poor yield. Hal's regulars are not only noisy, they're ready to drink. Air Force on one side of the room. Cameramen on the other. And what looks like a radiation survey team in between. Plus the ever-present prospector, back at the bar but eager for more conversation.

When the photographers come in, the prospector looks their way. Soon joins the tall one at the jukebox. Hal hopes the prospector's saying "No more Kay Starr," but no such luck. Unfortunately, from Hal's point of view, another "Wheel of Fortune." And another. Busy filling pitchers, the bartender doesn't have a moment to sip his tepid coffee. He watches the prospector join Mike and his friends, though. Everyone's talking at once about the Ruth fiasco. Even Sally, flirting as usual, can't get the men off target tonight. The radiation team members are loud. Especially agitated. Taking them a third pitcher, Hal listens.

"Might as well have turned off the radios."

"Couldn't hear a damned thing."

"Colonel Smith, cozy in the Plotting and Briefing Room, he could hear us."

"Nice not to hear him for a change."

"Yeah. But in the long run that makes more work."

"Do we really have to go out there tomorrow?"

"And measure all over again?"

"That's affirmative."

"Oughta be in bed, instead of in a bar."

"We're not at Boy Scout camp."

"Besides, the major'll never hear us coming back to the dorm. He's got better things to do than stay up and count noses."

"Yeah. Like getting those radios fixed."

"I know what we can say if he gives us any heat."

"What?"

"Combating radiation."

"Huh?"

"That's what we're doing. Combating radiation with beer."

"That's silly."

"No, it's true. Remember what happened to Dennis?"

"Of course. He's on a permanent Las Vegas vacation 'cause his badge turned red."

"As did his neck."

"'Cause he didn't tape down his hood."

"And 'cause he's never had a beer. At least not for years. Doesn't like the taste."

"So what's the connection?"

"If Dennis was a beer drinker, he'd still be on the job."

"You've lost your mind."

"Nope. It's the hops. They hop all those gamma rays right on out of our systems."

"Prove it."

"Easy. Dennis doesn't drink beer, and the radiation got to him last month. Last year, too."

"So?"

"In contrast, you're not incandescent, are you?"

"Of course not."

"Then it's working."

"What's working?"

"The hops. Hopping."

Hal can't resist groaning, though he wonders about poor Dennis. Kind of a cowboy. Used to be a good customer. Canadian Club and 7 UP, with a squeeze of lemon. Never a beer. Turning away from the raucous rad table, Hal moves toward the Air Force lieutenants. They're loud, too. Just as frustrated. The two helicopter pilots were in on the communications snafu. Hovering here and there. Didn't know where to be because they couldn't hear anything from the ground. Waste of time and fuel. Hell of a way to run an outfit. They'll have to be in the air tomorrow, too. With headaches. Their buddy, who flies an F-84G aircraft, gets the day off. He buys another round.

When Hal first went to work at Cactus Springs, he couldn't pinpoint anyone's exact atomic testing job. Three months at the bar, and he knows a lot more. The men were tight-lipped at first, at least until someone pours a third beer. Hal happily obliges. He's background now. Part of the furniture. If the drinkers notice anyone, it's Sally. She happily obliges, too. The two synchronize like clockwork, circling the room, urging everyone to buy more booze. Hal's far more effective than last year's dud. Clarence. Who ever heard of a bartender named Clarence? Acted just like his name. Easy to replace. Hal, on the other hand, fits right in.

"Thirteen minutes. I was only in the air thirteen minutes. Stupid tiptank malfunction. Down I come."

"How many planes up there this time?"

"I dunno exactly. About two dozen."

"Nine red, white, and blue Tigers, for sure."

"Tiger Red 2 got four penetrations."

"Lucky stiff. I only got one."

"That's 'cause you're a Tiger Blue. End of the line. Always."

"Better a Tiger than a Catnip."

"For sure. I was up there for nearly two hours, and didn't get a whiff."

"I'm still ticked off about my Snooper. Hope they get that tiptank fixed."

"Let's change the subject. How 'bout a little pool?"

"Rotation?"

"Sure."

Snooper, two Tigers, and a Catnip take over the empty pool table. Choose up sides. Begin to play. Hal pauses to watch for a minute or two. He loves pool. Never gets to join in, at least not here in Cactus Springs. A couple photographers wander over, plus a rad specialist, and an engineer. The prospector follows. They all watch together. When Kay Starr winds down in the background, the rad man moves quickly to the jukebox. Shoves in two quarters. Ten plays. Patti Page. No Kay Starr. Snooper pockets the nine ball. Trick shot. Ricochet. His partner, Catnip, cheers. He's on a run. Ten. Eleven. Twelve. Straight through to the finish. They win.

Now everyone wants to play. The two Tigers give way to two photographers, who promptly lose the next game. They laugh, and order another pitcher. The two Tigers try again. Without any luck. They stand aside, replaced by a pair from the radiation team. Watching the pilots carefully, the prospector finally edges alongside them, holds out his glass, asks them about their lousy day.

"Just routine," is the answer.

"Except the decontamination process took too damned long. Always does. Hard to sit inside, canopies closed, while they haul away the cloud samples. Stuffy as hell!"

"Then we're supposed to climb out without touching anything."

"Almost impossible in full gear."

"Dangerous?"

"Riskier to touch the plane than to fly into the cloud."

"Flying's the best part."

"In and out of all those colors. You feel like you're in the *Wizard of Oz*."

"Here come Wally and Todd. Ask 'em about the rainbow."

Two latecomers join the men standing near the pool table. Hal doesn't remember seeing them before. Doesn't take long to figure 'em out, though. One's a pilot, flies a C-47 nicknamed Skytrain. The other's a photographer, who takes pictures from a perch in the plane's nose. He's got the best job, to hear him tell it. Ribs his fellow cameramen. Wears an honorary Air Force cap. Talkative. Eager to boast. The prospector soon joins the conversation. Flatters Todd, who's even more talkative than Mike.

"Tight up there?" the prospector asks.

"Wedged flat on my stomach. In the stench." Todd sniggers.

"Stench?"

"Good old C-47 perfume. Leather and hydraulic fluid. Pilots love it. Makes me wanna puke."

"Hard to do. In the nose of a plane."

"Yeah. Damned uncomfortable. But worth it. Great pictures."

"Movie camera, or stills?"

"Movie. To track how the cloud climbs upward."

"So you fly over the cloud."

"First we aim right over ground zero. At the zero hour. Then make a pass directly back."

"Though the cloud?"

"No, before it rises as high as we're flying."

"How high's that?"

"Ten thousand feet."

"How long does that take?"

"Just a few minutes. Maybe five."

"Sounds tricky."

"It is. Have to time the shock wave, too. That's more worrisome than the cloud."

"Why?"

"Shock wave can bounce you around pretty good. Even tear the wings off a plane."

"So how do you avoid it?"

"That's Wally's job. The trick is to be heading away when the shock wave hits, so it slams into the aircraft tail first. If it gets you from the side, you're a goner. That'd make too much torque, and the wings couldn't stand the stress."

"So you fly over the blast. And then you're gone."

"Yep. We take off about an hour before shot time, hang out about 16 klicks south of ground zero. Then shoot in at the last minute. Only takes a few minutes."

"Hey, Todd. You're talking too much."

"Not a problem. Mike introduced me. Says this guy's okay."

"I don't mean to be nosy. I'm just interested." The prospector acts contrite.

"He's looking for gold."

"Us, too. In the clouds."

"Early prospectors around here, nobody ever found much."

"Except in Rhyolite. Big boomtown at the start of the century."

"Ever been there?"

"Sure. Lots of times. Almost a ghost town now. Just a few people living in a couple of old houses. Biggest building's the train station, still a real beauty. Starting to crumble, though."

"What's it look like?"

"Been to L.A.?"

"Plenty of times, mostly work-related."

"Well, Rhyolite's train station looks like L.A.'s. Same architect."

"Oh. I've only been to the L.A. airport. Never Union Station. I should go there sometime. Look around."

"Do you fly in often?"

"'Bout once a month."

"Go to Lookout Mountain?"

"How in hell do you know about Lookout Mountain?"

"I thought everybody knew."

"Not supposed to."

"Where, exactly, is it? I forget."

"Hollywood Hills, near the big sign."

"Todd, shut your mouth."

"It's okay. I'm not saying anything this guy doesn't already know."

"Hollywood Hills. That's Laurel Canyon, isn't it?"

"See? I told you he already knows."

"Todd, just shut the hell up."

Hal is listening as intently as the prospector. Give these men a few beers after a dusty desert day, and they can't seem to stop talking. He wonders, for maybe the hundredth time, about the prospector's angle. He's clearly milking the photographers for information, but what he's getting is pretty superficial. The other night, though, he was in the corner with the same guy as before, the one who makes all the gestures. Hal still hasn't figured out the connection. Doesn't know what the man does for a living. Or if he even works at Mercury. Unlikely to be here if he doesn't, though. Only Cactus Springs customers are the locals, military and Proving Ground men. And occasional drive-throughs, like the salesmen last week.

Sally swings her hips as she passes him. Nudges Hal with her elbow. Wonders why he's just standing there when there's so much work to do. Hal busies himself, wiping tables, busing glasses. He puts on a pot of fresh Maxwell House, knowing some of the men will need coffee before they leave the bar. Especially the ones who have to work out on the playa tomorrow.

Hal grins. Two regulars lean against the bar. Not regular drinkers, just regular customers. The one named Howard orders a bottle of Southern Comfort. Ugh! Ralph, a couple of six-packs of beer. They'll haul their stash back to Mercury, as they do every week. Never miss. Say they're bridge players. Need to wet their whistles while they play. Or afterwards. If they lose. Howard says he rarely loses. Ralph isn't quite so sure. They're good sports, both of them. Hal enjoys chatting with the two.

After they leave, he comes out from behind the bar, until Sally holds up her hand. Motions him backwards. Calls for three more pitchers. Two Schlitz. One Coors. And some icy mugs. Not many left in the icebox. If this keeps up, he'll have to wash dishes. Nights like this, they could use a busboy. But then, Hal thinks to himself, no excuse to clean up the tables. He'd miss the conversations. Never get to know customers. Never learn what they're thinking about. And talking about. Those photographers. Just can't keep their mouths shut. Flyboys aren't much better, though they never reveal any technical details. Air Force'd muster 'em right out of the service if they blab about their planes. Hal's nearing Todd and Wally and the prospector now. They don't look like they've missed a beat, though their words are more slurred than before.

"So next week's an air drop. Dixie."

"Coming in from Albuquerque."

"What time?"

"I dunno exactly. Somewheres after sunrise. And we get to fly right in behind her. See the blast. Take photos. Then chase on through before the cloud rises. And the shock wave hits."

"Gotta time it just right."

"You bet. Not a problem for Wally. He's a real pro. Trust him with my life."

WHEN DIXIE ROLLS IN from Kirtland Air Force Base, Wally's C-47 is right behind the B-50 bomber. And Todd's got his camera clicking away. Mike and Jackson are peering out their trailer window, trusting that their remote-control Rapatronic triggers are working well. Five of the other photographers are out on the playa, filming the airburst and subsequent mushroom cloud. The prospector? Doing whatever he does when he's looking for treasure. Somewhere in the desert. Watching the sky. Sally, too. She always gets up early on shot days. Loves the shapes and colors. A potpourri of colors. Hal taught her that big word. This morning, Hal's indifferent, sound asleep. Late trip back from Las Vegas the night before. He needs to get some shut-eye before the evening's onslaught of Cactus Springs customers.

THE BIWEEKLY LAS VEGAS MEETING went well. Hal met Patrick at the usual time, 11 A.M., in the casino coffee shop of the Last Frontier. After the breakfast crowd, and before lunch. Choosing their regular booth in the corner, Hal took the seat with the best view of the room and ordered a cup of black coffee. He liked the extra space, so he could stretch out his legs. He set his Stetson on the bench beside him. Patrick arrived a few minutes later, held up by a last-minute phone call, he said. Nattily dressed as always, wearing a blue blazer, white shirt, and red tie this sunny April morning, Patrick smiled at the waitress and ordered coffee with cream, plus a sugared bear claw.

As soon as the waitress turned away, Patrick got right to business. Pulling a legal pad from his briefcase and setting it squarely on the table, he looked over at Hal. "What have you got?"

The answer turned out to be lots of bits and pieces but nothing substantial. Hal started out talking about the photographers, how overly talkative they are and how indiscriminately they blurt out semi-classified information. Like where Lookout Mountain might be and what it might contain. Patrick frowned, and made a note. While he wrote, Hal pulled an envelope from his shirt pocket and lifted the flap. Inside were two napkins, covered with writing. Hal explained how one cameraman named Mike had diagrammed the details of both blast line photography and high-speed Rapatronic reverse image filmmaking. And he observed that it was a good thing Mike wasn't a scientist, or he'd be drawing nuclear equations on Cactus Springs cocktail napkins. Patrick shook his head. The sketches were probably innocuous, but Mike ought to be more discreet.

Then Hal began describing the prospector. He'd talked about the odd duck before, last month, after shot Annie, but now he had more information to disclose. For one thing, the guy was hanging around the bar more and more evenings, and sidling up to more and more different customers. He could just be cadging free beer, or he could have more ominous intentions. Hard to tell, at this point. Hal shared Sally's observations with Patrick. The shifty eyes, which Hal had noticed too. And the way the prospector smelled, or didn't. She even thought he might be younger than he pretended. Then the bartender added his own thoughts about the fellow's ingratiating ways. Patrick asked lots of questions about the jobs of the men the prospector liked to sit with—no pattern there. And about the total lack of information Hal had been able to get out of him. Nothing added up.

Patrick looked over at his partner and said, "You've got to get me more."

Hal's eyes twinkled and his mouth twisted into an edgy smirk. Shifting onto one hip, he reached in his Levi's pocket, pulled out a film canister, and flipped it across the table. Patrick caught it on the fly. Then Hal explained how he took the pictures, surreptitiously, in the bar. He pretended the flash on his Argus was only working sporadically, and asked the photographer crew if anyone could help him out. They were delighted. Mike wasn't all bad after all. He had the flash mechanism fixed in no time. Of course Hal had to try the Argus out, right then and there. Make sure everything was okay. He chuckled. He'd used up a whole roll of film. The prospector ducked his head, but Hal was pretty sure he'd gotten at least a shot or two of his face. Couldn't be absolutely sure, because the pictures were still undeveloped. Patrick could attend to that, and then follow up.

Patrick wrapped his fingers around the canister with its precious cartridge inside. Maybe they could get a line on this guy after all, either stop worrying about him or start tracking him. Whichever. "Anything else?" Hal paused, then flashed a wicked smile. He rummaged around in the jacket folded beside his Stetson. Carefully, he reached into the right-hand pocket, extracting a beer mug wrapped in more paper napkins. If the photos gave them any kind of lead, fingerprints would help even more. Then Hal reached into the left-hand jacket pocket, and removed a second glass. Just in case, he'd pilfered the one used by the man with the animated gestures, the one who'd twice talked with the prospector in the corner. If the talker's a government man, his prints'll be on file.

Patrick can't decide whether to laugh or applaud. Hal's always on the ball. "Anything else?"

The bartender responded slowly. Unlike the New Mexico Cantina, where altogether too much classified information leaked out in the '40s, the bar in Cactus Springs didn't attract many 1950s physicists. The few Hal had met dropped in only occasionally, mostly to buy a bottle or a six-pack. Almost none of them lingered for long. Unlike the photographers and the Air Force, who seemed to show up every chance they could. According to Hal, if the prospector was looking for a mother lode of information, he wasn't striking it rich. What Hal was overhearing were just casual indiscretions. There just didn't seem to be any spying going on, at least no obvious surreptitious connections.

Except maybe that first contact the prospector made last month in the Cactus Springs bar, and the repeat a week ago Wednesday. If the man had a security clearance, they'd soon know his identity. Still, that conversation might have been meaningless. With the prospector, who could tell? Unfortunately, Hal hadn't been close enough either time to hear anything that was said. Moreover, the man hadn't shown up again. Except for the possible fingerprints, that was a dead end for now.

Another couple of months on the job, though, until the end of Upshot-Knothole, Hal might learn something more. Not much point in staying around Cactus Springs after that. The Proving Ground would pretty much put itself into cold storage until the next round of atomic tests. And every physicist would head promptly back to Livermore or Los Alamos.

Patrick nodded. Maybe their operation would pay off. Maybe not. So far Hal was just gleaning blabbermouths. Nothing more. But the prospector angle was troublesome. Better keep Hal on-site through the rest of the season. Patrick dropped the film canister and the envelope with the two napkins in his briefcase. Then he added the wrapped glassware, gingerly. The notepad followed, and the meeting was over.

Sliding out of the booth, Hal jammed his Stetson onto his crew cut, picked up the bill, laid two dollars on the table. Leaving the coffee shop together, he and Patrick walked past the ubiquitous bank of slot machines. Hal dropped in a nickel, pulled down a handle, got no return, and shrugged. At the door leading outside into the sunshine, the two men paused. There, Special Agent in Charge Patrick O'Neal shook the hand of Special Agent Harold Burleson, the former turning toward his FBI office suite up Fremont Street, the latter heading toward the nearest Laundromat and then back to Cactus Springs.

"Maybe this week will be the jackpot," Hal said as they parted.

Dixie

Dixie flies in from Albuquerque on a B-50 aircraft. Released at 33,190 feet, she drops to a mile-high 6,020 feet above Yucca Flat before she explodes. She falls right on target. Because she is built with a newly designed tamper that percusses the fissioning plutonium, she detonates so violently that her cloud steams clear into the stratosphere. Because she explodes in mid-air rather than dropping all the way to earth, that cloud behaves differently. Less desert soil mixes with the mushrooming energy and the fine-grained atomic fallout spreads itself more widely. A light rain drizzles a small amount over St. George, Utah, along with some weaponry detritus. Soon the jet stream begins moving Dixie's remains so quickly that tracking planes fall behind. She picks up speed, heading for the East Coast. Before long, radioactivity reaches Long Island, Providence, Hartford. That evening, Boston measures 1,200 milliroentgens—nineteen times the amount of radiation the area would normally receive in an entire year. No one bothers to tell the Bostonians.

Archie

The old man lay curled against the cold. Beneath his faded mustache, as he breathed faintly in and out, soft snores ruffled the silent midnight air. Turning on the narrow cot, he tugged at a thin blanket that provided little warmth. He coughed a little, turned again.

A sharp bark, a second, and then a third, broke into whatever dreams were ranging through the worn-out cowboy's unconscious imagination. A buxom barmaid gave way to a horrific stampede gave way to hounds baying. He sat up with a start, swiveling his thin legs toward the floor and automatically groping for his weathered Levi's, his red wool shirt, his Stetson, and his boots. Shaking his head, he cocked one ear toward the door. Beyond, the sounds of frantic barking and savage, frightened yelps pushed through the stillness of the night. More urgently now, the old man stumbled across the chilly room.

Outside, he inhaled the night in one deep breath, then flicked on the flashlight in his hand. The beam caught the red reflected eyes of two dozen beagles, each one voicing a cacophonous dismay at the Nevada desert outside their narrow cages, cages eight in a row, stacked in piles of three. The biggest and loudest of the canine tribe bellowed from the top, angry, and suddenly even more afraid, now that the bitch had seen the man's silhouette in the dark.

Snapping off the light, dropping it into the desert dirt, the caretaker looked beyond the beagles, his eyes focusing on another, more distant, pair of luminous eyes, yellow, glossy, refracting the night. But before he could swing his rifle to his shoulder, the eyes flickered. And disappeared. A flash of haunches, a fleeting figure, and then nothing in the darkness.

Tempted to fire a shot at the receding shape, the man sighted down the barrel, curled his finger on the trigger, sighed. More trouble than it was worth; a waste of ammunition, too. Gunshots might bring the others running. If anyone happened to be within earshot this time of night. If anyone actually could hear a shot over the sounds of the wind that was rising in the north. Not likely. But possible. Too late to shoot the cougar anyway. Long gone. And lucky.

The old man smiled to himself, secretly glad the cougar had loped safely away. Actually, he half wished the big cat had gotten to one of the precious

beagles. Predator swatting prey, a fate more natural than the one dead ahead
of the caged canines. Not that they'd know the difference. Damned dumb
dogs, locked up now for the rest of their lives. He smiled again, rubbing one
hand across his stubbled face and twisting his mustache between forefin-
ger and thumb. Bitches fighting off a cougar—just plain more natural than
bitches combating an atomic detonation.

Whatever instinct drove them crazy, the beagles bayed on and on. Grimac-
ing, their caretaker tried to shush them down. Talked to them, even hummed
a cowboy lullaby. He tipped his rifle, its safety back on, against the stairs and
jammed his flashlight into his hip pocket. A sliver of a crescent moon gave
off a faint glow, just enough so he could see to pace back and forth in front of
the cages, left to right, right to left, left to right. The unfamiliar terrain, the
catch of his boots on dirt, made him wonder for the thousandth time what in
hell he was doing here. The thought didn't linger, though, as a long-ingrained
routine took over his mind and body, only on foot instead of on horseback.
His voice rasping in his throat, the cowhand crooned the lines he'd been singing for decades. Softly, ever so softly, to mesmerize the animals.

> Desert silver moon beneath the pale moon light
> Coyotes yappin' lazy on the hill
> Sleepy winks of light along the far skyline
> Time for milling doggies to be still-ill
> So now the lightning's far away
> The coyote's nothing skeery
> Just a singin' to his dear-ie;
> Yo ti ho, tomorrow's a holiday
> So settle down you doggies 'til the mor-or-nin.'

While he was humming the refrain, the rusty tenor revised the final line.
Dogies, doggies, what the hell. Interchangeable at this point in his life.

Images of dusty cattle drives, parading through his imagination, changed
for a moment the dry desert dust into real short-grass prairie, and maybe
a stream, slicing alongside a cutbank, nice and clear. Cows bawling instead
of dogs baying, and sweet night air instead of sterile, withering cold. The
old codger suddenly was in his twenties again, lean and lithe and ready for
whatever man or beast might come his way. He could almost feel a horse's
cadence, caught between his thighs. Anchor, his favorite mustang; Sundown,

his precious gray; Redskin, his treasured roan. Riding drag, pushing cows along, heading for high country and quieting their fears.

Not so the barking beagles, whose fears seemed heightened by the lonesome cowboy's unfamiliar voice. Choking on a high note and coughing phlegm into the dirt, he spat, cleared his throat, and tried another verse.

Nothin' out there on the plains that you folks need
Nothin' out there seems to catch your ey-eye
Still you gotta watch 'em or they'll all stampede.
Plungin' down some 'roya banks to die-ie.

The irony wasn't lost on him. To die. That's what the day after tomorrow, or maybe the day after that, would bring this set of little dogie-doggies, barking hopelessly into the night. Dumb as cows. Less pliant, though, because even a lullaby won't quiet them down. Not at this hour, with the sour smell of feral cat hanging on the night wind and blowing past their cages. The top dog, if anything, bayed even louder, lifting her nose to the dark desert sky. Ah, hell, the old man thought to himself, let 'em bark. Who gives a damn anyway?

At the same time, whispered soprano sounds from the other side of his Quonset hut home joined the beagle chorus. More of the old cowboy's menagerie, secluded out here in a frigid Nevada midnight. The second set of captives, herded together in a rectangular pen instead of trapped in individual metal cages, were perhaps even more vulnerable to uninvited predators. Better check on those critters, too, the caretaker decided. Flicking his flashlight on with one hand and wiping spittle off his lower lip with the other, he lit his way around back, where a dozen sheep huddled pitifully against the far side of their makeshift corral.

Some corral. A couple of Army boys had hammered it together last week, using old boards and then stringing barbed wire across the top. Supposed to keep the sheep in and the nightlife out. So far, the jerry-rigged rectangle seemed to be working. And it didn't have to hold forever, after all. Like the beagles, the sheep won't be here much longer. Just another day or two, and then they'll be gone with the dogs. Before the next wethers and ewes arrive, there'll be time to shore up the sides of the pen and tighten the barbed wire overhead.

Sheep! Unbelievable! The cowboy slammed his palm against the brim of his Stetson, then pulled it back down over his forehead. Sheep! Not only was he stuck in the southern Nevada desert, but a purebred cowhand—albeit one in his seventies—had sheep to tend. Nary a cow in sight, unless he counted those three wild ones over by Tippipah Springs. One of the sergeants had spotted the trio there last month, and invited the old man to look 'em over. Always glad for a break from the monotony of his caretaking job, the cowboy was eager for an adventure, but the cattle turned out to be scrawny wasted Brahmas. Not much to look at. Real savvy critters, though, after a decade running free. Even when the sarge chased after them with his Jeep, and sent 'em stampeding away from the water, they didn't go far. Just heeled into the sagebrush, then turned around, their skinny sides heaving, and stared. And frightened. More like antelope behavior than cow.

Aside from those three, the cowboy was pretty sure there were no more cattle for maybe a hundred miles in any direction. The old man knew the government had bought out the Tippipah Springs rancher ten or fifteen years ago, long before talk of an atomic proving ground. They simply wanted to clear the area for military flyovers and gunnery practices. The home place was gone, torn down by the Army. Some of those old boards now built up part of the new sheep pen, and the rest were scattered in the dust. The sergeant said the brass thought they'd rounded up all the rancher's cattle, too, except three got away. Once he saw them, the sergeant wanted to corral 'em, but that turned out to be impossible. After running wild for more than a decade, those bony old cows weren't about to get themselves trapped. Tough as nails. The caretaker tipped his hat again, kind of in respect. Glad he didn't have to chase 'em down on horseback, that's for sure.

Maybe the Army wanted to corner the cattle to see if their eyes glowed in the dark. That was the old joke, told and retold, around Mercury. How soon until everybody's eyes glowed in the dark? More likely the Army wanted to capture the cows just to kill 'em off. Come to think of it, the Army wanted to kill off every living animal on the Proving Ground, though they never said so out loud. To the old cowboy's eyes, though, actions spoke louder than words. Any critter he saw was doomed in one way or another. Those worthless cows were physiologically interesting, however, because they were survivors. God only knows how close they ranged near the blasts. So the Army wanted to check 'em out, postmortem that is. A little necropsy, just to see how their innards had fared. What a waste. Even though their hides were mottled and their insides naturally stringy, the old cowboy couldn't help but wonder what those old cows would taste like. Better a steak than a laboratory toy.

But these scientists around here, they could turn almost anything that trotted or squeaked into an experiment of one kind or another. That day at Tippipah Springs, he and the sergeant had also gotten a quick glimpse of a burro and her young look-alike. The Army guy got very enthusiastic, saying there was talk of trying to catch burros, too. Apparently burros have useful parts. Lungs, for one thing. And balls. They're the same height off the ground as a man's, so the researchers want to check their post-blast potency. Recalling that conversation, the old man shifted uneasily in his Levi's, and decided to switch his attention back to the sheep. He flashed the light over their woolly backs, making 'em bleat louder and push harder against the pen's far side. He couldn't see anything wrong, just their instinctive fear of the dogs' nonstop barking and maybe an intuitive sense of the big cat nearby. Couldn't have spotted it, though, with the hut in the way.

Turning his back and hunching his shoulders against a wind that seemed to be blowing harder and harder by the minute, the shivering man crossed back to the beagles. He stood there for a moment, bracing himself, coughing and spitting as the dust curled into his lungs. Almost a caricature of an aging cowboy, he pulled a bandanna out of his pocket, wiped his face and mouth. Then he took one last look at the dog cages, picked up his rifle, and stepped back inside his quarters. Some bunkhouse. All by himself in a Quonset hut in the middle of nowhere. Not even a potbellied stove to keep him company.

He shrugged out of his wool shirt, then reconsidered. With the wind coming up and the dogs still barking, he wasn't likely to get much more sleep that night. Probably none at all. Might even have to go outside again. Pushing his arms back in his sleeves, he decided he might as well stay up, make himself a pot of coffee, warm his belly and his hands all at the same time. Humming a dogie-doggie tune under his breath and trying not to cough, he headed for the hot plate at the back of the barren room he now called home.

Fifteen minutes later, he was nursing a steaming mug. And still listening to the damned dogs. The baying had subsided, so he knew the big cat hadn't returned, but whimpers and occasional yelps still echoed outside. The bitch was the loudest. He shook his head, and wondered for perhaps the ten-thousandth time how in hell he'd ended up in a place like this.

Well, in truth, he knew the answer. And knew he was damned lucky to find a job. At his age. Too ancient for real cowboying, and too stove up. He looked at his hands cupped around his mug, his knuckles gnarled and swollen and aching in the cold. No more roping, no more dogie-ing for him. Better to be here in the southern desert, he guessed, than sitting in a rocking chair on a porch somewhere. At least the pay was decent, and not many places to spend the money. Might be he could save enough to get north again, back to Reno, where he knew the terrain. Flexing his right hand, the old man slapped it palm down on the rickety table. Knew the terrain, like the back of his hand.

He closed his eyes, not to sleep, but just to think. Once he'd been king of the cowboys up there, just like Roy Rogers, only for real. There he was—Archibald Irving Netherton—hell of a name for a cowpoke—folks always called him Archie—there he was, a Montana buckaroo in town for the rodeo, girls clustered left and right. He'd been a winner, even after he got bucked off that mustang and smashed his shoulder so bad. Ended up staying in Reno, and that was okay in the '20s. All those divorcées hanging around, looking for anyone in a Stetson and boots. He'd had his share, for sure.

Never got back to rodeoing after that. His shoulder never felt right, his left arm never quite as strong. So he found a job just south of Reno, in Washoe Valley, at a dude ranch. Eastern women, come west for divorces, stayed in the cabins there. Six weeks, long enough to claim Nevada residence so they could get a judge to set 'em free from a husband somewhere else, back home. Archie chuckled, remembering those women, year after year. Like standing alongside one of them automobile production lines, a conveyor belt moving those girls right past him. And he was the workman who tightened the screws. Susan and Maureen and Lurabelle and Joyce—an endless list that made him feel warm inside.

No beagles, no sheep in those memories, just sleek horses and soft, slender women, cantering beyond the pastures and into the hills. Hardly like work at all, to keep 'em occupied. Easier than the rodeo circuit, and not nearly as bruising. Easier than growing up on his dad's Montana ranch, too. Sure glad he got the hell out of Billings as soon as he could. Archie rubbed his jaw. He hated to shave, although the Army was pretty strict. When he looked in the mirror, he could see his daddy's eyes, red-rimmed and always tired. And the same handlebar mustache. Sometimes he wondered why he'd copied his daddy. "Guess it just grows that way," he'd rationalize.

Archie had won that war with the military. Told 'em he wasn't a soldier and he'd keep his mustache if he damned well pleased. A lieutenant had groused back at him, patiently explaining that facial hair might attract dust and that wasn't such a good idea out here beyond Mercury. In fact, it wasn't allowed. "Big deal," Archie had responded. "I'm an old man, and not much worried about what might happen in the future." It was true that everyone he met out here was beardless and wore his hair buzzed short. But Archie didn't care. Besides, the mustache kept his upper lip warm when he had to go out to check on his charges.

And what the hell were they up to now? The baying was ramping up again, the lead dog howling as loud as she could. The old man swallowed the last of his coffee and heaved himself to his feet. Better check 'em out again. Couldn't afford to get fired 'cause he was lazy on the job.

Downright ironic, to think about protecting those beagles. Why beagles, he wondered. Why not German shepherds or yappy little schnauzers? Better to kill Kraut dogs, the silent caretaker thought to himself. Probably the lab boys just wanted something mid-sized and easy to handle. Without much fur. Archie remembered the first set they'd delivered. He'd asked a lot of questions, which no one would answer. What kind of experiments on the beagles? Silence, followed by a cryptic sentence or two. Something about heartbeats and trauma, but no one would spell out any details. The lieutenant said it was too technical, but the mystery made the old man curious. Or downright nosy.

The shaved spots on this batch of beagles just plain intrigued him. He knew they were planning to attach some kind of sensors after they took the dogs out on the Flat. Then they'd stuff each dog in an aluminum cylinder, about twenty-six inches in diameter. Archie had measured one just the other day, trying to see how it worked. Open at both ends, it eventually would have a dog wedged inside. Some sort of neutron irradiation study, the old man had been tersely told.

Last time Archie had beagles they came back in a heap, all discolored and charred. Couldn't tell if they'd had sensors at all. So wasted, they were, that the science guys said the remains were useless. The cowboy caretaker was more than glad he didn't have to dig the hole to bury the stinking corpses. Instead of going back to a lab somewhere, they got dumped out in the desert. A guy from the Quartermaster Corps used a backhoe and then covered the dead dog pieces all up in an unmarked grave. Archie scratched his nose, remembering the ugly smell. A sweet, overcooked kind of stench. He'd taken one look at the critters and turned his back. Not before he'd seen that guy's dosimeter tucked in the pile of carcasses, though.

"What the hell's your badge doing there?" Archie had shouted. The guy had shrugged and spouted forth about how much he hated this godforsaken place. How he'd do anything to get away. How he thought the R count might go sky-high if he tucked his badge in close to the beagle bodies while he dug. Then he'd get transferred. Out of Nevada. Where he didn't have to worry about his balls drying up.

Some guys worry about stupid things. Archie made a point of not worrying. Too late in life for that, though every once in a while he double-checked his badge, just to be sure its color hadn't changed. But most of the time he didn't think about the effects of the blasts. In fact, he was looking forward to actually seeing one of those gadgets explode. Right in front of him. So far, Upshot-Knothole had all occurred on the playa to the north. Not here, near the makeshift zoo. But come May, that would change, when the atomic cannon was set to shoot off over Frenchman Flat. Then he'd have a front-row seat, if the Army'd let him stay and watch. Last year, before he came to babysit the animals, a couple of the devices had really blasted this place. Blew in the Quonset hut door and shattered the front window. But the cannon wasn't supposed to be as powerful as a tower drop, so maybe nothing would happen at all. Whatever, he wasn't about to fret. He'd just cross his fingers and hope he'd get to stay for the big show.

Not his job to worry. Not his job to handle dead critters either, or to even think about 'em. Usually the guys running the experiments took care of the corpses. That was part of the deal. Not that first bunch of beagles, though. They were practically incinerated. Not much fur, just bones and tattered flesh. He'd been told that the trick was to stash the live animals close enough to a blast to gather information but not so close they'd get totally cooked. Hard to know the right distance. Didn't always work as planned. Especially when the first experiments were just getting off the ground, the Army made a lot of mistakes. Typical, he thought to himself, though he'd never say so out loud. Instead, he'd just keep caretaking, whatever they brought him alive.

Archie glanced at his wristwatch as he stepped outside. Nearly 2 A.M. And getting colder. Seemed downright silly to make such a fuss about the damned dogs when they were all gonna be dead in a couple more days. He looked over their cages, humming slightly off key.

Still you gotta watch 'em or they'll all stampede.
Plungin' down some 'roya banks to die-ie.

No sign of the big cat. Long gone by now. He remembered one guy up north, years ago, who was fascinated by big cats. Said he was gonna write a book about one prowling the hills above Washoe Valley. Spun a lot of good stories, that guy did. Stayed in one of those divorcée cabins, after the divorce business went all to hell. To save his soul, Archie couldn't remember the guy's name. Willie? Wally? Walter? Something like that. And what was he going to call his book? "Tracking the Cat"? "Track of the Cat"? Something like that.

Seemed like a long time ago, before Archie lost his cowboying job to younger fellers. Boys better-looking. With stronger hands. He coughed, and spit more phlegm into the desert dirt. Good thing the aging cowhand stayed friends with old Pappy Smith. Smith and his sons owned one of the big Reno casinos, and all three of 'em liked a Washoe Valley getaway. Fair enough. Archie liked a Harolds Club getaway from time to time. After Archie lost his job and just when he was running out of cash, Pappy had gotten wind of all the goings-on at the new Nevada Proving Ground. He talked to somebody who talked to somebody who talked to someone else. And bingo! Archie had a new career. Had to go through the security check routine, but that was easy. Corporal First Class Archibald Irving Netherton reporting for duty, sir.

Hell, that First World War seemed like a million years ago. Nobody even talked about it anymore. And once the combat was over, Archie never had given it much thought at all, until he got out here in the middle of nowhere and found himself surrounded by uniforms. Glad he wasn't Army anymore, just an aging civilian trying to hold down a job. With that thought, the old man finished double-checking the beagles and their queen bitch. All was well, at least from Archie's point of view. The sheep turned out to be okay, too, though still spooked and all jammed together. Twelve, just like before. Nothing to worry about out here.

Except maybe the mice. Archie hated the mice. Twittery little creatures. Dirty, with bright shiny eyes. But he'd better examine them at least once that night, make sure they were nice and warm. They lived in something called the "mouse house." Fine-sounding name for a battered shed sitting on a fork-lift. Inside their little castle, the wind and cold shouldn't get to 'em, and the big cat couldn't get to 'em. Yep, they were safe and sound tonight. Tomorrow, somebody would haul the mice away, prob'ly right after the beagles. Mice never needed much prep, and they were easier to move than dogs. Some grunt would just fork the mouse house onto a truck and away they'd go. Off to see the wizard. Or to see the brightest damned light they'd ever laid eyes on. Most of the mice ended up really close to the blasts. And never came back alive, not one of 'em. But their handlers liked 'em overcooked. After an atomic shot, the mice'd get hauled directly back to Tennessee, so somebody in a lab there could check their innards. Knoxville, Tennessee mice, like Grand Ole Opry performing rodents! Archie just had to laugh. Hell, he'd bury the little stinkers alongside the beagles if he had his way.

Same with the rabbits inside. They came from out of town, too, like clockwork. Every couple of weeks a new batch of bunnies arrived. From Texas, no less. San Antonio. The latest bunch flew in just in time for Easter, or their own private Alamo. As long as he was wandering around in the middle of the night, and thinking about what he considered oversized rodents, Archie decided he might as well look at the rabbits, too. Their cages were inside the Quonset hut, in a cubicle all their own. So he left the twittering mice and headed indoors.

Clutching a fresh mug of coffee in his hands, and wondering one more time how a desert could be so damned cold, he pushed open the door to the little room where the rabbits were housed. Maybe because of all the barking, or maybe because the rising wind was beginning to whistle outside their Quonset hut quarters, they looked as spooked as the sheep. They were bouncing all around their cages, making little squeaky sounds and wiggling their ears back and forth. Because of a talkative technician, Archie knew more about the rabbit experiments than about what they were doing with the beagles. Apparently the rabbits were useful for their eyes. Optics like ours, he was told, even though they're red. "We just point 'em at a blast and see how blind they get," the soldier had laconically said. That must make their red eyes redder yet, Archie had thought to himself. He'd seen one bunch right after the Nancy shot. Some just lay there in the cage. A couple others were like billiard balls, ricocheting. Didn't know which end was up because they couldn't see a thing. Archie'd felt sorry for them. He kind of felt sorry for these Easter bunnies, too.

If he let himself, he'd also feel sorry for the beagles. Good thing they were kind of wild. Impossible to pet, and snarly if you got too close to a cage. Whatever they did to the dogs before they got to The Farm—that's what Archie called this place—The Farm—imagining capital letters. Anyway, whatever they did was apparently not very kind. It turned the beagles into little doggie monsters. Made him think of that silly new Patti Page recording about the doggie in the window. Humming under his breath, he tried to imagine Patti Page on The Farm, crooning to the pathetic waggly-tailed beagles outside. How much are those doggies in the cages? He bet they'd quiet down for her, even if they wouldn't shut up for him. Well, these doggies weren't for sale, not anymore. That was for damned sure. He cracked a knuckle, swallowed more coffee, and coughed.

And wished for monkeys. For weeks now, Archie had wanted someone to bring the monkeys out to The Farm. No such luck, though. They were all stashed over at Indian Springs, living with the flyboys. In fact, the monkeys themselves got to fly. As if they were pilots, by God. He'd found out about the monkey experiments in the cafeteria at Mercury, overhearing a conversation between two supply sergeants. Apparently the Air Force had these drone planes that operated by remote control. They'd set two monkeys in the cockpit and strap 'em in with seat belts. Then they'd line up mice behind 'em, two by two, three by three, four by four, little cages all jammed together, just like passengers on a big old transcontinental prop plane. They'd take off just as each shot occurred, and they'd fly directly into the mushroom clouds, trying to find out what might happen if a commercial pilot got caught unawares. Bad news, apparently, for passengers and crew. Archie knew at least one drone already had crashed that spring, wiping out the animals on board.

The sergeants in the cafeteria were still annoyed about the crash but were really chortling about the monkeys' antics beforehand. Seems it didn't take the last duo very long to figure out seat belts. Unhitched 'em almost as soon as they were snapped closed. Then they had two monkeys scrambling all over the insides of the plane, scattering mouse cages left and right. Total chaos! Monkeys swinging down the aisles, and Air Force guys chasing them back to the cockpit, and monkeys not obeying at all. Archie knew he'd dearly love to see a bunch of 'em get loose at The Farm. So far, though, no one had come up with a ground-based monkey experiment. The damned Air Force had a monopoly.

At the time, the story had made the rounds of the cafeteria, and made everyone laugh at the thought of those two hairy creatures swinging up and down the airplane's aisle. The story still made Archie smile. Brightened up the night. He looked at his watch again. Only 3:30. And he was hungry. Well, he knew there were three slabs of apple pie in his little refrigerator. Might as well eat one of 'em with the last of his coffee. And maybe feed the other two pieces to the pigs.

The pigs! Those were the critters he loved the most, and for good reason. Even an unredeemed old cowhand could grow to love the pigs. Not only were they the smartest of The Farm animals, but they were the most useful.

Not useful of their own volition, of course, but useful nonetheless. Archie opened the door to the room where they were penned and stepped inside. Almost immediately the shoats waddled toward him. Only been here a week. Already knew the routine. Scooping chunks of apple pie toward the pigs, the cowboy-turned-hash-slinger fed his charges a late-night snack. As he did so, he grinned, and thanked God once again for the Army's incompetence. Or its lack of farm savvy.

Last year, somebody in the military decided they ought to find out what kind of uniforms the grunts should be wearing when a bomb goes off. Wool? Cotton? Nylon? Orlon? Rayon? Like the manikins in the Annie shot that wore all different kinds of civilian clothes. Some melted; some didn't. Some charred; some were perfectly fine. So what should soldiers be wearing in the field? That was the question the military decided to answer later on in the spring.

But they couldn't use real human beings to experiment on. Not only was it too dangerous to put soldiers close enough to a blast to get any decent data, but they couldn't take any chance that a uniform might stick to some-one's skin. The answer, somebody decided, was pigs. After shaving, pig skin wasn't much different from human skin. That thought brought out a snort from Archie. The most fun he'd had all year long was when he'd helped shave the first batch. Not an easy task, because it took two guys to hold down a slippery pig and one to wield a straight-edge. Cute little pink guys, with snotty snouts and beady eyes, but barbering the slithery critters took the better part of a day.

Then the Quartermaster Corps showed up, with little pig uniforms made to scale. Watching those guys wrestle with the shaved pigs was even more fun than the barbering itself. Four Army shoats and as many Navy shoats. Four blustery Marine shoats, too. Even Air Force pigs, with special goggles. Somebody spent a lot of time sewing up their suits and organizing their gear. Measuring every seam, just so. And it was really fun to dress 'em all up. Little pig pants and little pig jackets and little pig helmets. Uncooperative, they wiggled like hell, but if you sat on 'em they were pretty easy to control. For sure, those pigs looked damned silly on parade.

Then the captain in charge of the experiment took 'em and stashed 'em out on Yucca Flat. Archie could have told them this wasn't a good idea, to leave pigs outdoors all alone overnight, but no one asked him and he'd quickly learned that he ought to keep his mouth shut around the Army lifers.

That first batch, bobcats ate three of 'em. Not the cougar currently prowling nearby, but cats with smaller tracks set closer together. And two more froze to death. After that, the Army bought heat lamps to keep their hairless pigs alive, and built sturdier cages to keep the wildlife away. Archie never got out there to see the damage, but the guys who did really had guffawed. "Pig pillage," they called the remains, so it took the Army a while to get their pig experiments squared away.

In the meantime, the pigs got fatter. And fatter. Now Archie was chuckling so loud that he couldn't even hear the beagles outside. Middle of the night, pitch-black, the wind never stopping, dogs barking up a storm again, and he was reminiscing about fat pigs. Pigs so fat they outgrew their uniforms. Before long, the cute little outfits didn't fit at all. Quartermaster was beside himself. It had never occurred to him the pigs might grow. Archie loved such Army boneheads. Typical. So then they had to get rid of the old pigs and order in new ones.

Meanwhile a couple of boys from Hawaii volunteered to put on a party. "Let's have a luau!" they said. Why not? What a great way to make the fat pigs useful. Those Hawaiians, they wanted to make the luau authentic. They even wanted one of their Air Force buddies to fly over to the islands and pick up plantains and palm fronds. A training run, they'd call it. At least some lieutenant had enough sense to put the kibosh on that. So they had to make do with stale lettuce and bananas. They dug this big pit and lined it with stones and hot coals. Wrapped up those fat pigs in burlap and roasted 'em on the spot. The project took all day, while the onlookers were counting the minutes until they could dine on succulent pig instead of Mercury hash.

Great idea, everybody agreed. But the Hawaiians didn't know Nevada geology. They used sandstone and it crumbled, getting the pigs all gritty. And the burlap had been soaked in creosote. So the pigs tasted just god-awful, sort of like succulent crunchy tarpaper. Archie had taken one sour bite, and spit it out. The boys ended up throwing the whole feast away, and had to make do with beer instead.

Archie smiled down at his new charges, a fresh set of thirty-pound pigs that had come in on Wednesday. He'd held the old uniforms alongside 'em yesterday morning, before the beagles got here. According to his old eyes, the duds already were looking kind of snug. That meant the Army was gonna have to hurry, or else these guys would get too fat, too. Archie's unvoiced plan was simple. He'd help 'em along. Like the enlisted boys, he craved another

luau, only without the sand and the creosote. So after hours, he was slip-
ping the new pigs some extra chow. The last thing he did before turning in
was offer up a double helping of slops. And during nights like tonight, when
a man couldn't sleep, he'd serve 'em a double double helping. Before long,
he supposed, someone was bound to question how many pie servings an old
man could really eat, but for the time being, he was ordering as much food
as possible. Pie, cake, extra sandwiches, Snickers candy bars. The pigs especially liked Snickers. The peanuts and caramel, or maybe the milk chocolate.
Whatever, they loved the gooey taste. Their caretaker, happily, was doing his
part to satisfy their appetites. If he succeeded, there'd be another luau soon.

Because he helped with the shaving and the first fashion parade, before
the first batch of shoats got too fat, Archie knew some technical stuff about
the pig playa laboratory. He learned that the experimenters always put their
pigs in three different places. Close up, kind of midway, and farther off. An
overly enthusiastic lieutenant explained how they were trying to get three
points on a curve, so they could plot their findings on a graph. One side
was damage; the other, distance. They called the result damage versus flux,
and made it all sound very scientific. That would be fine, if the pigs didn't
freeze, or get too fat, or die too soon. And if the atomic "gadget" went off as
predicted.

For Archie, that was another story. A couple of weeks ago, Ruth had been
a real dud that just kind of fizzled out and annoyed absolutely everybody.
Ditto Ray on Saturday. Same yield as Ruth, just 0.2 kilotons, Archie had
heard via the grapevine, hardly enough to cause any damage at all. The flops
had mightily annoyed the scientists, especially the physicists, who thought
their calculations were next to infallible. For the animal guys, on the other
hand, duds were tolerable. In their micro-world, the real significant problems
occurred when a blast was too big. Too much detonation, too much energy,
and zowie! No more beagles. Or pigs. Or rabbits.

Or whatever. An overly effusive explosion dumped whole experiments
down the drain, and cost money, too. Archie had heard the looies bitch-
ing about getting their fair share of the dollars. Lots of dough being spent
around here, but God help anyone who killed off the critters without getting
any results. Then the Army got real fussy.

"God help me if I kill off the beagles!" Archie muttered to himself. By now
the wind was actually rocking the Quonset hut from side to side, and the

dogs were competing to see which one could bay louder than the storm. Still no sign of daylight. Tossing another handful of unwrapped Snickers to the pigs—maybe he should buy his own personal supply, keep the charges off the books, fatten the new shoats up entirely on the q.t.—the old caretaker ran through his list of early-morning options. Check on the beagles, the sheep, and the mice one more futile time. Brew another pot of bitter coffee. Lie down on his cot and pretend to sleep. Sing another lullaby to his charges. The last thought made him feel more like the young stud of yesteryear, but he knew another ballad would just make him cough all the more. "Hell to get old," he muttered under his breath.

But he was lucky. Deep down inside, Archie knew he was lucky. Out here on the Proving Ground, in the middle of the action. Made him feel young again. Even part of the future. Like that idealistic young cowhand in Montana, fifty years ago, riding point and looking dead ahead.

Yo ti ho, tomorrow's a holiday
So settle down you doggies 'til the mor-or-nin.'

Sweet harmony to the beagle bitch chorale.

Ray

11 APRIL 1953 • 0445 HOURS

Of the eleven Upshot-Knothole tests, Ray receives the least attention. Scientists from Los Alamos smirk at the puny Livermore Labs experiment, a weak 0.2-kiloton blast that barely clears the desert floor. The inner fireball occludes at 18.2 milliseconds; the outer shell of heated air, at 162. Accounts differ—a cloud that climbs 8,774 feet or one that bubbles up to 12,800. Whichever is correct, the characteristic mushroom never appears. Instead, the cloud spreads out in black pennants that stream across the sky. Rather than looking nuclear, Ray resembles a pile of burning tires or perhaps coal smoke pouring from an industrial stack. Something "small and ugly," reports an eyewitness. For a while, thick blackness obliterates the Yucca Flat scenery and makes ground maneuvers difficult. At the same time the tracking planes have difficulty tracing the fallout because it dissipates too quickly. Indeed Ray replicates the black-and-white irony of an Escher lithograph. A more prosaic joker opines that this device's secret neutron material is rubber, set off with a coal tamper. The cadre of atomic scientists all laugh, but use Ray's relative lack of success to spur their nuclear imaginations.

Candi

"Cute," giggles Ginger, holding a wrinkled page up so her five cohorts can see. "Some short-timer must have spent his last hours printing it out."

"Or just a few seconds," Candi snickers. "Look at the sloppy printing. Red crayon, like grade school."

"The Atomic Angels EXPLODE with Music," Jane reads aloud.

"Explode, my ass," Ginger responds. "We're gonna deflate in this horrible wind."

Flicking her cigarette lighter, Candi grabs the homemade flyer and holds it to the flame. "I've never been so cold in my whole life. Never!"

"Freeze my tits off," Bobby Sue mutters.

"No tits, honey, you'll have to find a new line of work," Ginger chirps, tugging a tight blue middy over her ample bosom. "Then you'll really be out in the cold."

"Look out! You'll set the tent on fire!" Jane, always practical, shoves a number 10 can filled with sand toward the pretend campfire.

Candi drops the burning sheet of paper into the makeshift ashtray and looks around for more fuel.

Watching the bottom line of the flyer turn to ashes, Bobby Sue points to more silly words. "'Onstage at Times Square.' What's this New York nonsense? Aren't we still in the middle of nowhere Nevada?"

"I think that's what they call the Desert Rock parade ground. Times Square."

"Why?"

"Makes things seem more civilized."

"Hardly possible in this godforsaken place." Sylvia's ever-present homesickness bubbles to the surface. "I hate it here."

"Sylvia!" Ginger's playful voice turns solemn. "What's not to like about a khaki compound filled with horny men and we're the only girls in sight?"

That observation brings a faint smile to the pouting corners of Sylvia's mouth. "Well, I guess you might be right about the wildlife. But the scenery sure is ugly."

"Girls! Stop your chatter. There's a show to perform in fifteen minutes." Joey's voice, sounding urgent, comes from just outside the tent flap. "Finish getting dressed, and stop fooling around!"

"Better hop to," Jane tries to persuade the others.

Sylvia shakes her head and stares at the olive-drab canvas. "Whose bright idea was this, anyway?"

"Joey's. And the Maestro's. Anything for the troops."

"Good press for the Desert Inn, too," Jane sardonically observes. "Bet this was Mr. Clark's idea in the first place."

"Yeah. He eats up publicity."

"But he doesn't have to sing and dance from morning to night." Sylvia is still unhappy.

"And freeze to death in these skimpy costumes."

"We've gotta wear 'em again tonight, too. When we finish here, it's back to Vegas in time for the evening show."

"Brutal!"

"Couldn't they have picked a warmer day?" Shivering, Candi begins struggling into her black net hose. "Damn, it's cold."

"The . . . Boys . . . Will . . . Love . . . Us," Linda emphasizes each separate word. "We'll warm 'em up for sure."

"They're hot already. Did you see that cute sergeant manning the gate? All those muscles? Yummy!"

"I sure did. Said he was off duty at 11, just in time to catch our act."

"The corporal who waved us in here, he couldn't keep his eyes off Ginger."

"Hot . . . To . . . Trot." Ginger thrusts her chest forward and sounds as throaty and as sexy as possible in the nippy morning air.

"While we're turning into polar bears!" Candi's hands, tugging her left stocking, are still shaking.

"Aren't deserts supposed to be hot?" Bobby Sue drawls. "I should've stayed in Georgia."

Ginger shrugs, and starts pinning her tiny pillbox hat to her thick auburn hair. "Anybody got an extra bobby pin?"

Opening her night case, Jane pulls out a handful and tosses them on the cot.

"Honey, wait 'til that sexy blue-eyed corporal finds a hairpin in his sheets tonight. The boys'll razz him for sure!"

"Let's have some fun." Candi reaches into her purse for an old tube of lipstick, checks to see that it's almost empty, and then tucks it under the pillow.

Bobby Sue joins in, spraying a squirt of perfume on the corporal's wool blanket. "Magnolia Blossom. A bit of the Old South," she smiles.

Laughing together, the girls finish getting dressed, Linda and Bobby Sue in red, Sylvia and Jane in white, Ginger and Candi in blue. They squirm and shake themselves into their sequined bodices, hook their mesh hose to their garters, adjust their matching square caps, fix their makeup, and spray more perfume.

"Sure wish we had a mirror," Linda complains. "I can't tell if my hose are straight."

"You look fine to me," Jane responds, offering her compact. "Here, check yourself out."

"Inch by inch, that'll take all day," Candi teases.

"Five minutes, girls." Joey starts his countdown. "The show goes on in five minutes."

As if on cue, Candi and Ginger burst into song, trilling up and down a musical scale with a series of do, re, mi's. Jane and Sylvia join in, while Bobby Sue and Linda tap-dance from one side of the tent to the other.

"Hey, stop stirring up the dirt." Jane cuts off her singing in mid-note. "We don't want to look like girls from the Sands, all dusty and sweaty."

"Not a chance, honey. They're not in our league!"

Joey interrupts the merriment by flipping up the canvas flap. A windy blast of cold air accompanies his voice. "Come on, girls. Time to get moving."

Automatically, the six Atomic Angels fall into line and parade outside. Linda, Sylvia, Ginger. Bobby Sue, Jane, Candi. Red, white, and blue. Red, white, and blue. Snaking their way alongside a long row of look-alike Camp Desert Rock tents, they turn right and, without thinking, sway seductively toward the music. Ahead, the in-house Desert Inn band is blaring "I'm the Sheik of Araby" into the morning air. Immediately the girls begin mimicking the words of the song, pretending all together, in rhythm, that they're lifting tent flaps along the way.

The Army whoops its pleasure. Privates, corporals, sergeants, lieutenants, even a major or two. They push forward, shouting and stomping their feet on the dusty desert floor. Waving, the Angels trip up onto a makeshift wooden stage erected just that morning. The band, sitting down front on folding chairs, repeats the refrain and the girls sing along with Chas's slick clarinet. Bobby Sue's boyfriend sure knows how to play sexy.

"At night when you're asleep, / Into your tent I'll creep."

Every man within earshot claps and whistles and invites the Atomic Angels to do just that. Blowing kisses at their audience, the girls caper across the stage and wave some more. Red, white, and blue, red, white, and blue, they position themselves for the special show. The Angels agree that these boys, serving their country, deserve the very best performance anyone can give.

For the first half hour, the sextet, who often call themselves a SEX-tet, alternates between old favorites and numbers from their nightly routine. A little Glenn Miller, a dose of Benny Goodman, then Hit Parade songs sure to warm the soldiers' hearts. "Glow Worm," "Cry," "Wheel of Fortune," "I'm Yours." The girls dance their hearts out, especially to the strains of "Wheel of Fortune," which is one of their absolute favorites. The big roulette wheel they use onstage each night at the Desert Inn is too heavy and awkward to transport to Camp Desert Rock, but they're able to mimic their casino moves, spinning and twirling across the stage, acting like they're winning money with every pirouette.

The men love it. Throwing their caps in the air, they celebrate a welcome break in their dry desert routine. One or two brush away a tear when the band segues into "Cry," thinking of unfortunate sweetheart letters no doubt, but mostly everyone laughs and claps and sways and hums along with the music. Playing to their crowd of admirers, the Angels crave the attention. Even cranky Sylvia comes to life, cartwheeling with genuine enthusiasm.

During the second half hour, the Maestro, as the girls call the snotty band director who changes rhythms without warning just to keep them on their toes, chooses more martial music. The show ends with a gala finale, two trumpets blaring and a snare drum snapping out the beat. The girls' costumes play up the theme, as they somersault back and forth across the stage. Red, white, and blue; red, white, and blue.

> You're a grand old flag,
> You're a high flying flag
> And forever in peace may you wave.

Marching across the stage and back, the Atomic Angels wave and throw kisses at the adorable military men. "You're the emblem of / The land I love." Candi can't resist. Never missing a beat, she hops off the stage, grabs the nearest soldier, and plants a squishy smack squarely on his lips. Before the astonished private can recover, she's back in the chorus line, dancing in place, while the private's platoon shouts with glee at the lipstick smeared across his mouth. "Every heart beats true / 'Neath the Red, White, and

Blue." With those words, the girls' somersaults turn to handstands, feet kicking high in the air, skirts flaring to show plenty of leg. "Keep your eye on the grand old flag."

Everyone claps, as Chas's clarinet riffs and repeats the last musical line. "Keep your eye on the grand old flag." The red, white, and blue girls blow more kisses at the boys, who by now are shouting so loudly that no one can hear the instruments at all. Candi and Ginger, in particular, grin broadly, flirtatiously making eye contact with the men standing in front. When Candi winks at the boy she kissed, he happily shouts, "More! More! More!"

"Every heart beats true / 'Neath the Red, White, and Blue." They hadn't forewarned either Joey or the Maestro, but each Angel, amid much laughter and many lascivious comments, had tucked a miniature American flag in between her boobs. In unison now, they jiggle their breasts and pull out the tiny Stars and Stripes. The gesture is the highlight of the show. One enamored soldier leaps on the stage and tries to grab a flag. Another joins him, throwing an arm around Sylvia and lifting her off her feet.

"Enough, enough," Joey shouts.

"Encore! Encore!" The men respond, eyes sparkling and hearts lighter than before.

The girls and the band oblige, the musicians repeating the "You're a Grand Old Flag" chorus while the Angels kick-step back and forth across the stage. Red, white, and blue; red, white, and blue. Stooping toward the boys in front, and showing plenty of cleavage, the girls toss the remaining flags to the audience. Candi wishes there'd been room to hide half a dozen grand old flags instead of just one. The boys would love it, but alas, no new Stars and Stripes emerge.

When a final trumpet blast signals the show is over, the men won't stop hollering. If they had their way, the Angels would go on for hours. But the revue needs to hightail it back to Vegas in time for the evening performance. The girls prance away from Times Square while the soldiers clap and clap, unwilling to let them go. Most nights Candi is ready for the final routine, but today she hates to see the show end. She could flirt forever. Such fun, such wonderful men, she thinks as she heads for the canvas dressing room, throwing kisses all the way. She's not even cold anymore.

FOR DAYS after their Camp Desert Rock performance, the Atomic Angels gossip about the fun-filled morning. Even Sylvia, although she despised the long bus ride to Mercury and back, admits that the boys were darling and the show a success. Much as the girls like their Vegas lounge routine, they love the soldiers even more. Bobby Sue, thinking about her Duck-and-Drill dancing days back in Georgia, can't remember another time when the audience clapped and stomped with every song. Ginger thinks they ought to add the flag sequence to their Desert Inn routine, too, but everyone agrees the Maestro would have a fit. He was apoplectic about the innovation. Jane, normally more serious than the other five, is surprised at how much she enjoyed the boisterous show. Linda can't get the muscular gate sergeant out of her head, and even Sylvia snickers over and over again when she thinks about the brawny soldier hoisting her off the ground.

Candi feels particularly patriotic after the Desert Rock trip. Until the show there, she'd always called herself a loyal American, and she'd always supported the troops, but she'd never given much thought to what that meant. Suddenly she takes enormous pride in the name of their group. Atomic Angels! They're part of something larger. They belong to the fight against the Communist threat. Since none of the girls is old enough to remember details about World War II, or has much to say about politics or international affairs, they tease Candi about her newfound loyalty to the American flag.

"Maybe you just like pulling those little Stars and Stripes out of your bosom."

"Showing off your boobs."

"If we go back for another show, you can kiss that handsome soldier again."

"Or another one just like him."

Good-natured Candi takes the ribbing in stride, but she keeps bringing up the subject. Patriotism. What else can the girls do for America?

Linda has an idea. "We're Atomic Angels, so we could volunteer. Maybe sit in for the manikins at ground zero. At least there'd be better photos."

"Honey, we'd be killed." Sylvia interprets most things literally.

Jane rolls her eyes, then suggests, "We could volunteer."

"To do what?"

"I dunno. Fold bandages or something."

"That's passé. Fat lot of good bandages would do in an atomic holocaust."

"Maybe we could model a new line of protective radiation covering. You know, overalls and oxfords."

"Nah, too much cover-up."

"We could support atomic causes." Ginger has a faraway smirk on her face.
"How?"

"Drink atomic cocktails, for one thing. It'd be patriotic to support Atomic Liquors."

Candi snaps her fingers. "That's it! Atomic cocktails can be our inspiration. After a couple of those zingers, ideas'll flow as fast as the booze."

Suddenly all the girls are talking at once and everyone's eager to party. Usually Jane and Linda troop off after each show, complaining that they need their shut-eye. The others generally gather in the casino bar and join their boyfriends for a drink or two. Tonight, though, Jane and Linda agree to stay up late, and the girls all decide to do something different. "Atomic Liquors, calling to me," Bobby Sue drawls. "Suits my mood."

"Me, too." Candi seconds her friend's suggestion. "Let's go have a blast."

"We'll need a car. The atomic lounge is a couple of miles away."

"Jeff and Chas can drive us. Come on. Let's find 'em."

The girls don't have to look very hard. The boys are waiting for their dates just outside the dressing room door. The minute they hear the Atomic Liquors suggestion, they agree wholeheartedly with the plans.

"Two cars," Jeff decides. "Yours and mine." He nods toward Chas. "Meet you out front."

The drive to Fremont Street takes only a few minutes. Trooping inside the smoke-filled bar, the Angels and their dates gravitate toward a big table in back, near two pool tables in steady use.

"Atomic cocktails all around," Jeff majestically orders.

Joe Sobchick, the owner who renamed the bar just so he could attract such groups, nods appreciatively. He loves serving his own special blend to customers. Out-of-towners, especially, often order more than one of the potent combination. Vegas showgirls know how to party, too. He smiles at the playful group, already speculating that tonight will be lucrative.

"What's in here?" Jane pushes her swizzle stick from one side of her glass to the other. "I've never had one of these before. Tastes awful strong."

"Just fruit juice, dearie."

"And a little more." Chas can't resist.

"I'm serious," Jane continues. "Name the ingredients."

"Well, mostly grapefruit juice and pineapple juice."

"And?"

"Galliano and Plymouth gin," Jeff confesses. "Has to be Plymouth. No other brand will do."

Candi holds her glass up to the dim light. "Silly-looking." She glares at the shapely showgirl container. "Just plain silly-looking. Doesn't look like anybody we know."

"Tits too small?"

"Nope, honey. Too knobby."

Laughing, the Angels and their dates toast the evening, banging swizzle sticks against voluptuous glasses and downing the potent brew. By the second round, everyone's having a rollicking good time. In the midst of the gaiety, though, Candi remains strangely quiet, puffing on a menthol Salem and not saying much of anything. Finally, Jeff throws his arm over her shoulders and asks what might be going on inside Carolyn's pretty little head.

Candi scowls. "What did you call me?"

"Ah, honey, I'm only teasing."

"You know I hate my real name!" Candi stamps her foot. "Rhymes with crinoline, that's what Carolyn does. Reminds me of some dowdy old lady in Iowa. Candi. That's who I am now!"

"When did you change it?" Bobby Sue asks.

"The moment I caught the bus for Vegas. Candi sounds so much sweeter. And more alluring."

Jeff nuzzles his apology, nibbling on her ear and agreeing. Totally alluring. But he still wonders why his girl is so preoccupied.

Carefully setting her cigarette in an ashtray, Candi slowly stands up and lifts her glass toward the group. "We've got to think of something, something patriotic."

"But what?" Sylvia hasn't a clue.

Suddenly Candi knows the answer. "I know what let's do," she announces. "Let's go to Mount Charleston. Let's watch an atomic explosion. Firsthand." Inspiration has struck.

"Huh?" Sylvia is totally puzzled. "What are you talking about?"

"I want to see what those boys are facing, as close as I can get."

"You should have been here last year," Jane interjects. "And the year before. Those tests kept going off like firecrackers, and you could see 'em glow from Fremont Street."

"Water sloshed out of motel swimming pools."

"In the Sands, chandeliers bounced so bad they nearly fell off the ceiling."

"I was standing outside of Penney's when all the windows broke. Pretty exciting."

"How come that's not happening now?"

As usual, Jane knows the answer. "'Cause they moved the tests farther away. Now they're at Yucca Flat instead of Frenchman. I heard someone say that's better for Vegas. No more damage."

"If you get up early enough in the morning, though," Ginger adds, "you can still see a little glow in the sky to the northwest."

Candi has a better idea. "Why get up in the morning? Why not just stay up all night?"

"That's the spirit!"

"And besides, you girls are off the subject. We can drive to Mount Charleston and look straight out at the Proving Ground."

Linda chimes in, "But the road's supposed to be awful muddy, and I've heard the switchbacks are horrid."

"Switchbacks? What are those?" Bobby Sue has no idea what Linda's talking about. "Atlanta doesn't have switchbacks."

"Neither does New York, but at least I know what they are." Ginger scoffs at her Southern friend.

"Well, I'd still like to see a blast go off." Like a dog with a bone, Candi doesn't want to let go. "Switchbacks be damned, I say. Besides, Jeff and Chas are good drivers."

Hearing her boyfriend's name, Bobby Sue's upset. Wherever Chas goes, she goes, too, but she is not the least bit interested in seeing a mushroom cloud or anything else at five in the morning from the top of Mount Charleston. She thinks for a minute, then calls out, "Hey, Candi! It'll be cold."

"I know," Candi acknowledges. "But we can wear sweaters. Besides, we'll have Jeff and Chas to keep us warm." She flashes her best seductive smile.

Jeff, although flattered, is reluctant. "I've only had my new Cadillac for a couple of months. It'll get filthy if I take it up there. Besides, it's not even paid for. What if I run it off that awful road?"

Chas steps in with a solution. "Not to worry. Nothing can hurt my old wreck at all."

Bobby Sue buries her head against his chest. "Honey, don't say that," she whispers in muffled tones. "Anyway, we won't all fit inside one little old car."

"When's the next test scheduled?" Jane wants to know.

"I'm not sure. Its name is Badger, but I can't remember when they're set-ting it off. Lemme check." Chas pries Bobby Sue away and wanders off toward the bar.

"What a silly name—Badger." Candi laughs. "I wonder who thought that one up."

"So far this year they've been people. Annie and Nancy and Ruth. Then Dixie and Ray." A strange voice enters the conversation.

"How come you're so smart, to know all that?" Candi looks oddly at the tall, good-looking man standing nearby.

"I pay attention," he responds. "Besides, I work out at Cactus Springs, not far from Mercury."

"Doing what?"

"Pouring booze for the off-duty guys. Pretty rare to get a night off. Bus-man's holiday."

As he talks, Candi gets more and more interested in what he's saying. "Ever driven up Mount Charleston to see the flash?"

"Yeah, I was there for Ruth. Turned out to be a real dud."

"How's the road?" Bobby Sue can't resist asking.

"Okay if you take it slow. The only hard part's the parking. Not much room at the landing."

"The landing?"

"Angel's Landing. That's the best viewpoint."

Candi is positively gleeful. "That's the name? Angel's Landing? That's where we go on Mount Charleston? Angel's Landing? Per . . . fect!"

Bobby Sue catches her enthusiasm. "Us angels at Angel's Landing. Yay, team!"

"Saturday morning." Jeff, back from talking to the bartender, interrupts the girls' enthusiasm. "Saturday morning before dawn."

"Whoa. On a weekend. That's tough."

"We'll need to start out right after the second show."

"Right after shift change, you mean. I've gotta work that Friday night." Jeff, a pit boss at the Desert Inn, never misses a single minute on the job because he so desperately wants to get ahead in the casino business. "And I'll have to be back by midafternoon on Saturday. That's cutting it pretty close."

"We'll be hard-pressed to get there at all," Bobby Sue hedges. "I think it's quite a drive."

"That guy over there, he said it was pretty easy." Moving closer to Jeff, Candi gestures toward the stranger. "Come join us, and tell us more."

Chas pulls up another chair. "How long from here? Three hours, four?"

"About that. As long as the weather's decent."

"Great! Plenty of time. My old Chevy'll make it up there and back without any problems at all." Chas gives Bobby Sue's shoulders a squeeze. "What about the rest of you girls? Coming along? If you are, we need to find more cars and drivers."

"Not me!" Jane sounds definitive. "You're all crazy."

"Me, neither," Linda agrees.

Ginger isn't sure. She hems and haws, back and forth, until her boyfriend reminds her that she'd have to dance two shows Saturday night without any sleep at all. Edgar sure isn't buying in to that plan. "Hard for me to even hold up a slide trombone without any sleep, let alone play one," he says.

Off to one side, Sylvia pouts a little. She kind of wants to go, but a ghastly head cold is squelching her enthusiasm. She blames the Desert Rock performance for her sniffles. Candi was right—it was just too cold out there. Driving to Mount Charleston, to Angel's Landing, is crazy, especially if you feel as lousy as Sylvia does, though she has to admit the atomic cocktails are making her feel lots better.

So that leaves Jeff and Candi, Bobby Sue and Chas. Excitedly, the three eager beavers plan their excursion while the fourth still waffles. "We'll need to take blankets. And sweaters to keep warm."

"Don't forget flashlights," Jane cautions from across the table. "It'll be totally dark, until the bomb goes off."

"I wonder if we'll feel any heat," Candi muses. "From the blast, I mean. Does the air get hot?"

"Up close, at ground zero, you'd fry in an instant. Farther away, like on Mount Charleston, probably not."

"Honey, I'll keep you plenty warm." Jeff is now fully in the spirit of things. "But let's be sure and fill a couple of flasks. A little booze'll keep us warm."

"Brandy," Chas replies quickly. "Nothing like brandy on a cold cold night."

"Maybe the bartender here would mix us atomic cocktails. Get us in the spirit of the thing."

"I dunno," Bobby Sue hesitates. "They sure are potent."

"Sure are," Candi adds, slurring her words just slightly. "They make me wanna dance."

"Let's." Feeling lots better, Sylvia surprisingly jumps up from her seat and takes a turn around the nearest pool table. Ginger hops up, too, and almost immediately all six girls are bumping and grinding to the jukebox music. "Heart and soul, I fell in love with you," the Four Aces croon as the Angels mock a striptease across the barroom floor.

"Ladies, ladies, settle down," Joe Sobchick groans. "I don't have a license that allows dancing," though his frown turns to a smile when the pool players applaud and order more drinks.

"Ah, let 'em go." Chas laughs. "They're just having fun."

The girls tumble back into their seats when the song ends, while Jeff gives the bartender the thumbs-up. Time for another round.

Jane and Linda shake their heads. They've had enough. The other girls stop counting. They'll have awful headaches tomorrow, but nobody cares. Besides, Candi has another inspiration, this one even better than the first. Leaping up, she raps on the table with her swizzle stick. "Listen up, listen up!" Her words tumble. "Let's dance on the mountains. Take our costumes with us. Atomic Angels dancing at Angel's Landing. It's perfect!"

"Huh?"

"Dance. Up there, with the mushroom cloud as backdrop. Chas can provide the music. A Benny Goodman blast."

"We can't take our costumes outside the property. You know that." Bobby Sue is more game, now that she's on her third drink, but she's always afraid of getting in trouble with the Maestro.

"We can bribe the wardrobe girl and sneak our outfits out to the car. If we bring 'em back the next day, in time for the show, no one'll be the wiser." Candi seems have the whole thing worked out in her head already.

"We'll freeze if we wear our costumes up there." Bobby Sue hopes mentioning the temperature will deter her friend.

"No problem. We'll put on sweaters and coats and leggings over them, then pull off the heavy clothes at the last minute."

"And then what?"

"We'll dance!"

"Dance?"

"Dance, that's what we do. Dance." Candi hops up on her chair before Jeff can stop her, though he catches her in midair before she can step onto the table. The glass atomic cocktail girls shimmer and shake as he pulls her back down.

"Dance, that's what we do. Dance," Candi repeats, just before she lolls back in her chair.

TWO NIGHTS LATER, Candi, Bobby Sue, Jeff, and Chas, considerably more sober, are eager for their Mount Charleston safari. Candi is so excited that throughout the show she can hardly concentrate on her moves. She even falls out of one of her somersaults, flopping gracelessly to the left instead of bouncing straight ahead. She'll hear about that from the Maestro, for sure. But she doesn't care. She's just so thrilled about the upcoming adventure. Dancing at Angel's Landing. Watching an explosion across the horizon. Hugging, from afar, a mushroom cloud.

After the final strains of "You're a Grand Old Flag," the girls hurry back to their dressing room, everyone talking at once. Candi and Bobby Sue are in a rush, pulling tights and sweaters over their Atomic Angel costumes as quickly as they can.

"What if Joey catches you?" Jane frets. "Remember, we're not even supposed to take our costumes home, let alone to Mount Charleston."

Candi snorts at Jane's worrywart question. "When the boss hears the good publicity, he won't care one whit!"

All the girls laugh, except Sylvia, who's still pouting about her head cold. She thinks they need a white-outfitted dancer to go with Bobby Sue's red and Candi's blue. But staying up all night and then dancing half-naked in the early dawn is just crazy, especially if you can't stop blowing your nose.

While Sylvia rationalizes, Candi and Bobby Sue put on their coats. Ready to leave, they hug their pals and smile their good-byes. At the last moment, Candi, reaching for the bag of tiny flags she bought for the Desert Rock show and hid in a dressing room drawer, stuffs her coat pocket with little Stars and Stripes. "Let's take the rest of these. We'll hand 'em out to anybody who's on the mountain in the morning."

"Great idea. Remember how much the boys loved 'em at Desert Rock?"

"That's 'cause they saw where the flags came from, you ninny."

"No matter, the flags are good publicity, and patriotic, too." Jane grabs another handful, thrusting the flags at Bobby Sue. "Y'all be careful on those switchbacks," she teases her friend, mimicking her Southern drawl. "Y'all be careful now."

The two adventurers flee, giggling together all the way down the long hall and out to the fountain, where Chas's white Chevy waits at the edge of the oval drive.

"Hop in, girls!"

Jeff jumps out. Sweeping his arm in a wide arc, he ushers Candi into the backseat. After helping Bobby Sue into the front alongside Chas, Jeff runs around to the far side and joins Candi.

"All set. Let's go!"

"We're on our way!" Chas shouts, raising one hand high in the air.

Bobby Sue gently lifts his clarinet case and lays it on the floorboard, then snuggles close to him, patting his knee and urging him to drive faster. She's checked with someone at the casino, who said they'll need to hurry in order to get there before Badger blasts off. Chas, who trusts the atomic stranger's information, is more relaxed. "We'll be fine."

In the backseat, Jeff puts one arm around Candi and reaches for something on the floor with the other. He has a wonderful surprise. That morning, before shift, he'd gone to the Army surplus store and bought an old kapok sleeping bag. Unzipping it, he wraps the bag around himself and his date. They'll be plenty warm, he'll make sure of that. So grateful is Candi that she doesn't even scoff at the olive-drab color, so reminiscent of those dingy tents.

The route turns out to be about as long as predicted. They make good time heading out of Las Vegas on Highway 95. As soon as they turn off to the west, though, Chas has to drive more slowly. Most of the time they have the road to themselves, but occasionally they overtake another vehicle. Passing someone else in the dark isn't easy. Bobby Sue clutches Chas's arm a couple of different times, while Candi cringes a little in the backseat. Jeff solves the problem by screwing the top off a flask of brandy and passing it around. Candi takes a deep drink, as does Bobby Sue, and immediately both feel better about the drive.

Soon they reach the mouth of Kyle Canyon, where a sheriff's car blocks the way. Chas rolls down the Chevy's window, and calls out to the deputy. Maybe they're too late.

"No problem, sir," the deputy replies. "I'm just keeping people out of the canyon. Road's confusing in the dark. Turn right here, and follow the switchbacks up the mountain until you find a lot of parked cars. Another ten miles or so. You'll be there in about an hour."

"An hour?" Bobby Sue gasps. "That's barely inching along."

"That's right, ma'am." The sheriff leans toward the car. "It's a narrow road. And bumpy."

"Is it dangerous?" Bobby Sue still doesn't know what to expect from switchbacks.

"Not if you stay in the center," the sheriff gestures in the dark. "Just keep away from the drop-offs. Some places, it's a long ways down."

"Honey, you all be careful!" Bobby Sue makes sure Chas has her attention. "I sure don't want to be an angel flying off the landing!"

"Not a chance," he assures her. Rolling up the car window and handing the flask back to his Southern belle, he shifts the car into gear.

The switchbacks turn out to be steep but easy to traverse. The Chevy has no trouble in second gear on the dirt road, and even Bobby Sue stops worrying after a while. No one's coming downhill, so Chas can easily steer in the middle, away from the edge. There's nothing to worry about at all. Candi, meanwhile, is bouncing in her seat. The brandy makes her more antsy and eager than ever. She's counting the minutes now, thrilled to finally see an atomic explosion. Jeff nibbles on her ear and moves his hands up and down under the sleeping bag, trying to distract her. But to no avail. Candi talks breathlessly, a mile a minute, guessing what the bomb will look like, guessing what Angel's Landing will look like, guessing how many other people will be there, guessing how they'll react to Angels dancing. She can hardly wait.

When the crew finally reaches their destination, the number of cars is a surprise. After so many isolated miles, no one expects to see so many other people, even though the stranger had warned that there would hardly be room for parking. Nearly three dozen vehicles are wedged beside the road. Most of them have their engines running, while the passengers use the heaters to keep warm.

"I hope we have plenty of gas." Bobby Sue arches her eyebrows.

"We do." Chas gives her a kiss.

"I can't see a thing." Candi states the obvious. "It's so dark."

"I think the landing's over there. Past those scrubby trees and up on that little knoll. If we leave the car just after four o'clock, that'll give us plenty of time before Badger's set to go." Whispering in Candi's ear, Jeff adds, "Meanwhile, I promise you won't freeze to death."

The four of them hunker down and wait. Candi keeps checking her watch, and even shakes it to make sure it's running. Jeff wants to tease her, but knows enough to keep his mouth shut. Up front, Bobby Sue and Chas are very quiet, unless heavy breathing counts for noise. Candi's too distracted to smooch. She can't even close her eyes. Finally she can't stand the inactivity.

"Let's go," she decides. "It must be almost time."

"Okay." Jeff acquiesces. But he warns, "It's cold out there."

"We'll warm up by climbing that hill." Candi slides out of the car, tugging Jeff by his hand. "Come on, you two in the front seat. Time's a-wastin'! Grab the flags."

"And the clarinet."

Outside, the temperature feels frigid. Candi quickly buttons her coat and pulls the collar up to her ears. She trudges up the hill, following the dim path lit by Jeff's flashlight. Bobby Sue and Chas, clarinet case in hand, trail behind. Near the top, a crowd mills along the edge of a rocky brink. The drop-off isn't hideously steep, but Candi does a double take. For sure she and Bobby Sue should dance away from the edge. Almost everyone has brought a folding chair. She imagines a stage, right in front of the viewers, with Badger's flare in the background silhouetting the dancing figures. Swanky, she thinks to herself. She checks her watch one more time. Four twenty. Fifteen minutes until detonation. Time now to announce their intentions.

After Jeff calls for quiet, the words bubble out of Candi. "We're the Atomic Angels from the Desert Inn," she announces. "At least, two of us are. I'm Candi, and this is Bobby Sue, and we mean to dance by the light of the blast. Right here, on Angel's Landing, in honor of our country and our brave soldiers in the trenches down below. Chas here, he plays the clarinet. He'll be the orchestra. And we'll be the show. Well, Badger will be the real show, but we'll be the encore. You'll see. You'll love it."

A few people murmur reservations, but most just laugh and wave to the dancers. Off to one side, a cluster of nuns stare uneasily in their direction, as if dance plans were blasphemous. Are the nuns up here to protest, or to celebrate the atomic test? Candi isn't sure. Sure weird, though, to see the nuns so bundled up in black when Candi and Bobby Sue are about to strip off most of their clothes.

Jeff looks at his watch. Five minutes. Almost time. Both girls shed their coats, their tights, and finally their sweaters. And wait. Tapping their toes. Shivering.

At 4:35 A.M. sharp, exactly as scheduled, Badger drops from its tower and explodes in the distance.

Looking toward the Proving Ground, Candi holds her breath. Even though she can't actually see Yucca Flat in the distance, she stares where Jeff points. First a faint, dim yellow glow glimmers like the flicker of a flashlight, barely perceptible, then more urgently spreading up from the horizon. Suddenly, before Candi can take another breath, an enormous orange balloon of color changes the night to day. It blasts high in the sky, a light so bright she can see the individual goose bumps on her arm. A crystal chandelier, lit with a million candles, swinging in the night air. Brighter and brighter, and brighter still. Watching in astonishment, Candi trembles. Then Chas begins to play his clarinet. Softly at first, as if its seductive notes are a heavenly accompaniment to the cacophony below. Then more loudly, insistently inviting the girls to dance.

Before they know it, Candi and Bobby Sue are moving their arms and bending their knees in rhythm. Ballet, rather than calisthenics; smooth pirouettes and gentle arabesques instead of handstands and cartwheels. Chas's music sounds soothing patriotic notes. "My Country 'Tis of Thee," and then "O Beautiful for Spacious Skies." As the girls dance, the sky changes colors, the yellows and oranges giving way to a long white afterglow that shapes itself into a mushroom cloud. All together, as the backdrop blossoms, the girls and the cloud represent the colors of the flag. Bobby Sue in her red costume, Candi in blue, and the atomic whiteness behind. Jeff, tempted to put his hand over his heart, can't believe the impulse.

Two professional photographers emerge from the crowd, elbowing each other front and center. Each wants desperately to capture the scene on film, a front-page photo for sure. One catches the girls just so, sensuous bodies silhouetted against the atomic afterglow, provocative smiles on their faces, celebratory arms thrust high in the morning air. Jane was right, the publicity will turn out to be priceless. Desert Inn Atomic Angels dancing on Angel's Landing, exalting the greatness of America.

Someone begins applauding, and before long everyone joins in. Chas picks up the pace, fluid notes from his clarinet tumbling together, while the girls whirl faster and faster. With "You're a Grand Old Flag," they leap high in the air and spin effortlessly back to earth, their very motions imitating the cloud's movements behind them. At the red, white, and blue climax, as if on cue, both girls reach for their bosoms and pull out tiny flags. Candi hands hers to the photographer on the right; Bobby Sue, to the one on the left. Then they each clap their hands for more. Jeff obliges, taking a handful from his overcoat pocket. Still in rhythm, the dancers snatch them and begin tossing flags to the other spectators.

Although more subdued than the Desert Rock soldiers, this audience whoops and whistles, too. Even the nuns begin to smile. Soon more than a dozen people are waving tiny Stars and Stripes in the air as the mushroom cloud climbs higher and higher, drifting off into space. As it ascends, the atomic vapors whiten. Soon the initial yellows and oranges have all but disappeared, leaving the bulging cloud an eggshell shape, an oyster shade. In perfect harmony, the girls, clad in their red and blue outfits, stand out even more patriotically against the sky.

Candi's spirits soar. She feels like she's a special atomic ingredient, part and parcel of the detonation's incomparable energy, part and parcel of the cloud now wafting across the heavens. She thinks she'll never come back to earth. Never. Perhaps she'll float away with the fissioned atoms. Blow gently east. Higher and higher still. An angel in the sky.

Badger

18 APRIL 1953 • 0435 HOURS

Badger hits the ground with a vengeance. The explosion turns out to be more brilliant than any of the preceding Upshot-Knothole tests, uniquely so. Spectators think its mushroom cloud flares twice the size of any earlier shot, but they are puzzled by the lack of a shock wave. Badger is ominously silent, as if the 2,800 military men who are watching have gone suddenly deaf. Badger's huge cloud is peculiar, too. A spectrum of yellows and oranges, rather than the more typical purples and reds. The afterglow lasts a long time, casting shades of apricot and tangerine across the sky, until the mountains east of Yucca Flat take on a perverse kind of alpenglow, with the shades and hues reflected instead of refracted. In the midst of all the color, a dingy white cloud emerges, pushing pomegranate and peach aside and taking over the dawn. As if for emphasis, the nearby Joshua trees burst into flame, red Roman candle punctuation marks on the flattened desert floor.

Liz

"I've never seen anything like it."

"Me neither. And I've been in this business forever."

Crouched alongside a pregnant ewe in the confines of a wooden chute, the two men shake their heads. Jeb Stevens holds a clump of wool in his fist, wool that too easily pulls away from the ewe's shoulders. Doc Hamlin is looking at her mouth, where black scabs cover her lips.

"When I try shearing 'em, the fleece just falls apart." Jeb's voice sounds agitated, higher pitched than usual. Although the Stevens operation isn't a marginal one, this crisis could be costly.

"Where were you trailing?" Doc asks.

"Same place as usual. Over the hills to the west."

"Much forage?"

"Nothing but sagebrush and juniper. Too dry this winter. The sheep had to be real scavengers."

"See anything out of the ordinary?"

"Nah. Been trailing that country for more than thirty years. Looked just the same as always, only drier."

The vet's daughter, Liz, sitting on the top rail of the corral, listens soberly to the sheepman's words. More words strung together than normal. Usually Jeb Stevens says very little, just a sentence or two now and then. His cousin is even quieter, so shy he never looks anyone in the eye. Now Jacob stands off to one side, his head bent toward the ground, ready to push another ewe into the chute as soon the current patient is released. He is listening as intently as she is.

A thousand questions race through Liz's mind, but she keeps quiet, too. No one cares what a fourteen-year-old is thinking, not today. Usually her dad knows the answer to everything anyone could ask about medicine and animals, but this morning he seems at a loss. Just keeps shaking his head as he examines the sheep. She wonders if Pops might have some ideas. Because arthritis and a gimpy hip tie her grandfather close to home, he rarely goes out in the field anymore. But Liz knows he'll be intrigued by whatever is happening to the Stevens flock. She bets Pops has never seen anything like it either.

She watches her dad check the ewe's hooves, carefully lifting each one. "Badly cracked," he observes.

"That's the drought," Jeb interjects. "Animals as parched as the land."

"Let's look at another one."

"Sure thing."

With that, Jeb lifts the gate, pushes the ewe out into the far corral, and slams the gate back down. Almost immediately Jacob shoves another pregnant ewe into the chute. As the men turn her into place, she bleats her dismay.

Doc checks her belly. "Feels like twins."

"One piece of good news. But look at her coat." As he speaks, Jeb grabs another fistful of wool and tosses it on the ground in disgust. "Too much slippage. I'll be lucky to salvage much of anything."

"Have you called the county agent?"

"Yeah. Merrill's kind of worthless, but he said he'd come around later today."

"Good. I'd like to talk to him. Find out if he's seen this sort of thing before."

"He sounded blank on the phone, like it was all a mystery."

"He'll know if any other flocks have been affected, though."

"Yeah, but that's about all he'll know."

"I'll see if I can get Pops to make a house call. Run him out here this afternoon if his joints aren't creaking too much. He might have some thoughts about what's going on."

"I'd appreciate it. I trust your dad more than I trust Brother Merrill," Stevens quietly acknowledges.

"Okay." Doc looks up. "I'll check out half a dozen more sheep before I head home. Let me take some blood samples to send off to Salt Lake City. Might be some clues the lab can find." With that, the vet glances down and plunges a syringe into the ewe's rump. Again, she bleats noisily. Out in the holding pen, a dozen other sheep echo her tone.

That's the only part of the business that Liz dislikes. Hurting an animal. Her dad and her grandfather never cause pain on purpose. They're always trying to help. She hopes she'll be as good a vet someday. From the time she could toddle out to the barn, Liz has planned to be a vet, just like the men in her family. Her brothers, especially little George, sneer at her ambition. "Girls can't be vets," they say, repeating their disdain. Well, she'll show 'em.

That's why she traipses after her dad whenever she can. On the weekends and just about every afternoon after school, she hangs around the clinic. She cleans cages, shovels out the pens, even gets up in the middle of the night to dose a sick animal. If someone calls him out to a ranch, she coaxes Doc to take her along. Any opportunity to learn more about the vet business, Liz takes. Today she is fascinated.

Jacob jostles another ewe into the chute, and then another. More bleating and more loose wool. Doc takes some fleece samples, too, planning to send the wool along with the bloodwork.

"Tissue would be even more useful. Don't guess you want to slaughter any of these soon-to-be mothers."

"Guess not!" Jeb's voice suddenly sounds self-assured.

"Well, let me know if you lose one. I'd really like to include some tissue samples, too."

"Will do. But keep your fingers crossed that nothing else goes wrong. The J-S-J is going to take enough of a hit from losing all this wool."

"Yeah. I understand."

"So what's next?"

"That's all I can do for now. We'll be back in a couple of hours."

"Thanks, Doc. See you later. Sure hope Old Doc comes with you."

"He won't be able to resist." The vet turns toward his daughter. "Come on, Liz, make yourself useful."

Liz hops off the fence rail as he hands her his kit. She asks to carry the specimens back to the truck, but her father doesn't seem to want them out of his hands. He holds the vials as if they're precious. Maybe they are, if they hold the key to what's happening to the sheep.

WHEN THE HAMLIN TRUCK arrives back at the Stevens place that Saturday afternoon, three family members crowd the cab. Liz sits in the middle of the bench seat, her legs awkwardly straddling the gearshift. Her dad is driving, and her grandfather has wedged himself against the passenger door, his cane propped against his knee. As Liz had guessed, Pops can't resist checking out the puzzle.

Behind them, Doc's faithful companions Shep and Rags hang out over the old Ford pickup tailgate, barking their excitement. In front, a white government Chevy is making dust.

"Looks like Merrill decided to join the party," Doc laughs.

"Fat lotta good he'll do," Pops chimes in. "Just make a lot of excuses about poor forage. I'm thinking it's something else."

"Like what?" Liz turns to look her grandfather in the eye. But he's already staring out the window, checking out as much of the flock as he can see.

As the truck slows and turns in beside the Chevy, Pops takes a deep breath and glances back toward his granddaughter. "Might be something from all those tests out in the Nevada desert."

"I asked Jeb about that," Doc interjects. "He said the flock was far enough away to be safe."

"How does he know for sure?"

"Merrill said so."

"Merrill? What does that guy know about anything? I don't know why the county extension even hired him."

"Sure you do, Pops. He's got the family name, with relatives in high places all over Salt Lake City."

Pops snorts. Liz is ready to hear more gossip, but instead the two men throw open the truck doors. Sliding under the steering wheel, she climbs down after her dad and then runs around to the other side of the pickup. There, she gives a hand to her grandfather, who carefully leans on her shoulder until he gets his cane firmly set in place.

"Let's go see those critters," he says.

Meanwhile, Doc and young Merrill strike up a conversation.

"What's going on here?" the county agent asks officiously, dusting his Stetson on his knee.

"Didn't Jeb tell you on the phone?"

"Yeah, sounds like the drought's catching up with these guys."

"Maybe, maybe not." Doc knows Merrill's words will rile both Stevens cousins, so he's trying to get the guy to listen.

"What do you mean?" Merrill respects Doc's medical training. Even though he gives more credence to his own recent schooling at the ag school in Logan, he's at least willing to listen to Doc's opinions.

"Real strange symptoms. Blisters, lesions around the mouths. Serious wool slippage, as if the fleece were just falling off the animals."

"Must be something they ate."

"Okay, you're the expert. What?"

"What?"

"Yeah, what? What could they have eaten?"

Just then the men reach the Stevens cousins, who are waiting with arms akimbo, fists clenched to their sides. "About time you got here."

Merrill immediately sticks out his hand. "Good to see you, Stevens."

Jeb shakes hands perfunctorily, then turns to Old Doc Hamlin. "Sure glad you could make it. We're anxious to hear what you have to say."

Liz watches the exchange from her grandfather's side, and wonders if Merrill recognizes a brush-off when he sees one. Probably not. His youngest brother is in ninth grade, in her class, and Justin is just as dense.

Pops limps over to the corral, with Jeb on his other side. Liz climbs back up on a fence rail so she can see more of the milling sheep at once. For a long moment no one speaks. Then Pops waves his free hand.

"Let's get one in the chute and have a look."

A large black ewe, nearly ready to drop her lamb, finds herself penned alongside the elderly vet. Jacob shoves her closer, so Pops can take a look at her mouth. As Liz can see, two big blisters are hardening into scabs. Pops reaches through the railing and runs his hand down her spine. It comes away covered with clumps of black fleece, some of it tangled and some of it looking almost charred. He examines the wool closely, pulling the strands apart as he balances himself by leaning against the pen. Then he stands a little taller, trying to see past the ewe to the flock beyond.

"Push 'em around a bit, Jacob," he orders. "I want to have a quick look at as many as I can."

As soon as Pops makes his suggestion, Doc climbs up alongside his daughter. "I think I know what he's after. Look at the other black sheep. Compare those five with the grays, and then with the whites."

Liz laughs. "They're so dusty, it's hard to tell which are white and which are gray. They all look dirty."

"But I think Pops sees a difference. Check it out."

Liz looks carefully at the bleating flock. By this time, the pregnant ewes, terribly unhappy, are noisily voicing their displeasure. The din makes this morning's complaints sound relatively minor. Almost instantly she can see what her father means. The backs of the six black sheep look faintly seared, as if they'd rolled too close to a campfire. The white ones seem fine, though the two she can see the best have more of those lesions around their mouths.

Pops reaches out toward a young gray ewe. She dances away, but not before Liz spots a lightly charred pattern across her rump. The gray's steps frighten the others even more, and suddenly the whole flock is milling far too fast for the small enclosure.

"Better calm 'em down," Jeb warns his cousin. "Climb out of there."

Jacob obeys, settling onto the top rail on the other side of Doc. Merrill leans against the fence alongside Jeb and Pops, waiting for someone to say something.

No one speaks, as the flock slows itself and clusters at the far side of the corral. Then Pops lifts his cane and points to the nearest ewe.

"See that corduroy look along her back? Looks like some kind of burn to me."

Jeb frowns. "I see it, but I don't understand it."

Merrill chortles. "Doesn't seem to me like sheep get sunburned."

Doc wants to shout, "It's not from the sun, you fool," but he restrains himself. This is his father's show for now. Time enough for him to talk after the lab results come back.

Liz glances at her father. He winks back, and she knows exactly what he's thinking. Merrill sure is a jerk, and she's beginning to understand what might be wrong with the Stevens sheep.

Pops turns toward Merrill. "How about radiation? Any chance of these ewes getting a dose of Nevada fallout?"

"No way." Merrill is on firm ground, sure of himself as he recites the information he's been given. He can almost quote the government brochures by heart. "Immediate biological responses should not be expected."

"I have to agree with Merrill," Jeb Stevens grudgingly accedes. "Whatever's wrong, it can't be from the atomic testing. If it wasn't safe, they wouldn't be setting those things off over there."

"The guys at the Madison mining operation say the government didn't tell them the truth. They say they got all kinds of assurances, and then the radiation count went sky-high." Doc can't resist putting in his two cents' worth.

"That's north of here, though, and west. I think they're pretty careful about what they're doing." Jeb isn't ready to blame the government for his woes, not at all.

Merrill concurs. "Not a problem here. We're far enough away to be safe."

"What about where you were trailing, though?" Doc keeps pushing his point. "Isn't that pretty close to the Groom Mountains?"

Still not convinced, Jeb shakes his head. "No, we were ten, fifteen miles this side. And besides, we didn't see a thing."

"Not even a cloud overhead?"

"Sure, but it was sky-high."

"Anything drifting toward the ground?"

"Maybe it was dustier than usual, more dust in the air, but that's from the drought."

"Maybe not." Pops speaks mildly. "Maybe your problem isn't drought. Maybe it's radiation."

"Come off it, Dr. Hamlin." Merrill jumps into the conversation. "You know better than to suggest that."

"How else do you explain what we're seeing on these sheep? The burns. The wool slippage. The blisters and scabs." Pops's voice is patient, as if he were talking to a recalcitrant student. "It's a pattern."

"I think we need a lot more information before we jump to any such conclusion," Merrill reacts. "I'll make some inquiries, maybe ask a couple of government scientists to come take a look. They'll reassure you that it's nothing but drought. Meanwhile, I sure hope you don't go noising this cockeyed radiation opinion around town."

Pops and Doc nod in unison, as if they had already guessed what Merrill's response would be. Liz smiles to herself. When she gets to school on Monday, she'll see what she can find out about radiation and fallout. Maybe stop by the Cedar City library after school. She knows about the Nevada Proving Ground, of course, but she doesn't know much about the science. Like the Stevenses, she's just assumed that the current testing is safe. Now she realizes that her dad and her grandfather aren't nearly so convinced. Time for her to learn some facts.

"Hop down here, Lizzie, give me your arm." Pops is ready to leave. He's seen enough, and knows there's nothing more to be done until the lab results come back. A pity they can't get any tissue samples, but Doc had said Jeb's pretty adamant about not butchering one of his ewes.

Liz and Pops amble back to the truck slowly. He turns a couple of times, looking back at the flock as if to double-check his observations.

"Did you solve the mystery?" Liz begs him to say yes.

"Perhaps. But that young Merrill fellow, he'll do everything in his power to prove me wrong."

"I'm pretty sure Dad agrees with you. He kept nodding his head while you were talking."

"Oh, I'm sure he's thinking the same thing. We talked about it before we left home."

"So what happens next?"

"Wait a while. Get the reports back from the lab. See if the sheep recover. Listen to what the government boys have to say."

Just then, Doc catches up with his father and his daughter. The three generations of Hamlins smile at each other. "That Merrill," Doc can't resist saying. "He's something else."

Pops grins, and so does Liz.

ON MONDAY AFTERNOON she settles herself in the public library. During her free period she had tried to find some atomic testing information, but the high school librarian wasn't particularly interested. Miss Hill made Liz watch a silly film called *Duck and Cover,* the same one they'd already seen in class the month before, and then she lectured Liz about the importance of everything that's happening at the Nevada Proving Ground. "It's the battleground of the Cold War," Miss Hill repeated over and over again, "keeping America safe from the Red Menace."

The librarian at the public library is a little more forthcoming. She's another Merrill, so Liz isn't altogether sure about the accuracy of her information, but at least she knows some facts about what's happening this year at Frenchman and Yucca Flats. Miss Merrill shows Liz a stack of newspaper clippings taken from the *Las Vegas Review-Journal,* and lets her read about the mushrooms blooming in the desert. Liz is especially intrigued by one reporter's flowery phrases describing the "boiling purple fireball" and the "low thumping rumble across the valley below." After she reads several articles assuring the population of the test safety, she copies down the headlines to show her dad and her grandfather. "Atom Test Poison in Air Minimized," says one; "Scientists Claim Utahans 'Safe from Radiation,'" announces another. That one was written right after the Groom Range miners complained. She wonders if her family would agree.

That night at dinner, she shares her findings. Lots of "feel good" phrases, not much in the way of facts. Her two younger brothers scoff at what she's doing. Her dad promises he'll try and find out some more details. Pops just nods.

"Like I suspected," he says, "they're not saying much about what's floating around in the air."

"Should we worry?" Liz's mother, Diane, frets about her family's safety.

"Not as long as our wool isn't falling out," her husband teases.

"Or worse," Pops mumbles under his breath.

Pretending she didn't hear, Liz excuses herself from the table so she can go and read some more.

LESS THAN A MONTH LATER, Utah's sheep problems are compounded. The telephone rings while the Hamlins are eating breakfast.

"I'll get it."

Liz, who isn't all that fond of her Cream of Wheat anyway, jumps up from the table.

"For you, Dad. Jeb Stevens again. He sounds even more upset than before."

Doc trades his spoon for the telephone, and listens to the voice on the other end of the line. When he finally hangs up, he looks toward his wife. "Jeb's got more trouble. I need to get over there."

"Can I go, too?" Veterinarian wannabe Liz begs her father.

"It's Tuesday. You need to go to school."

"I learn more when I'm with you," Liz cajoles.

Pops, always amused by his granddaughter's wily ways, coughs into his napkin. He knows she'll persuade her father. She always does.

"It's not going to be pretty," Doc observes. "The ewes are birthing and they're having problems."

"I don't mind. If I'm going to be a vet, I need to see what's real."

"Girls can't be vets," her brother George heckles his older sister for the thousandth time. "Don't waste your energy."

"Can, too," Liz retorts. "I'll get into vet school. You just wait and see."

"That's a lot of years in the future," their father reminds them both. "Think you can handle a real emergency?"

"Just pregnant ewes?"

"Sounds like more than that."

"Please, Dad." Liz insists.

"You won't throw up? The situation sounds kind of nasty."

"I've never been sick before. Remember that time when Mr. Larimore's horse got so cut up on the barb wire? There was blood spurting everywhere, and I was fine."

"You'll need to stay out of the way." Doc hesitates.

"I will. I promise."

Doc rarely can resist his daughter's pleas. "Okay. Come on. Diane, will you call the school and make excuses?"

His wife hides a smile, as if she'd known all along what he'd decide, and Liz throws her arms around her father, giving him a big hug. She follows him out of the kitchen. At the last minute, though, she can't resist turning and sticking her tongue out at her little brother. He's always such a pain.

Before Liz and Doc leave the house, Doc does some double-checking with his father. They step into Pops's bedroom, so Liz can't hear what they're saying. But both are frowning when they emerge.

On the way over to the Stevens place, Liz tries to gather more details.

"What exactly did Mr. Stevens say?"

"It sounds like something's wrong with the lambs, like they're not formed just right."

"Are they dying?"

"Almost as soon as they drop." Doc sighs. "And the ewes are acting weird, too."

"What do you think's wrong?"

"My guess is more radiation poisoning, probably left over from the dose they got while they were trailing."

"How can you be sure?"

"I can't. The lab tests didn't reveal much of anything. But now we'll have plenty of tissue samples. Sounds like a lot of dead sheep."

At the Stevens ranch, Doc doesn't bother to stop at the main house. Turning the truck down a narrow two-track, he drives over the ruts as quickly as he can. He parks under a big cottonwood, tells Shep and Rags to stay put in the truck bed, and grabs his kit, motioning to Liz to follow.

"Remember," he repeats his instructions, "you stay out of the way."

Liz murmurs a quiet "yes, sir" and nods her head in agreement, kind of. Doc gives her a quick hug in return, then steps ahead of his daughter so he'll be first into the lambing shed. She follows close behind, eager to see everything.

It's the stench that registers first. The terrible, acrid, biting smell of blood and putrid flesh. Liz puts her hand to her mouth, but holds herself steady. Reaching in her hip pocket for the red bandanna that always hangs there, she clasps it over the bottom part of her face and takes shallow breaths of the rancid air. She also pulls a piece of Wrigley's from her pocket, unwraps the gum quickly, and jams it into her mouth.

To her left, near the open part of the shed, an uneven stack of corpses, dead lambs piled as high as her shoulder, leans against the wall. She moves away from it, loath to look too closely at the rotting flesh and blood.

To her right, Mr. Stevens and her father bend over a ewe that is struggling to drop a lamb. From what Liz can see of the three protruding legs, the lamb looks unfinished, more like a fetus than a sheep. Two of the legs have no hooves, just rounded, seeping malformations instead. When the lamb finally emerges, its head is misshapen, too, nose angled off to one side, ears turned sideways. Doc spends some time examining it closely, checking its nostrils, palpitating its thin chest. Liz can actually see its heart beating erratically through its transparent skin. As the heart slows, and stops, Doc shakes his head. Mr. Stevens, holding the remains at arm's length, carries the tiny carcass over to the stack of corpses and tosses it on top.

Just beyond her father and the struggling ewe, Liz can see another mother trying to nurse a wobbly new offspring. But the newborn won't nurse. It stands as if in a stupor, frozen almost, unable to move. No one is paying attention to the pair, so she tiptoes over, intending to help. Just as she reaches for the lamb, it totters over, shudders once, and sprawls in the straw, unmoving. She drops her handkerchief, the stench forgotten, and tries to lift the lamb upright. To no avail. It lies dead at its mother's feet, until the ewe abruptly moves away from both Liz and the lamb. The ewe bleats softly—distrustful, distressed, and deeply confused.

Through the tears that are, by now, rolling down her cheeks, Liz can see her father and Mr. Stevens attending another birth, one that might be successful. She wants to help, but knows better than to get too close. Once the lamb starts nursing, however, her dad motions her over. "Keep an eye on this one, Lizzie," he says. "Keep it on its feet. It might be okay."

She nods. "Go on to the next ones. I'll stay here."

"How are *you* doing?" Liz's dad notices the tears streaking her face.

"I'll be all right," she assures him. "It's just so overpowering. Worse than I ever imagined."

"I know, I know. We just have to do the best we can."

Across the shed, Jacob Stevens is hard at work, too, trying to save as many tiny lambs as possible. He's having more luck as he moves from one sheep to another. That evening she'll remember to tell Pops—the white ewes with white lambs are doing better than the blacks and grays.

She checks over the lamb she's supposed to be watching. No malformations that she can see, except it's strangely potbellied, almost bloated. She sits down in the bloodied straw, props the lamb against her shoulder. Wiping its muzzle with her handkerchief, she urges it back to its mother's milk. The tiny lamb complies, and begins nursing again. Liz dries her hands on her bandanna. The poisonous smell doesn't bother her much anymore, though she reaches in her pocket for a fresh stick of spearmint.

Another lamb, this one a gray, looks like it needs her attention. It stands statue-like, barely moving and uninterested in its mother. Liz moves over and crouches alongside the newborn, trying to hold it upright and steady. Then she glances down at its hooves—where its hooves are supposed to be. It has only three, the fourth a mucous-covered, reddish-colored stump. Its twin, already dead, is faceless, its eyes unformed, its nose without nostrils. Before she has time to register the details of the grotesque body, the other lamb falls beside it. Twins, dead. Liz looks at the mother, notes the burn pattern on her spine, now healed over so it's almost invisible. She'll remember to tell Pops about that, too.

After what seem like nonstop births and deaths, for some reason there's a midafternoon letup. While Liz sits near still another ewe and her apparently healthy twins, she listens to the men talking about the day's events. Her father is certain that the malformations and the horrendous deaths are caused by atomic radiation; Jeb Stevens still isn't convinced. Jacob, silent as always, simply hovers nearby, gnawing on a piece of straw and rubbing his hands against his thighs.

"Tissue samples, they'll prove my point," Doc insists.

"Not likely." Jeb disagrees.

"Let's get some experts down here to check things out."

"Who? Merrill?"

"Merrill, yes. But some state officials, too. Maybe the AEC boys as well."

"They won't be bothered."

"They'll bother if we make some noise. Maybe we ought to invite a news reporter up from Las Vegas."

"I dunno, Doc." Jeb is unsure. "I hate to make a fuss."

"But we're talking about your stock, your livelihood." Frustrated, Liz's dad stiffens and throws up his hands. "You can't just pretend it's not happening."

"Okay." Jeb capitulates. "I'm willing to let people have a look, but we can't leave all these dead lambs stacked in the shed. It already stinks to high heaven in here."

"You shouldn't destroy the carcasses, not until we've had time to examine them more fully."

"Yeah, but they can't stay here. The maggots are already spreading."

Liz knows Mr. Stevens's observation is true. She's already spotted knots of white crawling in and out of the rotting corpses. Maggots can infect the whole flock, can debilitate the healthy ewes and lambs, too.

Her father frowns. "Either way it's a problem."

"Well, I'm gonna get these carcasses out of the way. You take what you need, get some samples, do whatever you have to do. But I'm not gonna let these sheep rot in my shed one minute longer." Jeb gestures to his cousin. "Can you push the 'dozer close enough to shove 'em outside?"

Jacob shakes his head. So does Doc.

"Then let's pull the flatbed up close," Jeb continues. We can stack 'em side by side and haul 'em to the dump."

"County won't like that," Doc observes mildly.

"Then we'll bury 'em right here. Jacob can dig a hole at the far end of our property, and we'll just dump 'em in. Cover 'em up by nightfall. No one can complain about that."

Liz can tell that her father doesn't agree with Jeb. But she also can tell that he can't think of a way to change the sheepman's mind. More than seven hundred dead lambs pose a real problem for everyone.

Jacob is heading out to the flatbed when he stops short. Squirreling down the two-track, Merrill's white Chevy is speeding toward them.

"Did you call him?" Doc inquires.

"Yeah, right after I talked to you this morning. He said he had to get out to the Bransons,' that Mark and Louella were having trouble, too. Said he'd come by later. That means now, I guess."

"Since he's in a hurry he must have bad news."

Even though she doesn't much like the Merrills, Liz decides her dad is being too harsh. Her mom at least thinks Mr. Merrill means well. She believes he just doesn't seem to think things through, that he'll be more thoughtful when he gets a little older. When she said so, Pops shook his head.

Now Merrill jumps out of his car, slamming the door shut with his elbow. "How's your flock?" he asks Jeb with a flourish.

"It's a disaster," Jeb replies. "Lambs born without hooves, without eyes, without nostrils, lambs dying, ewes not able to give milk." He gestures back toward the shed. "Look at all the dead ones. We're ruined."

Merrill walks over to the bloody stack of lambs. "Just like the Bransons. Their lambs are malformed and dying, too."

"When I was out there a couple of weeks ago, their flock was in pretty good shape," Doc interjects. "Not as much wool slippage as the sheep here, and not as many blistered muzzles."

"They were trailing a couple of canyons north of us," Jeb reminds the other men.

"Maybe ate the same weeds as your flock," Merrill responds helpfully.

Liz can hardly believe what she is hearing. Surely Merrill doesn't think some bush or shrub or grass led to this horror. She looks down at her hands, at the dried blood crusted underneath her fingernails. She's been around farm animals all her life, watched them get born, nursed them when her dad needed her. She's never heard of anything as gross as what she's seen today.

When they didn't think she was listening, when they thought she was inside studying when really she was sitting under an open window, she'd overheard her father and her grandfather talking about the blood work Doc had sent to Salt Lake City. Nothing showed up, the lab couldn't find any abnormalities. But that hadn't convinced them their theory was wrong. Both were insistent. Three weeks ago they thought the sheep were showing signs of severe radiation poisoning. Now the ugly births surely are confirming their suspicions.

THAT NIGHT, Liz hears them talking again. This time their voices are louder than before, as if they're more certain they're correct.

"Got to be coming from the Proving Ground," Pops says firmly. "Got to be poison in the air."

Liz knows the proper words. Gamma rays and beta rays. She'll tell him later.

Doc agrees. "What else could cause such malformations? Heads without features. Legs without hooves. It was god-awful, Pops. Just god-awful."

Pops lowers his voice. "How'd Liz take it?"

"Like a trooper. Sat right down in the muck and tried to help."

"She'll be a fine vet someday, son, a fine one," Pops whispers.

"I know, I know. Diane and I already are putting away a little money, try-ing to save up for her tuition. She's smart enough to get a scholarship, but we plan to help out, too."

Liz smiles at what the two men trust is a secret. She's already heard her parents talking, several times. She knows about the special fund. She knows they plan to send her away to school. She also realizes her dad wouldn't take her along on calls like today unless he was really sure she'll be okay. Her eyes briefly well with tears, but she quickly brushes them away. And she is okay, unless she dwells too much on the twisted, stunted lambs.

A WEEK LATER, Doc actually brings up the subject of skipping school. "I know I shouldn't suggest this," he begins slowly, "but Pops thinks you ought to come along and listen while the government scientists look at the Stevens flock."

"Do I get credit or the blame?" Pops chuckles, innocently buttering a piece of toast.

"I'll call school again," Liz's mother volunteers. Her tone of voice implies collusion, as if everyone had already discussed and settled the matter.

"Me, too!" George interrupts. "If Lizzie skips school again, I get to stay home, too."

"Not on your life," his mother replies. "I've already packed your lunch."

This time Liz, controlling herself but inwardly gloating, doesn't stick out her tongue.

Once again the three Hamlins jam themselves into the old pickup. Once again Shep and Rags jump in back. Liz isn't surprised that her grandfather's going to the Stevens place today. He's just as curious as she is about what the government men will say. And her dad can hardly contain himself. The Ham-lins want their theory proved correct.

Jeb Stevens is already talking with Merrill and two other men when Doc and Pops and Liz drive up. The visitors apparently are ag specialists from Salt Lake City. Doc recognizes one as Merrill's supervisor; Pops knows the other, a veterinary science professor from the university. By the time the Hamlins join the conversation, another government vehicle has arrived, this one with an Atomic Energy Commission logo on its door. Two more men emerge, one in uniform, the other wearing a suit that Liz immediately decides looks fool-ish in Cedar City, Utah. At least he isn't wearing a tie.

"Let's see what you've got," the uniform orders. Liz doesn't know his name, and doesn't care.

"I'm not sure why you called us out here," the suit adds. "I'm sure we'll be able to put your fears to rest."

Not likely, Liz thinks to herself.

Jeb Stevens leading the way, the men move quickly toward the enclosure where the sheep are penned. Liz and Pops follow more slowly. "Why are they here?" she whispers. "How can they put fears to rest after so many losses? That doesn't make sense."

"Shhh." Her grandfather puts his finger to his lips. "Just listen. You'll see what they're up to."

Now Doc and Jeb are describing the events of the month—the loose wool, the blisters, the hideous births, the incomprehensible number of deaths.

"How many deaths?" the suit inquires.

"Seven hundred and ninety-three for me," Jeb Stevens answers. "More like six hundred at the Bransons.' You can take a count up and down the valley. Probably close to five thousand overall."

The uniform turns toward Merrill's boss. "Get an accurate number. Guesses don't mean much."

"Will do."

While Merrill makes a note on the dingy pad of paper he carries everywhere, Liz nudges her grandfather again. "Is the guy in the suit in charge?"

"Looks that way, doesn't it?"

"If he is, then they must think they're responsible."

Pops grimaces slightly. "Wait and see," he repeats, his voice very low.

The conversation turns on numbers that mean little to Liz. The scientist has done a series of tests on the blood and tissue samples Doc sent north. He hasn't found much, except for some elevated thyroid counts. Doc argues with him, wondering how the lab tests can be so inconclusive. Surely they could glean more information. The scientist stands his ground, insisting that his findings are accurate.

Merrill's boss, cognizant of the insistent Salt Lake City newspaper coverage, is willing to investigate further. Another set of data surely will prove the problems have nothing to do with radiation. "How about another round of lab tests?" he suggests.

"Hard to do," Doc admits. "No more samples. Or else they've been contaminated."

"How so? Where are the carcasses?"

"Buried." Jeb spits out the word.

"Buried! Then how in hell do you expect us to investigate your inane allegations?" the suit snarls. "Branson burned all his dead lambs. Yours are six feet underground. There's nothing left to prove your claims."

Remembering her father's caution to the Stevens cousins, that they shouldn't bury all the remains, Liz wonders what he'll have to say. She can tell he's getting angry by the reddening on the back of his neck. But before Doc can add whatever he is thinking, Jeb Stevens takes one step toward the suit and looks him straight in the eye.

"Maggots. Don't you know anything about sheep or about dead animals? Maggots. We had to get rid of the carcasses or the maggots would have infested every sheep left alive." He coughs and clears his throat. "Had to save what we could."

The suit steps back a pace. "Without those carcasses, we can't do a thing."

The uniform concurs. Throughout the exchange, he hasn't said a word. But Liz realizes the uniform's job is to reinforce whatever the suit says, just as Merrill's assignment is to agree with the two men from Salt Lake City. Her dad, on the other hand, doesn't have to acquiesce to anyone. Instead, he points toward the flock.

"Let's take a look at the ones left alive. At least you can see the burns for yourselves. And the blisters."

Jacob opens the gate and slides into the pen. Moments later, he half shoves, half pulls a dusty ewe toward the group. Her lamb follows, bleating uneasily.

"He ought to pick a black one," Liz whispers to her grandfather.

Pops squeezes her arm, though he doesn't say anything in response.

The scientist leans over the fence, then joins Jacob and the sheep in the pen. He runs his hands up and down the ewe's spine. She'd been sheared a month ago. Since her new wool is already growing in, he has difficulty seeing any of the signs that earlier had been so apparent. He pries open her jaw. Liz can see that the blisters are mostly healed, that any scabbing has fallen away. The ewe looks perfectly healthy, if a bit underweight, as does her trailing lamb.

Doc motions for Jacob to pull over another. He does so, a gray one this time, with twins. Pops, still silent, squeezes Liz's arm again.

Once more the scientist checks over the ewe. He eyes her lambs, too, noting that they seem to be eating well. "Not much to see," he concludes. "No evidence of burns, no wool slippage, no lesions around her muzzle."

The suit halfway smiles. "That's it, then. There's nothing more to be done here."

"I don't think so." Doc raises his voice. "How do we account for what's happened? The loose wool and the blisters? And all the fetuses gone bad? Surely you don't think that's normal?"

"Poison plants of some sort."

"The drought's dried out the forage."

"Something they ate."

"Pity."

"No connection to the Proving Ground."

"Too far away."

"Can expect some losses in a dry year."

"No obvious radiation damage that I can see."

"So what on earth do you expect me to do?" Jeb Stevens's voice now takes on a plaintive tone.

The suit stands taller. "That's your problem, sir. It's out of our hands." Liz can tell he doesn't think much of men from the sticks. He sneered at Jeb Stevens, and he hardly listened to her dad. Now he's ready to go, already putting Cedar City out of his mind.

Jeb tries one more time. "My sheep, they died ugly. First time ever."

"Nothing to do with us." The uniform's voice is turning colder.

"The lab tests were all negative," the suit repeats.

"But look at the lambs. I could see the evidence with my own eyes."

The uniform can no longer contain himself. "What would you know about evidence, Mr. Stevens? You're just a dumb farmer. Nothing more."

Astounded, Jeb stares back at the arrogant man. Liz thinks the meddler looks like one of George's toy soldiers, overdressed and overblown. She'll be glad when the two men drive away. They don't belong here. Her father, clenching and unclenching his fists, looks like he wants to hit one of them. Finally the suit shrugs, voices meaningless condolences, and steers the uniform back toward their car.

But Doc isn't finished. "You'll be hearing from us again." His voice is firm. "The valley sheepmen have scheduled a meeting in the high school gym for Friday night. You're welcome to join us," he adds facetiously.

"We might just do that," the suit supposes. "If we're still in town."

"I'll be there for sure," Merrill's boss acknowledges. "Merrill, too."

The scientist needs to head back to Salt Lake City. "Prior commitment," he murmurs vaguely.

Then Liz knows that this is only the beginning, that her dad and all the sheepmen in the valley will take this fight further. Even Mr. Stevens, who so badly wants the government not to be at fault, can see that he and Doc and Branson and all the other men need to do more. The crack about being nothing but a dumb farmer, fighting words, has enraged Jeb Stevens. Now he and his cousin are ready for a fracas.

Pops nudges her toward their truck. "I think I'll take in that get-together, too."

"You, going out at night?" Liz can hardly believe what she's hearing.

"Why not? Can't let 'em get away with this. Can't let 'em think we're ignorant rubes, or that our animals are guinea pigs. Dumb farmer indeed! Besides, it sounds like they could use another vet's opinion."

"Can I come, too?"

"Sure, I expect there'll be a lot of women there. The wives, they'll scuffle when no one else will. In fact, if Jeb had a wife I bet he'd sing a different tune. She'd be nagging him into action, just like Louella Branson has been chewing on Mark every day this month."

"Mr. Stevens was sure annoyed at that stupid man's remark, but he doesn't want to blame the government. He wants to be a good patriot. And he doesn't want to think they're covering anything up." Liz pauses for a moment. "They wouldn't lie to us, would they?"

Instead of answering, Pops just squeezes her arm.

Simon

Three Marine HRS helicopters hover ten feet off the ground. Two wait eleven kilometers from ground zero while the third is six kilometers farther away. As protection from the atomic flash, the three helicopter copilots wear high-density goggles. The three pilots will duck their heads, hoping their visors shield their eyes. Simon drops from its tower on schedule and on target, but little else about Simon is predictable. The yield is huge, the equivalent of 43 kilotons of TNT when only 35 kilotons had been projected. The colorful cloud is gigantic, tornadoing to 44,000 feet, where the wind picks up at forty-eight knots. A Navy drone Skyraider aims for the top of the mushroom stem, where a pressure wave decimates its wing panels and sends it plummeting to the ground. Radiation, both visible and invisible, sails eastward, spreading quickly and closing highways. Commercial flight is banned across the intermountain West. The AEC quickly sends out word, however, that there's no need for alarm. Calling Simon a "miscalculation," Commissioner Thomas Murray reiterates the obvious. "Gentlemen, we must not let anything interfere with this series of tests—nothing."

Daniel

Five Chevys, a Studebaker and a Nash, two Plymouths, a Pontiac, a Cadillac, half a dozen Fords and a dozen pickups, one brand-new, another an aged Model T. A milk truck, a bakery delivery truck, a Greyhound bus carrying twenty-three passengers, a flatbed hauling coils of steel. Coming south from Alamo, a farm vehicle loaded with heifers follows behind a Bekins moving van. There at the intersection of Nevada Highways 93 and 91, the odd assortment of vehicles all line up together. Some from the north, others from the east, stopped by the makeshift roadblock that impedes their progress. Standing between a Jeep parked sideways and a sheriff's patrol car with flashing lights, an officer motions with his arms. No westbound traffic, headed for Las Vegas, can move forward until the sheriff and the U.S. government's two-man team of radiation monitors gives the okay.

Already warming up, the dry desert air seeps through the window cracks and heats up the already hot drivers. None of the vehicles has an air conditioner.

"Sir, you'll need to keep your window closed."

The man in the Cadillac looks uncertainly at the sheriff standing alongside his car.

"And the vents shut."

The man frowns.

"I'm sorry for the inconvenience, sir. We're hurrying this along as best we can."

The man rolls up his window, but the woman beside him is clearly agitated.

"Nothing to worry about, ma'am." The sheriff raises his voice so she can hear. "Everything's fine. We're just taking a few precautions."

Abruptly, the man throws open his car door and steps outside. Slamming it behind him, he stands jaw to jaw with the sheriff.

"No need to be upset, sir. Here comes the radiation specialist now."

A man carrying a portable Geiger counter moves close to the Cadillac. He runs the device's probe across the hood and then along the passenger side. A ticking sound grows louder, fades a bit, becomes louder still. At the trunk he pauses, then moves the detector slowly from back to front. Again the sound diminishes, then accelerates unevenly.

"Better get this one washed."

The sheriff inadvertently steps away from the Cadillac. The driver follows, arguing something about being in a hurry. The rad specialist intervenes, explaining the situation in delicate phrases. This morning's atomic test generated a minute amount of fallout. Blew some of it in this direction. Just a little; not much. Nothing to worry about, but the government wants to be sure that everyone stays safe. Can't be too careful. He recommends a car wash, at government expense.

The driver shrugs. He's persuaded. Safety, at government expense, is a good thing after all. A free car wash, a good thing too.

"If you'll just step back in your car, and drive to that service station over there, they'll have your Caddy scrubbed down in no time."

The government man and the sheriff nod at each other, while the driver climbs back in his car.

"Careful, sir. Try not to touch the side panel."

The car door closes, so the driver cannot hear the rest of the rad specialist's words.

"Four hundred! Hotter than a firecracker!"

"Highest so far today." The sheriff grimaces, wonders what else might be coming down the road.

The next vehicle is a Studebaker. Its driver pushes back a sweat-stained cap and smiles at the sheriff.

"This'll just take a moment, sir. Drive down from Alamo this morning?"

The driver nods.

"See the mushroom cloud?"

The driver nods again.

"Seems like some stuff might have fallen on the cars along Highway 93. We're just checking."

The rad specialist approaches. Again he walks slowly along one side of the car and then back along the other. He pokes the probe inside, checking, double-checking.

"Nothing here. This one's clean."

The sheriff motions the Studebaker to drive away.

"You're free to continue on, sir. Must have been driving too fast for that cloud."

The driver grins, unwilling to acknowledge aloud his appreciation for a state like Nevada. No speed limit posted on its open highways; no reason to drive slow.

The sheriff wipes his brow. The day is warming up quite nicely, but his winter uniform is too heavy for the morning air. He'll need to tell his wife to get out his short-sleeved shirts. He wonders how long he'll be stuck at this roadblock. The damned AEC expects him to be at their beck and call. Some bureaucrat phoned him at 6 A.M., all knotted up about a cloud drifting over the highway. Told him to get out there and wait for the mobile team high-tailing it east from Las Vegas. Told him to set up a roadblock near the local service station. Told him to make plans for washing down the cars. Told him to hop to, when these sorts of orders didn't seem at all like a part of his job.

It isn't his place to question the government, but he does wonder why they didn't just keep all the vehicles from driving into the potentially con-taminated area in the first place. They've known for days there would be a detonation this morning. Why not set up roadblocks someplace else? Hold everyone up in Alamo and St. George until the test cloud blows apart. Instead, they let all these cars come south and west across the desert. And now it's up to him to stop them, and if necessary to get them cleaned up. Doesn't seem like his responsibility, playing stop-and-go traffic cop along the highway. He has better things to do. The sheriff shrugs, and moves toward the Bekins van pulling alongside.

The rad specialist takes his time with the big truck, reaching the probe around each pair of oversized tires to check the underside of the trailer. All the time, his detector is clicking consistently, as if in tune with his motions.

"Another hot one." He signals to the sheriff.

The sheriff can tell the driver wants a free pass, but he directs the eighteen-wheeler toward the Texaco sign instead.

"Can't be too careful," he says.

At the service station, the thwarted travelers watch while two middle-aged men soap and rinse their vehicles. One holds a hose, spraying each car care-fully. The other pushes a long-handled mop over the roofs and sides, mak-ing sure the water touches every exposed surface. When they finish, a young Indian boy wipes the water off. The excess flows across the service station lot and into the local drainage ditch, where the muddy water soon evaporates into the dry desert air.

The woman from the Cadillac questions the Bekins driver, who frowns. This unplanned stop puts him behind schedule. He needs to be in Las Vegas before noon, and now he'll never make it on time. He knows he should have his truck washed down before he delivers the furniture inside. He understands that the government is just being vigilant. Clearly the monitors are looking out for his well-being. But he sure wishes he could be on his way.

The service station owner is more loquacious. Born and raised in Glendale, Nevada, he's lived here all his life except for a couple of years in Italy. He's an avid patriot, proud of his World War II service and eager to show off his knowledge about atomic testing and radiation safety. Today's experiment is the seventh of the Upshot-Knothole series. Supposed to be the biggest one this year, a tower drop, out on Yucca Flat. Wow—the government is building 'em giant-sized! His enthusiasm is contagious. Before long, the couple from the Cadillac, a woman driving a gray Nash, the milk truck driver, and a Fuller Brush salesman in a nondescript blue Ford are all listening. Then they're all talking at once.

"I overheard the government guy explaining to the sheriff. Sixteen, eighteen miles north and east of here. That's where most of the fallout occurred."

"Fallout? Should we be worried?"

"They say it's safe in small numbers. Most of the cloud blew on toward Denver. By then it was too high to do any damage."

"Damage?"

"Well, it doesn't exactly hurt anything," the Texaco operator announces authoritatively. "Not when it's in the air."

"Not so good for humans if it touches the ground, though," the salesman counters. "Look at what happened to all them Japs in Hiroshima and Nagasaki."

"Well, I'm not worried. What they're doing at the Proving Ground is perfectly safe." The service station man punches his fist at the salesman's arm. "Besides, we've got to keep ahead of the Russkies."

"Anything out there?" the single woman asks. "Anybody live where they think the contamination might have fallen?"

"Nah, just some Paiutes down along the river. And their sheep."

"Are they okay?"

"Sure. Jimmy came in to wipe down the cars. He didn't say anything about any problem." The man chuckles. "Of course, his English ain't too good."

"I don't mind the roadblock." The single woman changes the subject. "I'm glad they're taking precautions to protect us."

"Me, too," the salesman agrees.

Listening to the conversation, the cattleman wonders about his livestock. He doesn't say anything, though. The two washers finish his truck up by squirting a spray of water at the cows. "Lot of good that'll do," he mutters under his breath. He remembers the stories he's heard about beta burns, but he also recalls that those only occurred on horses out to pasture. Inside their trailer, his heifers ought to be okay. Another couple of hours, he'll have 'em to market. He smiles. He's just as patriotic as the service station owner, just as committed to celebrating the important tests taking place that year. He's proud to be an American, happy to do his part. Veterans of World War II, one in the South Pacific and one in southern Europe, both men applaud the work of the Nevada Proving Ground. Those scientists sure are smart. Still, the cattleman worries a little about the fallout and those beta burns. He's heard rumors around Alamo, and his wife got an earful when she was shopping in Caliente last week. Stuff about Groom Mountain and the Madison Mine. "Everyone was talking about it," she said.

A welcome voice interrupts his thoughts.

"You're all set, sir."

With a nod, the rancher climbs behind the wheel. Best not to fret about rumors. Now that so many vehicles are stopped here in Glendale, he expects little traffic. Ought to make good time, he thinks to himself, as one heifer lows in the background.

The driver of the milk truck isn't so lucky. The probe ticks noisily as the rad specialist rechecks the milk cans stacked side by side. Even after the washing, the gamma numbers are still too high.

"We'll have to do it again," the government man apologizes. "Don't want to take any chances."

The driver watches helplessly as the two workers begin hosing his truck a second time. They look like they're scrubbing a little harder, soaping the invisible contamination and hoping they'll get the milk cans clean. The Indian boy stands off to one side, waiting for the men to finish.

Back at the roadblock, the Greyhound bus pulls to the head of the line. Knocking on the door with one hand, the sheriff scratches his head with the other. No one said anything about buses. The sheriff can't decide. Get all these people off, or keep 'em inside. Tacitly, he looks toward the monitor for an answer. What's the protocol?

The rad specialist doesn't know. He's only been in Las Vegas for a couple of weeks, just since the last shot. Before that, he'd been up at the Madison Mine, keeping track of the gamma ray counts after the problems last month. Not likely to see a bus full of people out there in the middle of nowhere. Not likely to see another person, except for the four miners, who spend most of their time underground. No one's ever told him what to do about buses.

"Let me check the count. Then we'll decide."

As always, he starts at the front of the vehicle and moves slowly toward the back.

"Just under four hundred. Way too high. I'd better call this one in. Find out what the Las Vegas rad-safe officer recommends."

At the edge of the road, the sheriff stands silently while the monitor walks over to his Jeep. A quick radio check gives little additional information. Las Vegas has its hands full, processing those vehicles that passed through Glendale Junction before the sheriff arrived and set up this jerry-rigged roadblock. St. George is out of communication, at least temporarily. Alamo isn't answering either.

"I'm going to try the phone."

Walking to the booth outside Glendale's only store, the government man searches through his pockets for quarters. Finding two, he drops them into the telephone slot and dials his home office. No one answers.

"Guess we're on our own."

The sheriff knows they can't stand around all day. He knocks on the door of the bus, then swings up the stairs. Facing the passengers, he tugs at his hat and clears his throat.

"Nothing to worry about," he assures the twenty-three pairs of eyes that stare at him. "We're just taking some precautions."

"Does this have to do with those tests they're doing in the desert?" one elderly woman asks.

"I thought that place was miles away," her companion adds.

"Northwest side of Vegas," a man calls out from the back. "A lot of mountains between here and there."

"The wind came up a bit strong this morning," the sheriff admits. "Blew some of the big cloud over this way." Then he repeats himself. "Nothing to worry about, though. We're just taking some precautions. Probably not even necessary, but the government wants to make sure everything's okay."

The sheriff motions toward the door.

"Why don't you all just come on outta there? Stretch your legs while we check everything out."

The diesel engine idles noisily as the passengers shove toward the front of the bus. Some carry satchels; others leave packages behind. A young girl clutches her mother's hand, sneezing as she pushes past the sheriff.

"Are you sure there's nothing to worry about?" the mother frets. "My girl's allergic. To dust and pollen."

"She'll be fine," the AEC man reassures her. "This'll just take a few minutes."

The sheriff reaches in his pocket and finds a dime. "Here," he says. "I'm pretty sure you'll find some licorice in the store next door."

Mother and daughter smile. Exiting the bus, they walk together across the asphalt. "Don't leave without us," the mother cautions the officials.

"Not a chance," the sheriff responds. "We'll take our time making sure everything's okay."

The passengers disperse, some to the tiny market, others to gather in the shade of the Texaco station. There's not much else to see in Glendale Junction. A two-lane string of hot pavement extends east and west. A narrower road dead-ends in from the north. As far as anyone can see, mesquite and sand. Not a very hospitable place, though the locals are trying to be nice. One passenger remembers there's an interstate highway planned for the future, just a little to the south. "It'll skip the town completely," he recalls, pushing his straw hat back off his forehead. "Probably kill this place off. No cars stopping, no people. Not much business around here without the cross-country traffic."

Other passengers nod, acknowledging the emptiness around them. Like an emphatic exclamation point, a dust devil swirls up from the desert floor. The twining alkali and dirt spin off toward a desolate horizon.

On one side of the service station, at the edge of Highway 93, an ancient truck is parked just off the road, its weight heavy on three nearly bald tires. Two Paiute men, one elderly and one a generation younger, are working on the fourth tire, which is totally flat. Inside the Model T, an aged Indian woman sits silently in the passenger seat. Beside her, a three-year-old squirms, trying not to complain. Outside, the rest of the family observes while the men wrestle with the wheel. Initially stopped by the roadblock, they pulled out of line when their tire lost its air. Now they're like actors in a play, something else for the roadblock victims to watch while they wait for their vehicles to be cleaned.

The Paiutes are oblivious to their audience. Hoisting the car on a trembling jack and lifting off the tire, the younger man carries it over to the service station owner without saying a word. He gestures. The owner frowns. He gestures again. The owner holds out his hand, palm up. The Paiute pulls a fistful of crumpled bills from his pocket, sifts through them, separates one from the rest. The owner takes it, and leads the man and his tire inside the service bay. Wiping his hands on his faded shirt, Grandfather nods his approval. The rest of the family is indifferent. Two boys play in and out of the cast-off tires at the back of the station. The third, fascinated by the spray of water coming from the hose, watches the decontamination process intently. To him, it's just a game. A little girl clings to her mother's skirt. Grandmother remains silent.

By now the rad specialist has climbed into the bus and is walking down the aisle. He pauses alongside the last rows of seats, probing under the footrests and into the corners.

"Count's too high," he says, moving back toward the front. "Can we get a vacuum in here?"

"Probably not," the sheriff replies. "Unless the Texaco owner happens to have one handy, there isn't a shop vac for miles." Turning toward the driver, he asks, "Can you fit this thing into the space where that milk truck is parked? As soon as it leaves?"

"Easy," says the bus driver.

"See if there's a vacuum handy, too."

"Sure. Happy to. Can't be too cautious."

"That's for sure. There's really nothing to worry about. The count's a little high, but it's nothing dangerous."

"Great. My boss'll be happy to hear that when we're two hours late."

Shutting the door of the bus, the driver maneuvers it around the side of the service station. He's confident the wash job will only take a few minutes, maybe a little longer if they take time to vacuum. Meanwhile, a few of his passengers cluster in the shade while most of them want to see what the market has to offer.

The market's owner is delighted by the influx of potential customers. Welcoming, he waves several of them inside. "Fresh oranges. A string of licorice. A packet of Wrigley's." He's happy to oblige.

No one seems overly concerned about the stopover. One man worries that his daughter will be waiting for him at the bus station in Las Vegas and that she'll be too hot. Another rubs his hands together, anticipating the blackjack tables waiting for him on Fremont Street. The two elderly women who knew about the tests look forward just as eagerly to the slot machines.

"Good for us to wait a while," one admits. "We'll save our money for this evening."

"Slots right here in the market." The store owner helpfully gestures toward two battered Lucky 7 machines. "I can make change."

"Better not get started," the elder sister says to the younger.

"Maybe just some nickels?"

The passengers find various ways to keep themselves busy. Licorice. Slot machines. Hostess Twinkies. Icy bottles of Coke. Some, hoping they'll hurry, watch the men washing off the milk truck a second time. Others are content to make conversation with their fellow bus riders. Pleased that the government is watching out for their well-being, everyone boasts their patriotic bona fides.

"The cloud last week. Ever see such pretty shades of red?"

"Bigger than Bikini. That's what Walter Cronkite said."

"Those atomic scientists, they're really doing a bang-up job."

"Yeah." Several of the passengers laugh and nod their heads.

Before long, the milk truck is fully washed for a second time. While the Indian boy wipes down the sides and dries off the windows, the service station owner shouts toward one of the two men on the monitoring team. "All set over here."

The rad specialist strolls across the road and gives the truck a cursory inspection. Probing across the hood, he finds the levels have dropped significantly. Near the back and among the milk cans, the numbers remain higher than he'd like. Not much more can be done, though. Not much point in standing here all day in the hot sun, washing and rewashing the same vehicle. He waves at the driver.

"All finished here. When you get to Vegas, though, better have those cans wiped down again. Can't be too careful."

"Will do."

Eager to be on his way, the driver hoists himself into the cab of his truck and starts his engine. As soon as he pulls back onto the highway, the monitor motions the bus into place. "This is a big one, boys," he says to the workers. "Make sure you get all of it."

They nod silently, and begin hosing down the silver and gray bus.

Meanwhile, the rad specialist turns to talk with the service station owner. "Have you got a big vacuum in your shop?"

"Nah, just a small one for cleaning up the dust."

"That'll do. Can we use it on the inside?"

"Why not flush the bus out with a shot of compressed air? My line ought to reach that far."

"Not supposed to. They've found that a compressor blows too much contamination into the air around us. Regs tell us not to use one. A vacuum cleaner is safer for everyone."

"How about the guy doing the vacuuming?"

"Not a problem if he wears gloves."

The service station owner snorts. "Not many gloves in the middle of the Mojave Desert. My boys with the mop and the hose have the only two pairs in town."

"There's an extra pair in the Jeep. We'll make do."

"Think it'll do any good, just vacuuming the seats?"

"Hope so. It's a little hot in there."

"How hot?"

"Nothing to worry about. Just want to take precautions." The monitor repeats his phrases as if the words are a mantra he's memorized. Then he clears his throat. "You mind going inside and vacuuming it out?"

The owner declines. "I'd better stay out here and look after the customers." Neither the government man nor any of the passengers points out that few customers can come to buy gas as long as the roadblock stays in place.

The rad specialist swivels toward the bus driver. "You mind?"

"Not part of my job description, but I guess we'll never get to Vegas unless I help out."

"Thanks. Shouldn't take long."

The World War II veteran hauls his vacuum from the service bay of the station and hands it to the driver. "This ought to do the job."

Ten minutes later, slapping his borrowed gloves against his pants, the driver exits the bus. "All done."

The rad specialist comes back from his station near the sheriff, having just waved three cars past the roadblock. The numbers seem to be coming down now. Nothing much to worry about anymore. He walks around the bus, hearing a few clicks but not too many. Better climb inside, he decides. Half-heartedly, he meanders down the rows of seats, hoping the Geiger counter stays still. It doesn't. At the very back, between the seats and along the floor, the count is still elevated. He shrugs. Probably needs blowing out. It'll take more equipment than little old Glendale Junction has handy. Pulling a pad of paper from his hip pocket, he jots down some notes. He'll have to write a report when he gets back to the office. Not likely to encounter such wide-spread fallout in the near future, but he'll be asked to make some recommendations. A vacuum cleaner in the field? Not likely. But maybe the AEC higher-ups can think of something.

Smiling, he tucks the probe under his arm and returns to the waiting bus driver.

"All set?"

"You can be on your way. But be sure you tell the boys at the depot that this Greyhound needs another bath."

"Is it dangerous to drive that far?"

"Absolutely not. You and your passengers will be just fine."

With that, the government man backs away from the bus and watches the passengers begin to file toward its open door. Might not be perfect, but the insides are much cleaner than before. The short drive on to Las Vegas, not more than a couple of hours, shouldn't be a problem. They'll be there in no time. He's done his job as best he can. Now, on to that flatbed carrying the rolls of steel.

The truck turns out to be the hottest vehicle yet. Over four hundred, especially inside the coils. "Hard to wash this one down."

By now the sheriff is ignoring the rad specialist's running commentary. Talking to a driver or a passenger, the patter keeps repeating itself, and the sheriff finds himself mimicking the words. Nothing to worry about. Just a precaution. Better safe than sorry. No reason to be concerned. Then, as he walks away from a truck or car, the monitor mutters about all the attendant problems. The milk cans are stacked too close together. The bus is too hot. The steel coils are too twisted. Studebakers are harder to clean off than Fords, but give him a good Chevy any day.

Exasperated, the sheriff wipes his forehead with his handkerchief. He'll be mighty glad when sundown comes. He wonders how his fellow officers are faring. He trusts they're just as bored as he is. Up in Alamo they must not be getting much traffic at all. How'd you like to stand all day in the hot sun with only eight or ten vehicles passing by? At least he can talk to some different people, even if he ends up saying the same thing over and over again.

A Nash convertible pulls into place.

"Better put that top up, sir," he orders.

"Is there a problem, officer?"

"Nothing serious. Taking some precautions. Can't be too careful," he replies.

Just then, the Jeep's radio crackles with static.

"I'd better get that," the rad specialist calls out.

He walks to his dusty vehicle, and listens.

"What's the word?" The sheriff sounds almost impatient. He's been at this damned roadblock for nearly seven hours. He's hungry, and he's too hot.

"Sounds like we're almost through here. Contamination levels are sinking way down." The monitor glances back at the Nash convertible. "Did you come from St. George or farther east?"

"Albuquerque," the driver answers. "Been hightailing it since daybreak." He looks over at the sheriff, who suddenly is more interested in his belt buckle than in the conversation.

"No need to put that top up, sir. You were too far east to catch any of the fallout."

"Fallout?" The driver latches on to the buzz word.

"Just a little dirty air. Nothing to worry about. We're just taking a few pre-cautions. Go ahead, sir. You must be eager to get to Vegas."

"You bet." The driver smirks.

As he guns his engine, the two rad specialists confer. One shakes his head. The other insists. The sheriff tries to hear what they're saying, but he's too far away. He moves a little to his left, motioning another Chevy and another Ford to go ahead. The Texaco lot is almost clear of vehicles. Time to call it a day.

At the edge of the road, the Paiute family is finished with their struggles. The flat tire, now patched, is on its rim and back on the wheel. The jack has been lowered, and parents and children have climbed into the truck bed. The sheriff, who hasn't paid much attention to them before this, walks over and asks what they've been doing.

"Been here long?"

Grandfather, again behind the steering wheel, rolls down the Model T's window and nods.

"How long?"

"This morning."

"Been in line all that time?"

"Just off to the side."

"Why?"

"Flat tire. Needed fixing."

"Okay now?"

"Seems to be."

"Where did you start?"

"Up the road. A couple of miles."

"See much dust?"

"Yes."

"Any get on the truck?"

"Some."

"Did you wipe it off?"

"Some."

"Any get on the folks in back?"

"Some."

"Better let us check it out."

The elder nods and takes the car out of gear.

The sheriff looks over at the two government men, who still are talking intently. Their tones are hushed. They pay no attention to anyone else. Finally the sheriff walks in their direction. He points toward the ancient Model T and gestures. "One more before we're through," he calls.

The monitors shrug. One turns to put his Geiger counter into the Jeep, but the other comes over toward the sheriff. "What's the deal?" he asks.

"They've been here a long time," the sheriff explains. "Flat tire, kept 'em from staying in line. Drove down from just north of here, where the fallout was heaviest."

"Live close by?"

"On the res, like I said, a few miles north."

"Wonder how much got dumped up there?"

"Want to check it out? Drive up there after we're through here?"

"Nah, got no orders to do so. The AEC's much more worried about the main highways. Those people choose to live up there. That's their problem."

"Still, we'd better wand their truck."

"Sure. Why not?"

The rad specialist ambles closer to the battered Model T. With the Geiger counter loosely tucked under one arm, he waves the wand in the air. The clicking accelerates, so he moves his equipment closer to the family sitting in back. The noise grows louder, more insistent. He bangs his fist against his gear.

"Sounds ominous," the sheriff comments in a low voice.

"Hotter than a pistol," the government man says under his breath.

"Better get 'em washed off."

"Won't do much good now. Not if they've been sitting there all day." He lifts his hands helplessly.

"Well, what should we do?"

"Tell 'em they're okay. Send 'em on their way."

"Doesn't seem right. Not after they've been waiting so long." The sheriff, who doesn't want any problems in his county, is concerned about what people might say.

The AEC officer, from out of state, doesn't much care.

The sheriff turns toward to the truck. "If you'll just drive over there, we'll have your vehicle washed down in no time."

Staring at him, the driver doesn't say a word.

"Sir, please, park your truck over there. And have everyone get out of the back."

An animated conversation ensues. Parents, grandparents, and children. All talking at once. The sheriff cannot understand a word. He's getting irritated. All day in the hot sun. He leans toward the truck. He's going to ask the driver for his license. The sheriff hasn't asked anyone else all day, but somehow these redskins are striking him the wrong way.

"May I see your driver's license, sir?"

The old man shrugs.

"I need to see your license."

Reaching into the pocket of his faded shirt, the elder pulls out a folded piece of paper and hands it out the window.

The sheriff reads off the name and address, jots words on a pad—Moapa Reservation—then hands the license back while the radiation monitor taps his foot impatiently. "If we're going to wash this guy's truck, let's get going."

The sheriff agrees. "Right over here, sir. And get everyone out of the back."

Another conversation ensues. Then, one by one, the children, followed by their parents, climb over the tailgate again. The grandparents get out of the car, too, as the three-year-old dances toward her mother. Two boys head back toward the pile of tires; the third one goes toward the hose and its spray.

The rad specialist looks inside the empty truck bed, sees white dust coloring the black Model T. He thinks about the vacuum cleaner. But the service station owner has long since taken his equipment back inside his building. Even the two workers, tired from scrubbing down so many other vehicles, look ready to quit.

"One more," he says, pointing toward the truck.

A couple of squirts of water, a halfhearted pass with the mop, and the men are finished. They choose not to look in the back.

"Going to do anything about the truck bed?" The sheriff can't resist asking.

"Not much point," the government man replies. "Probably stuck to their clothes. And likely as not, the fallout probably drifted down on wherever they live, too. So not much point in worrying about this old Model T."

The sheriff nods. "Not much point."

The family, still chattering with one another, settles back into the truck. At the same time, Grandfather is listening to the government man's conversation with the sheriff. The AEC official, paying no attention, doesn't even know the old man is there. The elder, standing perfectly still, watches until everyone has found a seat.

"Where's Danny?" Grandfather calls out.

"He was here a minute ago," his daughter-in-law replies. "Danny!" she shouts. "Daniel! Come here this instant!"

Grandmother leans out the passenger window of the aging Model T. And echoes. "Daniel! Come here!"

The small boy, his blue jeans muddy and his white T-shirt striped with brown desert dirt, appears alongside the old black pickup.

"Daniel, where have you been?"

"Making a better ditch," the boy answers solemnly. "So the water from the hose goes into the lake."

"What lake?" His mother looks puzzled.

"The lake I made from the water. You know, from the hose. Over there." Danny gestures toward the clean-up men, the makeshift arrangement.

Exasperated, his mother frowns. "Come here. Let's wipe that mud off you." She pulls out a tattered red bandanna. "Daniel, disappearing like that, you'll be the death of me."

The boy climbs over the truck's tailgate and drops beside his mother. She scrubs his cheeks with her bandanna and dries his hands as best she can. Grandfather settles himself back behind the steering wheel and puts the key in the ignition. The old engine coughs once, then catches. Shifting from first to second gear, Grandfather pulls onto the black-topped highway, heading east. The children bounce happily in the truck bed, glad to be on their way.

The sheriff, eager to shut down the roadblock and get home to supper, is glad to see them go.

Encore

A great blue heron lifts from a leafy branch of a cottonwood tree and heads toward the western edge of Upper Pahranagat Marsh. Like all such birds, he looks awkward, as if a giraffe were taking off and attempting to fly, until his legs lengthen behind him, his trajectory straightens, and his wings catch unseen currents in the air. Then he's a streamlined projectile, more graceful and far more controlled than the aircraft carrying Encore, as it turns out. The lumbering B-50 drops Encore off target. Fortunately, the gadget doesn't land atop the 2,475 military personnel crouching in the trenches but instead flops uncomfortably nearby. For the first time, the men are allowed to look directly at an atomic explosion, to see what resembles a giant flashbulb going off. The white light momentarily blinds the observers, who then comment on the subtle shades of pink that tinge the edges of the resulting cloud. And that cloud differs from its predecessors. Pinched in the middle, it resembles an hourglass more than a mushroom, a shapely figure more than a squat cauliflower. By the time the air-borne particles reach Pahranagat, the heron is in the air again, carrying dead reeds back to his nest.

Roger

"Eight hours and counting."

"Surface winds?"

"North-northwest, three knots."

"Mid-cloud elevation?"

"Directly out of the west. Twenty-five knots."

"Predicted top of Simon's cloud?"

"At forty thousand feet? Winds still out of the west. Stronger, though. Thirty-five knots."

"Foresee any problems?"

"No, not really. Not according to the current graphs. Ten or twelve hours from now? I can't promise perfection, but everything looks stable. Besides, it's a Nevada crapshoot until we see the yield. How big a bang you boys set off, that's key. I do know the winds at present are a-okay. Ditto the cirrus clouds. No precipitation in sight. No front coming through. No change expected between now and shot time. Simon ought to be fine."

"No problems whatsoever?"

"According to the data, no weather problems at all."

"Anyone have any reservations? Are we set to fire in the morning?"

One at a time, each man in the CP-1 conference room nods his assent. First the Air Force colonel, then the Army lieutenant colonel and his smiling staff adjunct, the sober weapons development director, the civil effects bureaucrat, the Los Alamos physicist and the Sandia scientist, the technical liaison, the two Public Health Service officials. The test manager, sitting beside the test director. Around the table, everyone agrees. And finally, Roger Harmon from the U.S. Weather Bureau repeats an endorsement. "No weather problems at all."

"Then Simon's a go," announces the test director. "We'll meet back here at 0300."

Picking up his charts and sticking his slide rule back in his shirt pocket, Roger reaches for his coat. It's cold outside, and windy. He needs to get back to his Mercury office, to check and see if new data have come in from any of the nearby field sites. Beatty. Tonopah. Las Vegas. St. George. By morning, the wind speeds could be close to the outside limit. He needs to keep an eye on that, but maybe he can grab a little snooze on the cot in the corner before the next report arrives.

Sleep turns out to be impossible, though. The two teletype machines and the facsimile recorder clack nonstop, a grating screech of a rumble that Roger never notices by day but drives him crazy at midnight. Besides, he wants to review the latest charts. Brewing fresh coffee, two lumps of sugar, no milk, Roger pulls his chair up to the long metal table that holds the new graphs and numbers. Frank, the Air Force technician who works as his assistant, has plotted those numbers meticulously. On a large Nevada map, Frank has drawn a parabola east from Yucca Flat that defines the cloud dispersal if current conditions hold true. Roger traces the lines with his index finger, recalculating direction and distance. Everything's normal. He might as well relax.

Tamping fresh tobacco into his pipe, he lights it, tips his head back, and slides down in his chair, dreaming about the Montana fishing trip he and his wife will take as soon as the Upshot-Knothole sequence ends. A bubbling trout stream, a perfect cast, a creel filled with cutthroat and maybe a big brown or two, a campfire that night with fish roasting hot on the coals, cowboy coffee instead of this government-brand gunk he's drinking now, the Milky Way overhead, cloudless, and nary a thought of atomic testing.

His reverie is short-lived, however, because 0300 comes all too quickly. In the hour preceding the final pre-shot meeting, Roger again refigures his calculations. The numbers remain near the edge, but he is confident in the computations at hand.

The other men are more than eager to give the go-ahead.

"Hot spot anywhere?"

"Three hours out, a hundred-micron particle size. Might be as low as fifty. Just nuisance value," the Sandia physicist adds.

"The trajectory?"

"Eight thousand feet over Madison Mine; ten thousand feet over Pioche."

"Might lose a few windows in Caliente. Nothing serious."

Listening to the men interpret his numbers so cavalierly, Roger fingers his unlit pipe. The conversation bothers him a little. Just "lose a few windows." Nothing but "nuisance value." To his way of thinking, atomic particles of any size, micron or not, sound like more than a nuisance.

"Last chance to abort." The test director's tone of voice is stern, insistent, compelling.

"Ten minutes and counting."

"Surface winds still out of the north-northwest. Five knots now."

"At forty thousand feet, where the top of the cloud will be?"

"Stronger. Now up to forty-eight knots."

"Predict any problems?"

"No, sir, no problems, assuming you boys have done your jobs." No one hears Roger mutter under his breath, "And assuming the yield prediction is as accurate as my weather forecast."

"Eight minutes and counting."

On Saturday, the 25th of April, at 0430 hours, Simon drops three hundred feet from its tower emplacement and explodes brilliantly. The subsequent brightness lasts more than three seconds, longer and more blinding than usual. The earth shakes, rolling underfoot, as if giant volcanic magma were pushing up from below. Listening to the deafening sound that ensues, watching waves of dust and blasted debris, spotting the elephantine size and shape of a growing mushroom cloud, every onlooker realizes that this is a big one.

In fact, Simon's yield turns out to be considerably higher than expected. Forty-three kilotons, to be exact, an explosion far larger than any previous Proving Ground stateside experiment. The fallout generated turns out to be greater than that from any previous test, too. The top of Simon's mushroom cloud blossoms to 44,000 feet, where westerly winds blow it rapidly toward the east. The voracity and the velocity alarm every AEC authority. When the resulting off-site fallout drifts over U.S. 91 and U.S. 93, and becomes apparent to the naked eye, the test director takes immediate action, contacting the local sheriff and ordering roadblocks on those highways. Every vehicle is stopped and checked for excessive radiation. Any deemed "hot" is washed at government expense.

Meanwhile, everyone is safe inside the control point, front-line operations center for atomic tests on Yucca Flat. Built of reinforced concrete, a one-story building with a basement below, the structure can withstand an atmospheric pressure of 0.6 pounds per square inch. Neither Simon nor any other gargantuan atomic explosion can do any real damage here. In the hour immediately following Simon's detonation, Roger tries simultaneously to stay out of the way and to listen to the myriad conversations. His voice louder than usual, the test director sounds agitated. His words carry, as he argues with some lawman somewhere, probably from eastern Clark County, maybe Glendale Junction, who doesn't want to be responsible for tending an all-day roadblock on the main highway between St. George and Las Vegas.

The test manager insists, finally slamming down the telephone and shaking his head. He hates surprises and he loathes bad publicity. Simon is generating both, pushing a stream of hot air, 300 roentgens per hour.

As the test director turns away from his long-distance argument with the sheriff, he spots Roger casually standing in front of a graph pinned to the wall. Crossing the room, he questions his meteorologist. "What the hell were you thinking, Roger?"

Roger jabs at the graph and then at the map alongside. "Data shows there shouldn't have been a problem."

"Well, the data was wrong."

"No, sir. The data was right. Simon's at fault, not the data. Biggest yield so far, that's what Los Alamos is saying. And the highest cloud, too. More debris and heavier fallout than usual, blowing more broadly than any physicist expected."

"Aren't such possibilities part of your calculations?"

"Absolutely. Should have been okay, given the data. Except Simon was huge."

"Well, in the future, we've got to be more careful. There's gonna be hell to pay about these roadblocks. Bad press and angry public. We've got to be more careful."

"I plan to be."

But Roger knows there'll be hell to pay if they postpone a shot. Los Alamos, Livermore, everyone hates to get off schedule. Those boys, they don't worry about nuisance value. They just want to get results.

WHEN THE ADVISORY PANEL convenes that evening, the test director is still incensed. His phone has been ringing all day, first with vituperative complaints, then with unanswerable questions about radiation levels and fallout danger. Although the public appreciates the government's concern for their safety, they're not happy about any ensuing inconveniences. A few reporters are even asking questions about health hazards. Fortunately, public relations people in Las Vegas take the lead. The AEC locals handle the minutiae of acceptable radiation levels and parts per thousand, and forcefully nip public concern in the bud. No one mentions the word "nuisance."

To make matters worse at the Proving Ground, an AD-2 drone crashes shortly after takeoff. Simon's excessive heat weakens the underskin of one wing. Shock pressure from the blast and a subsequent wind gust rip one wing off the drone, which immediately cartwheels into the ground. The Air Force is as unhappy as the public. They lose a lot of valuable instrumentation, not to mention a costly aircraft, although they learn key information about how close to a mushroom cloud a plane dare fly. Apparently not so close, Roger presumes.

"How many days until Harry?"

"Set for May second, a week away."

"He's a big one, too. Simon's size, approximately."

"Better delay. Got an angry bird colonel at Indian Springs. Irate people in eastern Nevada, western Utah, too. Need to do some cleanup here on the playa, and need to let everything beyond air out a bit. Blow that dust on outta there. The Las Vegas folks need time to get out some post-Simon good news, too. Successful atomic test trumps slight rain of fallout. Valuable scientific data obtained. That sort of thing."

"How about those folks complaining, the ones east of here?"

"They're fine. Just a little dusting. Won't stay long on the ground."

"I didn't know anybody lives out there in the middle of nowhere."

"A few, scattered."

"They're making a stink."

"Ah, that'll blow over. Just like the cloud."

"Let's postpone Harry anyway, just to be sure. Put him off another week or two."

"But we have results we want to obtain." The Sandia man never likes delays.

"You'll get 'em," the test director promises. "Later."

The test manager has a more pressing concern. "What'll we do about Encore? That's an airdrop, all set for the seventh."

"Airdrops are always smaller. Less magnitude of soil scavenging. Let's go ahead with Encore as scheduled."

Listening, Roger groans but doesn't say a word. "Magnitude of soil scavenging"? Jesus Christ!

"Change the order? Encore first and then Harry? Instead of the other way around?"

"That oughta work out just fine. Air-drop Encore on the seventh, as planned. Harry nine days later, on the sixteenth."

"I'll make the announcement."

"Los Alamos is gonna screech."

"Let 'em. The final decision's our call, not theirs."

No one asks Roger's opinion. While the others talk, he mulls over what he's hearing. Simon was so damned big. Twenty percent more yield than predicted. They'll all be more careful in the future. Right now, reordering the shots is the first priority.

"Anything more?"

"Not today."

"Let's get the word out, then. Encore on the seventh, Harry on the sixteenth."

"That's a go."

ENCORE is only the second Upshot-Knothole airdrop. As with Dixie a month earlier, a B-50 from Kirtland Air Force Base in New Mexico will carry the nuclear device west to Nevada. At the late-evening readiness briefing on May 6, every advisory panel member is tense, especially the test director. Remembering Simon, each of the men, no matter what his responsibility, wants Encore to be perfect. Unfortunately, the weather forecast is problematic.

"Whaddaya think, Roger?"

"Well, the front has moved to the east, with a trough and then a ridge of high pressure beyond. Behind, the weather balloon at the Death Valley station shows lots of wind over the Panamint Mountains. Gusty. Forty, fifty knots. Likely to increase by morning."

"Strong enough to abort?"

"Not yet. I'll have more data in a few hours."

"Costly, if that aircraft takes off and has to turn around."

Costly's not Roger's problem. His job is to calculate accurately the atmospheric processes. Convergence. Divergence. Vorticity. Condensation. He flattens his hand against the chart pinned on the wall. "Springtime in the desert. Never can be sure of these damned zephyrs. Can't promise anything 'til after midnight."

The panel formally reconvenes just as dawn begins glowing in the east. The B-50 left New Mexico an hour earlier, rapidly winging its way west toward Yucca Flat. Meanwhile, the early-morning winds are stiffening, raising a skiff of dust off the desert floor and swirling miniature dust devils into the air. The test manager stands at an open doorway, looking out at the playa. He shuts the heavy metal door quietly, then turns and says in an all-too-quiet voice, "Make a decision, Roger. The plane's partway here. We've got to resolve this now."

Roger taps his pencil on the table. It slips a little between his fingers because his hands are clammy. He examines his charts one more time, studying them carefully as if they'll reveal some secret he hasn't calculated before. "Two-hundred-seventy-degree winds at practically all levels. Two-hundred-thirty-degree winds at surface. The sky will be clear, with a little cirrus. No precipitation downstream. No inversion problems." He sees nothing new. The prognosis is still iffy.

"Yes or no?"

"It's up to you," the Army chimes in.

"A slight misdirection. A change of wind speed, degrees of wind distribution, whatever. There'll be trouble."

"We're out of time here, Roger. Do we need to abort?"

"Come on, Roger." Sandia Laboratories this time.

"Now or never."

"What's the word?"

He hesitates. The winds are picking up, especially above ten thousand feet. Switching directions, too, with a more southerly angle toward Las Vegas.

Roger's trapped in a catch-22. Unable to guarantee anything absolutely, he'll take a lot of heat if he says no. Lots of jabs about cost overruns and cowardly meteorologists. This one's a close call that could go either way. Roger decides it's better be conservative. Not take a chance.

He lays down his pencil and pushes his chair back from the table. Making eye contact with the test director, he shifts uncomfortably in his seat. "Cancel," he says softly.

"You sure?"

"Cancel. The winds are just too high. Fifty knots now, and rising."

The other men sitting in CP-1 sigh, but they follow Roger's lead. Protocol dictates trust in his decision. The word goes out. To the pilots: turn around and head back to Kirtland. To the scientists: retune your experiments. To the craftsmen: do whatever is necessary to put everything on hold. There'll be no test this morning in Nevada. Tomorrow at 0830 instead.

The disappointment is palpable.

No one speaks directly to Roger. He rolls up his charts, erases a graph from the blackboard on the east wall, crams his pencil into a shirt pocket, and jams his unlit pipe into his mouth. He needs to get back to Mercury, to turn his attention immediately to May 8.

But he's perplexed. What if tomorrow is as blustery as today? Springtime's always windy in southern Nevada. He wishes they would schedule the tests in the fall. There's more reliable weather in October. It's too unstable this time of year. As always, though, the Feds know better. Upshot-Knothole, from March until May. Maybe June, if they add that extra text they've been talking about. He shrugs into his coat, deciding to double-check every station this morning. He'll need the charts as up-to-the-minute as possible, and he hopes Frank comes in early.

THE ADVISORY PANEL reconvenes that afternoon, and again at 2200 hours that evening. Each time, Roger is fairly confident that his data show the wind speeds dying down. Encore will be okay as scheduled. The resulting cloud will drift into northern Arizona. No one living there, that's what everyone says. Not something they need to be concerned about.

"Weather at time of impact?"

"Light winds. North-northwest, one or two knots."

"Foresee any problems?"

"No, no problems."

On the morning of May 8, the B-50 again takes off from Kirtland Air Force Base. It flies without incident over the sparsely populated landscape below. Arriving at Yucca Flat slightly ahead of schedule, it drops to 22,000 feet and, flying at a magnetic heading of 245 degrees and at a speed of 250 knots, takes several practice runs above the drop area. All is well.

Seconds before release time, however, a mechanical linkage failure occurs in the bombing system. When the plane begins to drift off course, the bombardier frantically tries to disable the system. Too late. Mesmerized onlookers watch the device spin from the belly of the aircraft toward the desert floor below. More than thirty seconds later, the device explodes just above the ground, off target by 250 meters. No one applauds.

"Jesus Christ! Can't anyone get anything right?"

"Doesn't look like it."

"Airdrop, though, less desert debris."

"Less fallout, too." The men watch for a while, as the cloud spirals in the sky. Its rapid growth spurs the test director to say, "Glad it's going over Arizona. Better than repeating the Simon fiasco over Utah."

"Right about less fallout. Wrong about Utah." Roger shifts his weight uncomfortably.

"Say what?"

"Frank just handed me an update. The winds are shearing off. Unexpectedly. Cloud's drifting northeast into Utah again."

"You've gotta be kidding."

"Don't I wish. Damned cloud ought to be over Arizona, where no one lives. A slight wind shift, the numbers change. I hate to say it."

The men in CP-1 just shake their heads as the mushroom cloud skates above the Nevada communities of Hiko and Alamo and Pioche and Panaca and Caliente. Roger listens to the numbers. The bottom of the cloud reaches 29,000 feet; the top, 42,000. Almost as high as Simon, though not nearly as lethal. So Encore, unlike Simon, really is only a "nuisance value" causing a "few broken windows" here and there. Meanwhile, experiments like the "Evaluation of Wiancko and Vibrotron Gauges and Development of New Circuitry for Atomic Blast Measurements," the "Dynamic Pressure versus Time and Supporting Air Blast Measurements," the "Radioactive Particle Studies Inside an Aircraft," the "Gamma Radiation Spectrum of Residual Contamination Studies," the "Neutron Flux Measurements," and the "Residual Ionizing Radiation Depth Dose Measurements in Unit-Density Material" proceed as scheduled. The Department of Defense is pleased. Sandia Laboratories physicists and chemists are ecstatic.

The Forest Service is happy with their "Incendiary Effects on Buildings and Interior Kindling Fuels" and "Ignition and Persistent Fires Resulting from Atomic Explosions—Exterior Kindling Fuels" test results, too. Yucca National Forest, an oblong grove of fifty-foot-tall ponderosa pines and another two rows of smaller evergreens brought down from Mount Charleston, then replanted in concrete, blows violently to one side, like a green wave, and then bursts into flame. Now biologists have a vital benchmark, a clearer understanding of how forested areas might suffer in a nuclear holocaust.

With eight Upshot-Knothole tests under their belts, everyone—the military, the scientists, the engineers, the technicians, the craftsmen, the photographers, the Civil Defense authorities, and even the weathermen—are eager for the next shot. Harry. Now rescheduled for Saturday, May 16.

THE WEEK BETWEEN Encore and Harry is a busy one. More than nine hundred military personnel plan direct participation in trenches located 3,660 meters from ground zero, with another two hundred troops providing radiological safety, transportation, communications, and control functions for their exercises. The Second Marine Corps readies helicopters they will fly as close as possible to the detonation point. The 412th Engineer Construction Battalion and the 3623rd Ordnance Company place equipment and fortifications at 460-meter intervals, plus one 105 mm howitzer, which sits directly on the atomic bull's-eye. Twenty-six sheep are staked in the display area, where those that survive will be checked for radiation burns and contamination. One hundred and thirty rabbits are located closer to ground zero, between fifteen and sixty kilometers away. A cluster of beagles is caged slightly farther away. The litany of Harry's experiments includes "Bacterial Studies on Animals Exposed to Neutron Radiation" and "Long-term Studies on Dogs Exposed to Primarily Neutron Irradiation in Shelters." Harry will generate a superabundance of statistics and experimental evidence.

At 1600 on May 15, the test director calls the advisory panel to order. The test is planned for early the next morning, but this evening's meeting will be brief. It doesn't take Roger's expertise to know the weather outside is damp, windy, and unseasonably cold. Nonetheless, the test manager wants an official opinion.

"Rain. Might last another day or two. Front out in the Pacific, pouring weather directly our way."

"Any chance of a change?"

"Not likely."

"Twenty-four-hour postponement, then. We'll get the word out immediately." The test manager turns to the secretary sitting in the corner of the room. She takes his words down in shorthand, then meticulously reads her notes back. "The weather forecast for tomorrow morning did not give assurance that the data desired by the test organization scientists could be obtained. The test manager has postponed the detonation for twenty-four hours." When the test manager nods, she leaves to call Las Vegas 6350, a telephone number she has memorized by now. The official memorandum of postponement always comes from Las Vegas, from the Atomic Energy Commission—Department of Defense.

As Roger listens, he manages to suppress a smile. "The weather forecast for tomorrow morning did not give assurance" sounds like a euphemism for

"It's raining outside." Nobody mentions the people living downwind from the Proving Ground, either. They don't seem to count much, unless they complain too loudly to the AEC. "Data desired by the test organization scientists." Now that's more like it, he thinks to himself.

"We'll meet again tomorrow at 1600. Good chance to get some shut-eye tonight."

As the meeting breaks up, Roger wonders about the rabbits, who probably won't get any shut-eye at all.

THE NEXT DAY brings little change in either temperature or precipitation. At the afternoon meeting, the conversation follows the usual pattern, with Roger characterizing the ever-present cumulus clouds and wishing for cirrus. The long-range forecast, however, several days out, looks promising. "Not likely to get good test results on the seventeenth, though. Need this front to blow on through."

The Army man is dismayed. "Are you trying to tell me that we should postpone again? Delay for another day? Or maybe two?"

"Yes, sir."

"That's unfortunate. We're all set to go. Can't ask any more of the boys."

The test manager intervenes. "You'll have to deal with that after we're through meeting. If the Army's inconvenienced, that can't be helped."

"Well, there's too damned much uncertainty. That's for damned sure."

One Public Health Service man pokes the elbow of the colleague sitting next to him. "I've got an idea," he announces, hoping to break the icy impasse. "Let's rename the sucker Hamlet. No more Harry, except for public consumption. In CP-1, let's call him Hamlet."

Immediately the other Public Health Service official picks up on the joke. "To be, or not to be. That is the question."

Roger rolls his eyes and smiles. "I like it. I like it."

Everyone in the room laughs and nods. "Hamlet it is," the usually solemn test director agrees. "But don't tell AEC."

"Ah, they'll find out soon enough. They always do." The colonel looks around a room filled with Top Secret Q clearances, as if seeking a spy.

The test manager pounds his fist on the table. Once, twice. "Gentlemen. This isn't getting our work done. Postpone for twenty-four hours?"

"To be, or not to be?"

"Not to be, at least for now."

"Roger?"

Comfortable with a camaraderie he hasn't felt before, Roger nods his head. "Postpone for twenty-four hours."

"What about my damned animals? And the boys from Desert Rock?"

"To be, or not to be. That is the answer."

"Oh, hell, you boys are full of it."

The weather on May 17 shows improvement. Just not enough amelioration overall. By now, the entire advisory panel is on edge. A dozen rabbits froze overnight, and need to be replaced. The atomic soldiers and their support troops, although trained to obey orders without complaint, are sick and tired of getting up at midnight, trucking out to the trenches, then turning around and driving back to Camp Desert Rock. And the scientists, as always, are worried about losing experimental data.

"Hell," says the Sandia man, "without a little fallout we can't get decent sampling. We need a good-size ball of fire up there."

"Better from cirrus than cumulus. Looks like cumulus tomorrow."

"Harder for planes to penetrate."

"A mix of weather clouds with radiological clouds is a bad idea." Roger says what several of the others are thinking.

"We could shoot without sampling."

"Are you kidding me? What's the point?"

"The fractination of tritium, that's the point of this shot."

My God, Roger wonders, where do they find these words? "Fractination of tritium," indeed.

"I think we ought to postpone again."

"Alas, poor Hamlet."

"Is this guy ever gonna get on the ground?"

"Not unless Roger gives us better weather."

Roger, unlit pipe clamped between his teeth, doesn't answer for a moment. Then, slowly removing his pipe, he clears his throat. "I just bring you data," he slowly enunciates. "Nothing but the facts, ma'am, nothing but the facts."

"Hey, do you watch *Dragnet*, too?"

"When I can, where there's television reception."

"Back to business, boys." The test director, who doesn't own a television set, is uninterested in their conversation. "Is Harry—errr, Hamlet—to be or not to be?"

"Weak front coming in on the northwest coast of California. Should brush past us."

"And that means?"

"Still quite a bit of moisture in the air."

"Gentlemen, can we safely delay all the experiments one more day?"

Murmurs occur around the table. The Sandia man purses his lips, while the Army colonel shakes his head. Everyone is anxious to send Hamlet on his way, but no one is willing to take a chance with the forecast. If they shoot in bad weather, their long-planned experiments likely will come up short. Best to delay again. The consensus comes together slowly, reluctantly, almost unwillingly.

Listening to the conversation, Roger can't help but pay attention to the priorities. No one mentions the radiation pattern, though surely the test director and his staff are keeping potential problems in mind. Instead, it's cloud sampling, electromagnetic signals, seismic geophones, debris calibration, beta-gamma skin hazard, and aircraft vulnerability. All on-site or in-air operations. No one comments today about any post-test fallout, or any people in the way. The longer Hamlet gets postponed, the more focused they are. The Army on its troops. Los Alamos on the yield. Sandia on whatever dozen experiments Sandia cares about at any given moment. Roger on the weather. Maybe they think about those nuisances downwind, but not at any length. They've got to get Hamlet going.

The test manager interrupts Roger's train of thought. "We'll meet tomorrow at 2200 for another briefing. Hopefully, the weather will improve by then."

"So Hamlet's not to be?"

"That's correct, for now. We'll reschedule for the nineteenth. Are we in agreement, gentlemen?"

Even Sandia has to acquiesce.

As the advisory panel participants pack up their papers and prepare to leave the room, the test director puts a hand on Roger's shoulder. "Let's talk about this a little further."

"How so?"

"All these delays are causing real problems. Everybody's antsy, and I worry about the multitude of experiments. It's not good to keep putting Harry off."

"I know. But tomorrow's data show only slight improvement."

"A little better, though. That's what you said earlier."

"Yeah, a little better. But not a lot."

"We'll take what we can get. Why don't you type up the figures for tomorrow's meeting? That way we all can hold the data in our hands."

"Will do. Though that won't change anything. Still the same data."

"Maybe you can walk us through it in more detail."

"Absolutely. I'll be ready. You can bet on it." Smiling at his joke, as if Nevada weather were a crapshoot just like its casinos, Roger turns to go.

BY 2200 HOURS on the eighteenth, the tension is palpable. Roger's calculations are unlikely to put anyone at ease. Handing out the latest Mercury Weather Station memo, "Forecast Number 94," Roger avoids eye contact. He wishes the numbers were better. Still too much moisture, and he doesn't like the winds. They're just too damned strong, and it's difficult for him to plot an accurate cloud trajectory.

Roger walks the men through the data, detailing current weather conditions and outlining the prevailing patterns. He reports a six in ten chance that the cumulus clouds will soon be giving way to cirrus at 25,000 feet and that there's no measurable precipitation for a thousand miles downstream. However, while the surface wind speed is only five knots, the winds aloft are picking up. Thirty knots at 20,000 feet; fifty knots at 30,000 feet; a whopping seventy-five knots at 40,000 feet. The forty-eight- hour forecast is even worse, suggesting that by the day after tomorrow the wind speed will increase to eighty knots at 40,000 feet. Roger points out another alarming fact. At 37,500 feet the projected fallout will occur right over Glendale, Overton, and Logandale.

The test manager listens for a while, then interjects his thoughts. "Thus far in the series Overton's had no dosage; population 600. Glendale's had no 1953 dosage either; population 15. Logandale, no dosage; population 350. So we needn't worry. A little hot dust won't take anybody over the safe rad dose."

Roger shrugs. Apparently a thousand or so people don't count, not if nothing's been dropped on their heads so far.

"Besides, if Roger's correct, there's a fifty percent likelihood of a ten-degree shift in the wind. That'll take everything north, where even fewer people live."

"Worst-case scenario, we could tell 'em to stay in their houses."

"They're farmers, for God's sake. They'll be outside."

"But not for twenty-four hours straight. Besides, if you stay inside you receive a twenty-five percent reduction in dosage. We can notify the women and children."

"I'm uneasy." One Public Health official speaks for the first time, while his colleague nods tacit agreement. "We're talking about real live people."

"But how many?"

"Maybe a thousand. No more than two or three."

"I think we oughta shoot anyway. It's a calculated risk."

A "calculated risk"? Roger doesn't like what he's hearing at all.

"The forty-eight-hour forecast is lousy. I think we ought to go ahead. Best window is right now."

"Maybe we should approach this more cautiously. What if we shoot, and the laboratory doesn't get the desired results?" Sandia muses. "A sixty percent chance of cirrus isn't good enough for me."

"You mean you want to delay even longer?" Army demands.

"No, not really. I just want to be sure we get the best data. Especially from the cloud samples. That's really important. Crucial."

"Six in ten. That's good enough odds for me."

"Let's double-check later. Send an airplane up at 0200 to make a jaunt southwest, look at the cloud cover."

"I hate to be pessimistic. Let's plan on letting Hamlet be."

"Okay. We'll watch the weather all night."

"Your thoughts, Roger?"

He hesitates, thinking to himself that the damned clouds are too heavy. If the radiation mixes with the weather, that's a formula for disaster. But the data's right on the edge. Might be perfectly okay by tomorrow. A delay could make things worse.

"What say, Roger?" The test director again interrupts Roger's ruminations.

Tapping his pipe stem on the pages piled in front of him on the table, Roger finally nods. "Let's give it a try."

The night progresses with little atmospheric change, and little attitudinal change either. Everyone is eager to see Hamlet get off the dime. Willing, now, to forget about Simon's fallout. That's in the past; Harry's the future. Once the crew of the early-morning test flight calls back its findings, no one on the advisory panel voices a negative opinion. The cumulus is dissipating, replaced by thin cirrus at 38,000 feet. Shouldn't be a problem for Harry. Not at all. Roger and the Public Health Service people have minor reservations, but the enthusiasm of the other men overrides their silence.

In his mind, Roger runs over the available information. A lot going on up there. Surface winds from the north-northwest, but changing to south-southwest at twenty thousand feet. Back to north-northwest at thirty thousand, sixty to seventy knots. He knows there's no way in hell to know exactly where Hamlet's mushroom cloud might blow. Back and forth. Back and forth. To be or not to be. No way in hell he can guarantee much of anything this morning. Everyone else is determined, though. He'll give 'em that.

"Might as well get this over with," Roger concurs.

The test director nods. "Ten minutes, and counting."

"Three, two, one, zero."

AT 0505 HOURS on the morning of May 19, 1953, Harry plunges three hundred feet from its tower and explodes above the floor of Yucca Flat. The relative humidity is thirty-five percent. The pressure is 874 millibars. The yield is 32 kilotons. And the fireball lasts an unusually long time, seventeen seconds. The top of Harry's cloud rises to an altitude of 42,500 feet, higher than originally estimated by the scientists, and moves due east at 91 miles per hour, riding the strong winds that Roger feared. As the gargantuan mushroom shape weaves upward and sideways, it picks up the moisture that Roger expected in the atmosphere. The combination is lethal. Radiated desert detritus spins over eastern Nevada and then the heaviest particles begin to fall. Directly over St. George, Washington County, Utah. Population 4,562.

Harry

On one side of Snow Canyon lie the pale outlines of the White Hills; on the other, the darker tones of the Red Mountains. Punctuating the scenery, black lava from ancient volcanoes strews downslope in sporadic piles. A rainbow of earthtone colors, waiting for dawn. Perhaps the old sandstone shudders slightly from the atomic burst of Harry, two hundred miles to the west. Perhaps not. More probably the first hint of cataclysmic change comes three hours later, from above rather than below. A feathery cloud drifts slowly overhead, a beautiful cloud, with shades of apricot and peach. Particles almost invisible settle onto the boulders of Snow Canyon and onto the fields of the surrounding rural farms and onto the streets of the nearby Utah community of St. George. Then the particles grow larger, more palpable. The sandstone whitens, and the leaves on the trees turn pale, as a layer of radioactive ash floats down like fallen snow. Snow Canyon, appropriately named, now ready and waiting for Howard Hughes's ill-fated filming of *The Conqueror,* starring Susan Hayward and John Wayne.

Janine

"And thus the face of the whole earth became deformed, because of the tempests, and the thunderings, and the lightnings, and the quaking of the earth." Brother Orson's baritone conjoins the words, turns phrases into sonorous chords that roll mightily throughout the chapel. Mesmerized, his fellow ward members listen intently to his scriptural prose. Heads tipped, hands tightly clasped in their laps, the men and women hearken to the disturbing recital of the hours following the death of Jesus Christ.

Janine tries to pay close attention, but her children are shuffling restlessly beside her. Nudging young Richard with her elbow, she leans over and whispers a shushing sound in Thomas's ear. Katie, age four, pulls at the ruffles of her dress, while baby Lisa sniffles slightly. Beyond the wiggling Thomas, Will frowns. Disliking any interruption of Sacrament Meeting, Janine's husband expects model behavior from his family. Will's eyes meet his wife's. His forehead wrinkles, and he shakes his head almost imperceptibly.

Suppressing a sigh, she shifts her weight from one hip to the other, moves little Lisa from her left arm to her right, and puts her free hand on Katie's knee. Thus finessing Will's displeasure, Janine focuses on Brother Orson's choice of scripture, each verse more potent and prophetic than the last. Strung together, the sentences remind her of ominous times: the week just ended, with its atomic onslaught of St. George. Her hometown, where parents and grandparents have lived safely for more than half a century, apparently threatened, a sanctuary safe no more.

"And behold, the rocks were rent in twain; they were broken up upon the face of the whole earth, insomuch that they were found in broken fragments, and in seams, and in cracks, upon all the face of the land." Like a one-man symphony, Brother Orson's voice builds toward the climax. "And it came to pass that when the thunderings, and the lightnings, and the storm, and the tempest, and the quakings of the earth did cease—for behold, they did last for about the space of three hours; and it was said by some that the time was greater; nevertheless, all these great and terrible things were done in about the space of three hours—and then behold, there was darkness."

Clasping loving arms around Lisa's fragile shoulders, Janine squeezes her daughter gently. Even so, Janine cannot relax. She's been on edge all week, ever since Tuesday when that heinous mushroom cloud blew east from

Nevada and dropped its poison southward over Utah. Unsettled by today's speaker, Janine lets her mind drift back and forth between the desert to the west and the passages from *The Book of Mormon* that echo in her ears. Her imagination, momentarily, concocts a psychedelic picture. Not a blast of light and then three long hours of darkness, like Brother Orson forewarns, but a vision just as harrowing. The sun a yolk of yellow-orange, tinged with unearthly magenta tones. Quick alterations in weather and wind. Most terrifying of all, a gargantuan mushroom cloud billowing dark across the horizon, then pausing over St. George as if alien and alive. So unnatural in the springtime desert air. Janine does worry about her children growing up so close to the Nevada explosions, even though she rarely says so aloud. She remembers newspaper pictures of Hiroshima and Nagasaki youngsters, the horrendous burns and tattered flesh. Might Richard and Thomas and Katie and Lisa suffer from similar atomic blasts? Might her family pay a price she cannot comprehend?

Maybe the atomic testing is just that. A test. Of her promise to be a good wife. A test. Of her resolution to be a good mother. A test. Of her faith.

If only she were sure.

BROTHER ORSON'S WORDS, the chapel itself, her fellow worshippers, and even her family fade into the background as Janine's imagination teases and torments her. Scenes from the past five days unwind like the reel of a silent film, looping over and over and over again as if they were a recurring nightmare without end. "And thus the face of the whole earth became deformed, because of the tempests, and the thunderings, and the lightnings, and the quaking of the earth." The scriptural music drums a cacophonic background, while incidents from the past week of consternation and alarm, a horror movie without end, bombard Janine's memory.

TUESDAY MORNING, Janine woke with anticipation, not sure what the day might bring. She is always edgy whenever an atomic test is scheduled. What is happening in the Nevada desert is a mystery to her, especially after last week, when Will's milk truck had been stopped so long at the roadblock in Glendale Junction. Asked about the delay, Will shrugged his shoulders. The government takes precautions, normal precautions that any reasonable person might expect. That's what the sheriff told him. If there'd been any real danger, they would have embargoed his truck. And they didn't. Will is quite certain there is no cause for concern. The United States government, after all, is in the business of protecting its citizens, not causing them harm. Besides, he believes that America must, absolutely must, stay ahead of the Communists, and atomic testing is the best possible way to ensure the U.S.of A.'s premier position in the world's political arena.

Generally Janine agrees with her husband, but recent events have unsettled her. Why, if there were no danger, would the sheriff stop traffic for hours? Why would a government man spend so much time checking vehicles with a Geiger counter? And why was her husband's milk truck washed and rinsed and rewashed again? Will can't answer, not for sure, and neither can she. But she can wonder. Besides, Janine remembers the first atomic test ignited this year, and how its images alarmed her. Photographs from Annie showed manikin children tossed every which way, their manikin mother's head wrenched to one side, her legs twisted, and her bathrobe torn. Whenever Janine thinks about those stand-ins, she imagines how terribly they would have suffered had they been human beings. Real children, live children, maimed and crippled—or worse.

Still, she must admit that test days are exciting interludes in St. George. Her boys especially look forward to seeing an apocalyptic sky. Their teachers at Woodward School usually bring their classes outside to view the changing coronas of light and dark, taking advantage of a fine opportunity to preach patriotism. While the teachers justify this opportunity to connect current affairs with governmental largesse, Thomas and Richard and their friends just enjoy the break in their routine. Today would be no different, because Janine will say nothing aloud to diminish their excitement.

While Will showers, shaves, and dresses as quietly as he can, so the children can't hear his movements, Janine fixes hot oatmeal. She smiles when he comes through the door of the kitchen, thinking how handsome he looks and knowing how lucky she is to have married a loving provider. Even though his salaried job as a truck driver will never make them wealthy, she knows how hard he works and how loyal he is to his employer, as faithful to Donaldson's Dairy as he has always been to his family. Janine very much wants to confess her current concerns about their children, her foolish fretfulness about another countdown-to-zero day, but she maintains her silence. Instead, she squeezes Will's arm as he settles in his chair at the head of the table.

As she sets his hot cereal in front of him and before they can say a word, Janine hears a door slam at the back of the house, accompanied by a little-boy shout that sounds like Richard. Their sons are at it already, bickering over some toy or other. A minute later, Katie chimes in. Needing to go to the bathroom, now, Katie shouts her urgency at a door that doesn't open. Unable to wait any longer, she calls to her parents, hoping one of them will force the boys away from the only bathroom in their six-room house on West Street. For perhaps the thousandth time, Janine wishes the house were larger, fancies buying one of the two-story residences closer to the tabernacle or moving to one of the new brick homes on the hill. She says nothing aloud, however, for she knows that wishing for a bigger place to live is foolish. Will's salary will never be large enough to warrant such a move. Acknowledging that she even dreams of larger quarters, with a second bathroom, would only hurt his feelings, although they both realize that one more child surely would make their current home feel claustrophobic. Squeezing his arm once again, she drops her dish towel and trots quickly down the hall.

By the time the children are separated, dressed, and ready for breakfast, Will is already gone. Fortunately he drove from the dairy to Las Vegas yesterday, so he isn't scheduled to go there again this morning. Instead, he's handling a much shorter milk delivery route through the eastern half of town. Janine hopes he'll be finished by midafternoon, so he'll have time to spend with the boys after school. Thomas needs to work on a Cub Scout assignment, and she isn't much help with either reading maps or using a compass. Since she isn't very good at tying knots, either, Thomas needs Will's guidance. And Richard, as always, wants to tag along. Besides, if Will is in charge of the boys, Janine can take the time to fix scalloped potatoes for dinner, always a favorite. Planning her day, Janine will spend the afternoon at Relief Society, while she and her friends further their current charity project and the youngsters listen to the grown-ups gossip. Janine hides a grin as she thinks about the word "gossip." Will says that's what the women do whenever they get together without the men. Janine says no. But of course Will is right. Everyone will be agog about the morning's atomic test, and they'll swap eager opinions about Nevada's willingness to float fallout over Utah skies. Because the Simon cloud blew too close for comfort, all the women will be curious about today's pre-test prognostications and how the government will deal with any unpredictable consequences.

Janine hurries the boys through breakfast. She packs their lunches, tells Richard to change his jam-smeared shirt, finds a lost cap, urges Thomas to look after his little brother, and reminds them both to be careful crossing the streets. Stoically spooning lukewarm oatmeal into her mouth, and unfortunately dribbling it down her clean dress, Katie listens to her mother's directions. Today is laundry morning, a sheets-and-towels day. The sooner the boys leave, the faster she and her mother can strip the beds and get to work. Swallowing the last bite, she's ready to go.

Janine already has taught Katie how to gather towels and pile them neatly on the bathroom floor. The sheets, they strip off the beds one at a time, then pull the cases from the pillows. Together, mother and daughter carry four loads to the old washing machine on the back porch. Turning on the faucets, taking care not to overuse the hot water, Janine measures the Oxydol detergent carefully and then starts the first load. She'll be back shortly to operate the wringer, but for now the washer can work on its own. In the meantime, she needs to remake the beds quickly, with clean sheets. Propping Lisa where she can watch, Janine wishes one more time that Katie were older. Another few years, and she'll be a real help around the house. Now, she just jabbers nonstop and, as her mother only occasionally points out, gets somewhat in the way. Katie thinks she's helping, though, and Janine doesn't want to discourage her childish enthusiasm in any way whatsoever. All too soon the youngster will be a wife and mother herself, with weekly washing rituals in a house too small for her family.

Soon the first laundry load is finished. Janine shakes the sheets once, twice, three times, then puts the family's wet linens in a basket. In the backyard, Will has rigged a setup so Janine can hang the washing alone without much difficulty. She sets the pole in place, pulls four clotheslines back to the house, wrestles the loops over their separate hooks, and tightens the tension. Humming under her breath, and quite delighted that her chores are well under way so early, Janine begins to clothespin the sheets to the line, grateful that the unusually overcast sky doesn't seem to contain any precipitation to dampen her laundry. Repeating the ritual for the next hour and a half, she and Katie, with baby Lisa looking on, soon have the morning tasks under control. Janine even has time to pause for a moment, sitting in the grass with Katie while the two of them count the remaining wooden clothespins, first in four piles of three, then in three piles of four, finally in piles of six. Katie giggles at the game, as she always does when reciting her numbers, and reaches to push twelve together in a heap. As mother and daughter laugh, a lowering shadow begins to eclipse the morning.

Startled, although almost simultaneously realizing what is happening, Janine looks across her backyard. Beyond the two tall mulberry trees, arching from the northwest, she sees the by now familiar but nonetheless astonishing malevolent Nevada cloud sear the sky. Pulling Katie by the hand, and snatching Lisa up from her basket beside the back stoop, Janine walks a few steps to get a better look. While the rest of the sky is layered with dull, thin cirrus wisps, the dissipating mushroom cloud comes in luscious tones of persimmon and dirty shades of copper-gray. It seems to be charging through the air, surging much faster than the usual testing afterglow, as if being pushed by an energy more powerful than ever before. Apricot tendrils hang from the bottom of it, curlicue particle braids that turn darker and darker as they swirl along the horizon. Above them, the cloud stretches north to east. Katie clutches her mother's hand more tightly, pointing her other fist toward the sky and its treacherous trajectory. Janine's eyes follow the path, watching the cloud pull closer, closer, closer. She loathes the enormous elephantine shape, yet cannot take her eyes away from its colors, both beautiful and terrible all at once.

Soon the sky is heavily overcast, the May morning more night than day, an unnerving, unnatural phenomenon. Janine wonders about the rest of her family. Are the boys watching, too? Has Will paused, somewhere on his route? Despite her uneasiness at the shifting brown and black dusk with its hints of orange and peach, Janine stands steady with her two girls and watches a netherworld spin overhead. The ever-widening ebony whorls remind her of the Third Book of Nephi, where the world is described after Jesus Christ's crucifixion, the "great and terrible things that were done" when "the face of the whole earth became deformed." She even conjectures that she might hear thunder, see flashes of lightning, though she assumes the sounds are a figment of her imagination rather than the reality of an evanescing mushroom cloud. As the sky spins overhead, the ground beneath her feet feels unsteady, too. Does the whole earth pulse around her, as if the land were breathing, even gasping, fighting for breath, beneath her feet? She's not sure—perhaps it's another figment of her imagination. She's not sure of anything anymore, while the unnatural sky is throbbing so. She wishes Will were here, steady arms around the boys as she is holding the girls. The family needs his unflinching grasp.

At one point, Janine feels a flutter of dust, like dry falling snow on a cold winter night, and tastes something faintly metallic in morning air that smells almost putrid. She looks down at her faded housedress, and sees smudges of white. Dropping Katie's hand for a moment, even as she clutches Lisa more tightly, Janine brushes the eggshell layer away. Perhaps she and the girls should go inside, safely away from this hideous, unsettling cloud. She reaches for Katie's hand again, then pauses, remembering the laundry. Still a load of towels to clothespin tightly to the line. She'd better get her chores finished. Should she first take the girls inside? Katie, of course, doesn't want to go. She'd rather run across the lawn to the mulberry trees and then back to the house, making faded footprints on the whitened grass. But Lisa is crying now, and Janine detects a faint redness to her cheeks.

In fact, Janine herself feels hot, especially around the yoked neck of her yellow flowered dress and where her wristwatch band is tight. Scratching her arm, she sees tiny welts rising, like mosquito bites on a sultry summer day. She motions to Katie, eager to deal with Lisa and unsure whether or not staying outdoors is a good idea. So the three Carr women turn away from the murky, opaque sky and go inside. Once Janine changes Lisa's diaper and pours a glass of milk for Katie, she relaxes a little and decides to listen to the radio while she fixes lunch. St. George has no radio station of its own, but KNNZ from Cedar City comes in loud and clear. Rather than assuaging her apprehensions, or dismissing today's atomic wind as routine, the announcer's words turn out to be alarming. He issues a warning to all southern Utah residents, imploring them to stay indoors until noon and suggesting that they wash their clothes if they've been outside. Today's Nevada test, formally named Harry but already nicknamed Dirty Harry, is a big one, with an immense mushroom cloud blowing piecemeal in a southeasterly direction. Directly over St. George at ten o'clock in the morning, it is spreading farther to the east, drifting over Albuquerque and the Texas Panhandle and on toward the Atlantic Ocean. Meanwhile, the announcer urges that all Utahans take precautions, although he emphasizes the fact that the government's own radiation specialists believe there's no serious reason for concern. Dirty Harry is just a little larger than usual, emanating a cloud that is taking its own sweet time scattering into the atmosphere.

Hearing the announcer's words, Janine is upset. So she keeps busy, making an instant decision to do another load of laundry. Quickly she unbuttons Lisa's soft pink nursing gown and replaces it with another well-worn hand-me-down of Katie's. Katie changes her own clothes, donning a new bibbed skirt that she loves. Janine, too, picks out a clean outfit, then gathers all their clothes together. On the back porch, alongside the washing machine, she can see more of the telltale powdery white dust. After she sets the machine in motion, adding soap and the incriminating clothes, she grabs the broom propped against the kitchen door, wanting to get rid of the filth as quickly as possible. Filthy fallout, though even to herself she never says the word. Katie wants to help, but Janine turns her aside and sends her back indoors. This is a job for mother, not for little girls.

As she sweeps, she hears the telephone ring. The voice on the other end of the line is Will's. After listening to the radio while making his deliveries, her husband has stopped at Judd's Market to call home. Ten cents wasted, perhaps, but he's concerned about his womenfolk, checking up on them, wanting to be certain they're listening to the radio and following the announcer's directions. Janine is tempted to ask if he has decided the atomic tests are dangerous after all, but she knows better than to bring up the subject. Instead, she tells him that she and the girls are finishing laundry, that everything is under control, that they'll leave for Relief Society right after lunch. When she asks him if he saw the cloud, Will replies that probably every living soul in Washington County saw the cloud. Iron County, too. How could anyone miss it, with its fantastic shapes and its tropical colors? And no, he's not really worried about Janine and the girls or about the boys at school. He's just hoping they're taking the advised precautions, and he'll see them all tonight, after work.

Janine shakes her head, ever so slightly, as she puts the receiver back on the hook. Rarely does Will call while he's working, only after Thomas broke his leg and again when Katie had pneumonia, so the sound of his voice during the daytime unsettles Janine. Unable to tell exactly what her husband might be thinking, with the static on the phone line and his terse replies to her questions, she is uneasy. Yet almost immediately she's busy with the girls again, scrubbing their lunch dishes and getting all three of them ready for the afternoon gathering. While she fusses, the radio drones steadily in the background. Although the news is being broadcast from the north, the station's announcer has been in touch with St. George authorities, along with a radiation expert from Las Vegas. No one official has much to say, so he has little new information, other than the by now familiar admonitions and the simultaneous assertions that the eastbound cloud is no longer a concern. Janine pays scant attention to the repetitiveness, until she catches him saying Woodward School and referencing St. George. Evidently the local teachers, knowing nothing about warnings to stay indoors, took their students outside to watch the morning sky's contortions. Thomas and Richard must have seen the extraordinary light show, too, with its dark, debilitating colors. She wonders what they'll say when they get home, how Harry compares with the other clouds they've seen this spring. Whatever, she plans to follow the broadcast instructions, washing their clothes, making certain that everyone has a bath, even though that will take hours in their tiny house. Will won't like the wasted water, and the children will complain about the change in routine, but Janine trusts the announcer's calm voice. Precautions do need to be taken, just in case. In case what? She doesn't know the answer to her own question, as she rubs a reddish warm spot on her left forearm and wrist. Perhaps Relief Society conversation will enlighten her.

THE WOMEN gather at one o'clock, ostensibly to sort the children's clothes they've collected for the nearby Paiute Indian reservation. Recent news from distant Washington, D.C., reports that the United States Congress has introduced a bill to terminate the Shivwits's tribal status, and the families currently living on tribal land are terribly needy. The bishop has asked the Relief Society to gather outerwear and as many pairs of shoes as possible, so the women have a lot to do this afternoon. But first, Janine anticipates the gossip. When she arrives, sharply on time, half a dozen conversations are already under way.

Everyone has seen the cloud that enveloped St. George, and everyone has an opinion about its potency. Sisters Genevieve and Virginia, shopping at Judd's Market, were astonished to see the mushroom blossoming so close to St. George, right overhead, as if someone steered it this way. They're still excited now, talking nonstop about the beauteous colors and gargantuan shapes that changed by the minute. Patriotic to the core, the Smith twins repeat the enthusiastic incantations about atomic testing they've heard from their husbands. Most Latter-day Saint leaders, in fact, celebrate each detonation. The United States government, so mistrusted by nineteenth-century followers of Joseph Smith, is highly esteemed by twentieth-century male church members. The women respect Washington, D.C., too, but they're not wholly convinced that they're hearing the full truth about atomic testing.

Sister Elaine is especially alarmed. She confronted two white-overalled men at the intersection of Main Street and St. George Boulevard, right here, in the center of town, like moon men from outer space. One toted a Geiger counter, the other was writing notations on a pad of paper. When she asked them for an explanation, they waved her away. One told her to go home and stay indoors for a couple of hours, the other said there was nothing to worry about. But he talked over her shoulder while he was speaking, unable to look her in the eye. Sister Elaine mimics his tone of voice, his shallow insincerity, and emphatically states that she doesn't believe a word he said.

Listening while Elaine describes her encounter, Janine expects her own sister, Susan, to chime in, for she knows Susan has always been opposed to the Nevada Proving Ground. When she doesn't see her older sibling, she prods her sister-in-law, Mary, asking if she's seen Sue. Janine's mother knows the answer because she talked to her eldest daughter just an hour ago. Susan is taking the radio pronouncements very seriously and will not, under any circumstances, venture outside. Apparently she had been nursing a bout of morning sickness when normally she would be shepherding her children off to school, so she had been listening to the early-morning news. Susan heard about the mushroom cloud an hour or more in advance, long before the radioactive winds loomed over the St. George horizon. Alarmed, she kept her children home from school. Safely indoors, her family watched the cloud together through their living room window, a glass prism distorting the changing shapes and colors, as she characterized the view to her mother. Even afterward, she made her four daughters and two sons stay inside and forgo their classes. Her oldest two, already in high school, were irate, but Susan is refusing to let them go anywhere until she says the word.

Susan herself won't step outside the front door, either. Twenty-four hours—that's the time that must elapse before the air is safe, or so Susan says. Where she got the twenty-four-hours figure is unknown to Janine's mother, since the word around town is all-clear by noon, but Susan is immovable. Not even Relief Society can coax her outdoors. Janine can't remember anyone in the family ever being absent from a Relief Society meeting, except when nursing a sick child or giving birth to a new baby. Ever since she was a little girl, however, Susan has been obstinate, so today's firm stance is absolutely in character. When she makes up her mind about something, not even Relief Society can sway her decision.

Now Sister Mary searches for words, wanting to understand what caused the lingering pall in the morning sky, the irregular mushroom shape, and its awful barbaric colors. Listening to her sister-in-law, Janine can tell that Mary is upset. Like Janine, Mary has had a busy day, seeing her husband, Tom, out of the house in time for an early meeting, shooing their children off to school, then getting out the vacuum cleaner. Impossible to hear anything over the roar of the Hoover, let alone think about listening to the radio, so Mary hasn't heard the news. Only when the morning sky turned unnaturally dark did she realize what was happening. Now she's almost weeping. Married to Janine and Susan's oldest brother, she should know what to do in an emergency. Now she feels so guilty, letting her whole family go outside that day. Janine tries to calm her, while at the same time worrying that somehow she has let her own children down. Maybe Susan is smarter, at least about atomic fallout?

Mary feels conscience-stricken about her husband, too. Tom, as the principal of the local elementary school, let all the children go outside and watch the sky's display. He saw no reason to keep them indoors. It was his idea, in fact, earlier that spring, to use atomic testing days as occasions for civics lessons. Mary turns to Janine and speaks sotto voce. Might Tom be responsible for something awful? Janine doesn't think so. She's talked to Will, who alleges that everything dangerous floated high in the atmosphere, that the cloud blew through and dispersed before any damage could occur to anyone. Elaine, overhearing the whispered conversation, reminds them of the white-clad men. If there's no reason for alarm, what on earth were they doing in downtown St. George, just a few blocks from Woodward School?

Back and forth as they sort clothes, the women debate the issues. Sister Nancy detests the naming of one Upshot-Knothole test "Nancy" and another one "Dixie." The former is a personal affront; the latter, discourteous to their Mormon community. Their part of southwestern Utah is nicknamed Dixie because of its temperate climate. While the Atomic Energy Commission considers the name a compliment, the locals find it insulting, especially since Dixie precipitated a light rain over their community. Some residents insisted that the dusty mist contained debris from the test itself, though no one knew for sure because the government would neither confirm nor deny the rumor. Now Sister Nancy labels the Civil Defense response to Dirty Harry insulting, too, as if the poor isolated citizens of St. George were cannon fodder, nothing more. Not everyone agrees. The Smith sisters defend the Nevada Proving Ground and maintain that the government is a friend of the people. Elaine counters by insisting that what fell from the sky this morning was anything but friendly. Others are hesitant to express an opinion one way or another. Janine looks over at her mother, hoping to take a cue. But her mother sits quietly, matching pairs of patent leather shoes and putting them in boxes. She'll not join in the conversation, not when her daughter Susan contrarily stayed home and her own husband of forty years favors atomic testing so adamantly. Thus Janine is left to her own thoughts, and she wonders what she'll say to Will.

AS IT TURNS OUT, Will takes no time at all to pause and answer reservations she might voice or any question she might ask. He comes in through the kitchen door bursting with energy, detailing every event of the day. Watching the cloud from Rainbow Hill, later driving through a soft mist that stuck to his windshield, stopping back at the dairy where Evan Donaldson was fretting about his cows' strange behavior, pawing the pasture with their hooves while shaking their heads as if something were tweaking their eyes. In contrast, Will is worrying about very little, except he hopes the scientists got some good answers. The cloud, after all, is totally gone, billowing off to the east and evaporating into the heavens. The government sure knows its business, that's what Will repeats several times, first to his sons, who are celebrating a grand day of savoring long school recesses and sky-watching brilliant rainbow clouds, and later to Janine, who tacitly accepts his constant buoyancy.

Will's contagious enthusiasm is second only to the boys,' who barrel through the front door, tracking mud across the carpet. Only after they're tramping through the kitchen, leaving tracks on the linoleum, does Janine realize the damage done. May weather, in southwestern Utah, rarely leads to muddy floors, so the footprints puzzle her. When she asks the boys where their feet got so dirty, they lift their hands in meaningless gestures, as if they haven't a clue. Janine shakes her head, knowing that tomorrow's task, first thing after breakfast, will be to mop the kitchen floor. For now, she wipes futilely at the carpet while she tries to sound keen about the boys' escapades. A fabulous day, they both report, just peachy. Thomas begins with the fact that Jessie, a little freckled girl he despises, was late to school, and Miss Turlock scolded her, sent her to the back of the room, in fact, and made her practice penmanship. Thomas thinks this serves her right, and wishes Miss Turlock had kept the hated Jessie indoors when everyone else got to go outside to see the mushroom cloud. Richard is just as excited about his hours at school. Nothing as dramatic as Jessie being punished, but a day that began with a coloring session, which Richard loves, and soon bloomed into an early recess with its own kind of rainbow hues.

The boys' words come fast, tripping over each other as they vie to shout out the most vivid description of what they saw in the sky. A big wave, like Thomas imagines an ocean even though he's never seen one, a big wave that rolls and crashes. Lots of movement, lots of noise, rumbling right over the tabernacle and the new chapel. He bangs his hands together, then claps them over his ears. More entranced by the palette of unimaginable colors, Richard wraps his mind around the new words he learned from the teacher, like "magenta" and "mauve." Instantly he wants new crayons, a bigger set than he got for Christmas, a box with magenta and mauve. The boys boast about other things their teachers told them, Thomas more sophisticated with his fourth-grade vocabulary, Richard just trying to keep up, a tough task for a second grader who worships his older brother. Richard, in fact, lets the cat out of the bag, or so Janine characterizes his big blunder. That trite saying suits Richard's innocence exactly, when he unwittingly celebrates the mud puddles left from a peculiar midday shower on the school playground. Unused to rain in May, the boys happily stomped through the water at lunchtime, splattering their playmates again and again. After school, they managed to find a spot where puddles still pooled, on South Street, so they had been able to splash one more time. Finally, Thomas admits getting Jessie's dress dirty. The boys laugh.

Everyone's energy and exhilaration carries over. Thomas has already earned his Tiger and his Wolf Cub Scout levels. Now, to attain Bear status, he needs help from his father before dinner. In the backyard, Will and Thomas pace off their directions, north and west, out to the two mulberry trees and back, just as Katie and her mother had done several hours earlier. Richard tags after them, scuffing the grass with his shoes as he tries to listen to Will's explanation of south-southeast, the very direction the vagrant mushroom cloud took that morning. Katie climbs into the lowest mulberry branches and hides, although they know she's there because it's her favorite spot. The Carr menfolk ignore her, as is often the case when she wants to play. She always carries on, but the fellows have more important undertakings, measuring distances and getting Thomas ready for his Cub Scout paces.

When Janine finally calls the family to dinner, she's happy to see everyone having fun, although Katie complains that the mulberry is slippery this evening, and shakes tiny dust particles from her dirty jumper and blouse. Janine scolds her daughter, in a tone slightly milder than the one she used when chastising the boys earlier, but Will, practical as always, points out that she can throw Katie's clothes in with the boys,' so Janine relents. No matter, because laundry must wait for morning. The children need baths tonight. Not enough hot water in the heater for both tasks, though Will doesn't say so and neither does his wife.

Janine, in fact, has little energy to pursue either activity. She's tired, and after supper she takes time to sit down for half an hour before she washes up the dishes, nursing the baby during a peaceful moment in a normally bustling routine. Lisa is fretful, however, as if she isn't feeling well either. Janine's supper isn't settling in her stomach. Usually scalloped potatoes are one of her favorite casseroles, but tonight she's gaseous and uncomfortable and eager to put the baby down. When she suddenly runs outside, unable to use the bathroom because the boys are in the tub, Will quirks an eyebrow in her direction. Janine shakes her head, knowing exactly what he's speculating. He's thinking about morning sickness, like Sister Susan's, only in the evening, and hoping that's the reason for her sudden illness.

His wife intuitively understands that what she's experiencing is quite different. After four children in ten years, she knows exactly how a new pregnancy is supposed to feel. Not this ache-all-over sensation, her head throbbing and her skin hot to the touch, not this mind-numbing weariness. For the umpteenth time, she looks at her arm, the very place where she brushed off the powdery dust that morning, and appraises the scarlet hue, as if she were sunburnt and windburnt all at the same time. The tiny welts have vanished, but her arm itches just the same. Her neck is prickly, too, so much so that she stews about the irritation. She prays to her Heavenly Father that nothing bad comes of staying outside to watch the sky's contortions, "the terrible darkness upon the face of the land."

After the children are bathed and clad in fresh pajamas, after her stomach has plenty of time to digest what little remains of her supper, after she and Will go to bed, Janine still feels nauseous and queer. Normally the Carrs are as healthy as horses. Except for the occasional head cold and Katie's babyhood bout with pneumonia, illness is an unfamiliar state in their household.

Bruises, broken bones, and occasionally sprains, yes; but internal illnesses like stomachaches and fever, almost never. Their forebears, after all, pushed handcarts thousands of miles across prairies and mountains to reach Utah's promised land. Both Janine and Will flaunt their vigorous ancestral heritage, and both maintain that any physical shortcoming is almost an insult. Nonetheless, Janine's tongue still tingles with that rough metallic taste and her stomach is roiling inside and her aching bones quiver beneath the beehive quilt that covers their bed. Will broaches the notion of morning sickness, but his wife brushes him away. No morning sickness ever caused her to feel this debilitated. Laying a cold washcloth across her forehead, Will can think of nothing else to do. Lisa wants to nurse again, and he is of no help whatsoever.

By midnight, nothing is improved. Janine staggers to the bathroom every half hour or so, Lisa cries almost steadily, and Katie is feeling ill, too. She complains of the same symptoms as her mother, although her head isn't pounding in quite the same way. Miraculously, the boys sleep through all the commotion, while Janine watches Will pace restlessly beside his womenfolk, obviously wondering if he should wake Brother Greg, longtime friend and family doctor. He has never before phoned Greg in the middle of the night, and he hates to do so now because he trusts that these crazy symptoms will be gone by morning. That's what he says to Janine at 2 A.M., after she climbs back into bed and moans ever so slightly. She realizes that today is a scheduled milk run, so Will needs to be at work by 4 A.M. at the latest. She feels sorry for him. After an almost sleepless night, he now faces a long drive to Las Vegas and back, but she can hardly face the thought of fixing his oatmeal, let alone getting the boys off to school. Hesitantly, she asks if her husband might take a day off work, to help out while she feels so rotten. Will looks at her with that familiar wrinkled brow, an odd look this time, one that implicitly says he cannot believe she actually thinks a day away from the dairy is a plausible idea.

She does know better. Financially, the Carrs need every dollar Will earns, and besides, a frivolous day off might even cost him his job. The St. George economy is perilous in 1953. Even though Will has worked at the dairy for six years now, ever since he returned from the service, and he's an exceptionally safe driver and loyal employee, he must never irritate his employer, Mr. Donaldson. There are other men willing to rise at dawn and deliver milk, other men ready to do whatever is necessary, other men who could be hired in his place. Will conveys all this to his wife in a single glance. Her response is to stumble out of bed, almost eager to see him on his way, although she still doesn't know how she'll find the energy to deal with the boys.

She manages. Thomas, never having seen his mother ill, is particularly well behaved. Fortunately, the baby sleeps through the boys' breakfast, having hiccupped her distress for so long that she is finally out of lung power, and Katie stays in her room until they're gone. When Janine tries to get her daughter up and feed her breakfast, at least a piece of toast, she's lethargic and pushes her mother away. Relieved in a way, Janine settles back in the living room, slowly sipping a glass of milk, Lisa at her side. She knows she should get going, do the children's laundry and mop the kitchen floor where the boys tracked in the mud, but her energy escapes her. She takes another swallow, then turns on the radio, tuned to the Cedar City station. Today the announcer is playing an interview with a radiation specialist from Las Vegas, a man who has been checking the gamma- and beta-ray levels in the surrounding communities. So that's what Sister Elaine's moonwalkers were doing downtown. Somehow this doesn't make Janine feel any better, as she listens to the rad man, as he's called, insist there's little cause for alarm and reiterate the same bromides about washing clothes and taking precautions that Janine heard yesterday. He adds something new, however, advising St. George residents to monitor their milk intake.

Janine looks at the half-empty glass by her side, and wonders why he's talking about milk. He doesn't explain, and the rest of the interview is innocuous. She drinks her milk anyway. It soothes her stomach, and she knows it adds needed calcium for Lisa. To her way of thinking, a real warning should be just that—a real warning, with red signs at the market dairy section, and newspaper headlines, and definitive words instead of platitudes on the radio. Today's newspaper prints no more useful information. Primarily the headlines tout the success of the Harry blast, while the ensuing articles mention some wariness about the path of the mushroom cloud but sound no fearful alarms at all. The government insists everything is under control. Precautions, yes, like washing clothes and reducing milk consumption and scrubbing fresh vegetables from the garden, though it's too early for anything except strawberries and peas. Otherwise, the news on the second page of the *Daily Spectrum* is benign. Monitoring intake levels indeed—that just sounds pointless and futile to Janine. Surely the government doesn't recommend that St. George mothers cut off their children's milk supply.

The interview over, the announcer summarizes the rad man's recommendations. He also itemizes a set of minor symptoms that families should note, signs all too familiar to Janine. Aching bones, a slight fever, nausea, chills, as if these are everyday irritations. Almost clutching Lisa, Janine checks her baby's hot, dry brow. She can't call Will. He's on the road to Las Vegas. She hesitates to phone Brother Greg, whose busy schedule is always overbooked. Besides, what can he possibly prescribe? She doesn't want to worry her mother, and certainly not her sister or her sister-in-law. All from the same pioneer stock, the women in her family would put aside her trepidations, tell her to get up and get busy, the children need their clothes washed and the kitchen floor can't mop itself. Worse yet, Susan might point to the obvious: staying outdoors yesterday, watching the ugly seductive cloud gyrate across the sky, was not a smart decision.

Janine closes her eyes, just for a minute, rocking Lisa in her arms and keeping one ear attuned should Katie call from the back of the house. As she rests in the half-waking state that happens when one's temperature climbs higher than normal, a malevolent vision takes over her brain. A convoluted cloud, a helix of Satan, twists into the stratosphere and then settles back to earth, swallowing St. George and all the neighboring communities in midnight shades of ebony and smoke. Just like *The Book of Mormon* predicates: "And thus the face of the whole earth became deformed, because of the tempests, and the thundering, and the lightnings, and the quaking of the earth."

Janine wakes from her nightmare with such a start that she bumps Lisa, who immediately begins squalling. The baby's cries drop to a whimper as Janine rocks her daughter gently, and before long Lisa is asleep again. So is Katie, when Janine looks in on her other girl. Neither's forehead, in fact, is as hot as in the middle of the night, or even earlier this morning, and both seem to be resting comfortably. Janine feels much more like herself, too. She bends her head, again prays to her Heavenly Father, and thanks Him. Just as the earth's quaking passed with yesterday's cloud, so today suddenly appears much brighter.

THE NEXT TWO DAYS, in fact, pass rather quickly. By the time Friday morning dawns, Katie is on her feet and eager to be entertained, Lisa's temperature is actually subnormal, and almost all of Janine's energy has returned. Her arm still itches a little, and the leathery swath near her wrist looks as if she had burned herself in a careless moment by the kitchen stove, but her stomachache is totally gone and the spring is back in her legs. Questions about poisonous radiation still plague Janine, though, questions that neither Will nor the local news can answer. As she does her morning chores, she thinks about her bedtime conversation with her husband last evening, when she conjured images of Hiroshima and Nagasaki. Will brushed away her apprehensiveness, pointing out that the Nevada blast took place more than a hundred miles away and that the Carr family in St. George lives well outside critical radiation limits. Will's trust of the federal government remained unwavering. A follow-up question about the possible cause of Janine's sudden illness and the reason behind the girls' high temperatures fell on deaf ears. If there was a connection, Will saw it as nothing more than a minor inconvenience, nothing worth Janine's alarm. Even when his wife waved her reddened arm in the evening air, Will remembered that Janine stood too close to the barbecue last Saturday night. The bruise on her neck he dismissed totally, shaking his head at her uncharacteristic hypochondria.

Needing to talk things out, although she would never admit that her husband doesn't listen, Janine hopes she'll find more sympathy from her women friends. Every Friday morning, she and her sisters, along with their mother and a dozen other women from the community, quilt together while babies gurgle by their sides and preschool children play happily in the corners. Today they are meeting at Sister Susan's, whose big house has more room than anyone else's. Susan, her Relief Society absence unmentioned but not forgotten, welcomes the women one by one, offering orange juice and cookies to her friends and their children. While everyone is getting settled, Janine stares briefly out the plate glass window, wishing for the twentieth time that she had kept her own children indoors. Too late to cry over spilt milk, she thinks, trying to push her regrets to the back of her mind.

Nobody says much at first, as the women seat themselves in their chairs with their quilting frames, each busy at her stretcher with the task at hand. Janine reaches for a sky-blue cotton square, and Mary takes a piece of white wool. Sister Susan prefers a black-and-red flannel one. When she incidentally remarks that her square reminds her of Tuesday morning's sky, everyone immediately begins talking at once, each recounting her own personal experience with the otherworldly vision. Ominous, black, devil-spawned, horrific. No one has much new to add, at least not about the cloud itself, but the women soon turn the subject in a new direction, voicing their apprehensions about the fearful aftermath. Everything Janine has been thinking, and more, surfaces in their discussion.

A few, like Sister Miriam, repeat what they've been told by their husbands and cannot understand why the others are so agitated. Sister Susan disagrees with such passivity. Angrily, she counts on her fingers the mistakes made locally in the past week. Insufficient warnings to stay inside, no procedures for cleaning up any fallout, belated concern for the schoolchildren, indifference to the citizens of southern Utah. Sister Mary adds her two cents' worth, repeating Brother Tom's frustration with the test itself, which he believes never should have occurred. He's been applauding the experiments all spring long, but he's convinced that when the velocity and wind direction changed so suddenly, they should have put Harry off for another day. He's so angry, in fact, about the schoolchildren going outside on Tuesday that he's beside himself. Mary resoundingly defends him, repeating and repeating that her husband would never endanger anyone, especially the children in his charge.

Susan fingers a newspaper article that has her husband particularly upset, something from the *Los Angeles Times* saying that since not many people live in southern Utah there wasn't much damage done by Harry's freefall through the skies. Susan is irate, as are most of the women around the table. Susan reads aloud the entire article, which goes on to itemize possible radiation dangers, her voice rising with each paragraph. Listening to the list of symptoms, Janine idly rubs her forearm, scuffing her skin. Hopefully the radiation is sloughing off, too. When she looks at her hand, she notices that her fingernails are discolored, as if they were bruised as well. Darla, Susan's next-door neighbor, interjects symptoms of her own. She, too, was doing her laundry on Tuesday, so she, too, was outdoors most of the morning. She's been feeling poorly ever since. Unlike Janine, who's definitely better, Darla still aches all over, and her eyes remain puffy and swollen. She hasn't had a decent night's sleep ever since that cloud dropped down on St. George, and as a result she's exhausted. And why is her hair falling out? That's not normal, not normal at all. She doesn't care what any old newspaper article says. Whatever blew in from Nevada must have been bad, must have poisoned them, Darla is sure.

Listening to her friend talk, Janine thinks about the excess strands of brown on her comb that morning. On Katie's as well. Across the table, Brother Orson's wife, Sarah, discreetly checks the curls cascading down her back. An odd look crosses Sister Sarah's face. Always so proud of her thick black tresses, she flutters her eyes rapidly, as if blinking back tears. A telltale strand adheres to her hand when she picks up a piece of quilt and hastily sets to work again. Janine rubs her own brow, and pulls a smallish clump away. And notes her ugly fingernails again. Surrounded by friends and family, she suddenly feels terribly alone, so lost in a maze of facts and fiction. She feels like sobbing, no longer knowing true from false, no longer knowing what to believe. Looking over at Katie, happily playing with her young cousins, Janine prays that her daughter will not suffer from Tuesday's outdoors washday. She repeats her prayers to herself as she gives an extra hug to baby Lisa, whose forehead again feels warmer than usual, and thinks of her two sons happily at school this Friday morning. Counting her blessings, Janine bows her head.

BROTHER ORSON'S VOICE intrudes. "And in one place they were heard to cry, saying: O that we had repented before this great and terrible day, and then would our brethren have been spared, and they would not have been burned in that great city Zarahemla."

PAST AND PRESENT COALESCE, as this Sunday's calamitous talk breaks Janine's nightmarish reverie to pieces. "O that we had repented" jars her awake, dislodges her from quilting bee to chapel. Embracing Lisa more tightly, she instinctively reaches for Katie's hand. The boys, she sees, are paying attention to the apocryphal Chapter 8 scripture, too, as is Will, his head bent slightly toward the front of the room. Her husband seems unaware, in fact, that his wife's mind had strayed, that now she is disoriented for a moment, staring fixedly at her family, while Brother Orson intones verse 25, a reiteration of 24. "And in another place they were heard to cry and mourn, saying: O that we had repented before this great and terrible day."

Janine's heart desperately begs for forgiveness. She repents her maternal laxity, allowing her children to suffer the destructive forces of Dirty Harry. She promises her Father in Heaven that she'll cherish her family even more from this day forward, always putting their welfare before her own backyard curiosity. She vows eternal faith. "And it came to pass that it did last for the space of three days that there was no light seen; and there was great mourning and howling and weeping among all the people continually; yea, great were the groanings of the people, because of the darkness and the great destruction which had come upon them." Janine bows her head once more. She knows that the Third Book of Nephi, after these portentous passages, will go on to describe how her people will be led beyond the darkness. Jesus Christ will descend from the heavens, "the light and the life of the world." Mournful cries will be silenced, darkness lifted, the chosen saved. "Therefore let your light so shine before this people, that they may see your good works and glorify your Father who is in heaven."

And so Janine assumes, as she listens, that her family will escape the darkness of the week just ended. Though she may no longer trust the government, she trusts the future for her children. Brother Orson's next words seal her optimism completely: "And blessed are all the peacemakers, for they shall be called the children of God."

Grable

25 MAY 1953 · 0830 HOURS

Fired by remote control, the artillery shell shoots out of the big gun like a bolt of lightning. The recoil rocks the cannon's tonnage as if it were a child's toy. A twenty-second trajectory carries the ordnance seven miles across the desert floor. There, five hundred feet in the air, the projectile detonates. A sharp crack, and then a burst of white-hot air almost immediately turns dirty gray as a wispy mushroom cloud forms quickly. Ten, twenty, thirty thousand feet high in a matter of seconds. Through the greasy smoke, an unusual double fireball can be seen, one that flashes from red to peach and then takes on the gray pallor of the cloud itself. Grable makes history, the one and only atomic shot fired from a 280 mm cannon first nicknamed Amazon Annie, later glamorized as Atomic Annie. Three thousand soldiers who watch from their bunkers and trenches make history, too. Tipping their heads back, they see Grable's towering vaporous cloud, topped by a blue-tinged ice cap, drift safely away. Blinded by the flash, the three dozen rabbits caged nearby see nothing at all. So the rabbits miss the cloud's reversal, as it floats back over the soldiers in the artillery's wake.

Matthew

Finally—a few minutes of free time.

Got to Las Vegas about noon yesterday. Off the train quickly, then stood around in the hot sun for a while. Couldn't see much of the city, but it sure sounds like fun! Noise everywhere. Coins ringing, jackpots galore. Neon flashing, even in broad daylight. Put some nickels in a slot machine at the depot. Lost three bucks.

When the buses finally arrived, we were ready to roll. The drive from LV to Camp Desert Rock turned out to be weird, through miles of dusty flat without any trees. Just a few skinny cows trying to find grass. Nevada's the strangest place I've ever seen—hardly any vegetation anywhere. Just some scrubby bushes scattered here and there. Worse than Texas, and definitely not like Wisconsin, that's for sure.

The Rock isn't any better. The only green things are the tents. They're lined up in rows, along pretend streets, with latrines in cement blockhouses at the intersections. Pretty primitive. A sergeant assigned us to our new homes. I'm in Block 5F, along with the rest of the boys from the Midwest. Via Fort Hood.

Not much here in the way of amenities. A cot, four blankets, a pillow and a pillowcase apiece. A string of electric bulbs gives us some light after dark, but it's still hard to see. I'm writing after dinner right now. Probably have to quit when the sun totally disappears. Besides, it's getting colder. Boys who've been here longer clued us in: Be prepared to freeze. They suggested padding our beds with newspapers. I haven't found any yet, and damned near froze my butt last night. More of the same tonight, I suppose.

Can't complain, though. I can't wait for next week!

Right now, everything is just routine. Reveille came early this morning and dawn felt just as cold as midnight. At breakfast my eggs congealed as soon as they flopped on the plate. Plenty of food, but it all tastes the same. I miss Mom's cooking. Her housekeeping, too. After breakfast cleanup we did more cleanup chores, like sweeping the tent out when the floor is just desert dirt. I can't believe the dust. It's everywhere! Even in my mouth when I brush my teeth, like gritty tooth powder, only brown instead of white. Spit and polish is a joke.

All day long, more and more boys arrived at the Rock. Someone said that three thousand soldiers from all over the country are going to participate in the upcoming maneuvers. Glad we got billeted early. Jeremy, Ethan, Leo, and I are assigned to the same company, along with about 175 other grunts. As soon as everyone gets here, they'll tell us more about what we're supposed to do.

DIDN'T WRITE ANYTHING for the last couple of days because nothing much has been happening. Some lectures, and a lot of standing around. Today got better, much better. Just before lunch, some dancers from the Desert Inn put on a show for us. They even brought a band. Live music, especially the clarinet, was good to hear, but not nearly as sexy as watching those girls twirl around. We clapped and stomped and whistled something fierce. They just kept dancing and blowing kisses. I loved it! Short red, white, and blue skirts and tight little tops and bouncing sequins. Just made you want to hug one of 'em! Jeremy tried, but failed.

They didn't stay long. Had to be back in Las Vegas for their evening show. Nice break, though. After they left, a major met all afternoon with our company. Most of what we heard is classified, so I guess I can't write it down. But the exciting part is fairly common knowledge. We get to participate in the Amazon Annie exercise!

She's a 280 mm artillery piece that can fire an atomic projectile. We're going to watch her shoot her wad. The newspapers—yeah, I finally got some to pad my blankets—say she'll fire that projectile about seven miles before it explodes with an atomic blast supposedly equivalent to more than 15 kilotons. That ought to be some explosion. Bigger than any fireworks I've ever seen!

The major handed out a little pamphlet to each of us and told us to study it carefully. That's what I should be doing right now, before lights-out. No one else seems to be reading it, either. Jeremy's playing his harmonica. Ethan's writing to his girlfriend, like he does almost every day. Leo's trying to figure out how to make his bed warmer. One blanket on the bottom and three on top? Or two and two? Newspapers between the blankets or underneath?

If Susie were here—that'd fix it! I'd be warm all night.

SPENT YESTERDAY AND TODAY in class. Might as well be back in school. Learned about what's called CBR Warfare. That's Chemical, Biological, and Radiological Warfare. Sounds like both the United States and Russia have huge quantities of deadly gas and germs stored away somewhere, just waiting for an ugly war. We're supposed to be prepared. Fat chance if air particles we can't see are bouncing all around us! Glad I'm mustering out real soon.

We also learned about alpha and beta and gamma rays. After hearing all the particulars, I studied my pamphlet pretty carefully. Sounds like we'll be fine if we're careful. No one in my company is worried at all. They've given us all badges—dosimeters—to wear clipped to our collars. That way, they'll know if we're hot!

Saw several films, too. Two made by the Civil Defense people, the others by the military. Lots of pictures of atomic blasts. I know the real thing will be bigger and better. I'm already tired of sitting around and listening to warnings and reassurances, back and forth but mostly the latter. I'm ready for some action.

I can't wait!

GOT SOME ACTION, but not quite what I expected. A bunch of us piled into three Jeeps and headed off for Beatty. Scruffy little one-horse town, fifty or sixty miles from the Rock. Beer, slots, and floozies. The girls weren't much, kind of old and overused, but the booze sure tasted good. Put my usual three dollars in a slot machine and had a little luck. Made ten bucks off a row of sevens. Spent it all on beer. Back in camp now, writing this by flashlight. Kind of woozy. Hope I feel better in the morning.

NEARLY MISSED MASS. Forgot it was scheduled before breakfast so the priest could get back to Las Vegas. He came out to Mercury yesterday afternoon to hear confessions. I didn't go. Too busy.

I confess. Haven't been in a while. Head pounded all through Mass. Couldn't take communion. Father Joseph would be disappointed. I'll make amends when I get home.

AS USUAL, out of bed at the crack of dawn. Just as cold as ever. Right after breakfast—more congealed eggs—we crammed ourselves into the backs of Army trucks that bounced us over to Frenchman Flat. I know we drove past Amazon Annie, but I didn't catch a glimpse. Captain Jameson promised we'll get to see her emplacement tomorrow or the next day. I sure hope so.

Today we practiced maneuvers. Over and over again. In the heat. This place is unbelievable. Freezing at night and sweltering by noon. A regular temperature roller coaster. The captain made us keep our jackets on the whole time today, so we were really sweating up a storm.

Sure happy we didn't have to dig our own trenches. They've got a backhoe that scoops out the dirt. Long, narrow rows, sort of mid-chest deep. Reinforced with two-by-fours, tarpaper, and chicken wire, as if that'd provide any real protection. Shouldn't cave in on us, though. Ethan and Leo and Jeremy and I've been assigned together. Our trench is supposed to be 4,570 meters west of ground zero. Or so they say. But if they've never fired an atomic blast from an artillery piece, how can they be so sure where the projectile will land? Anyway, now I've got my own trench, just like I've got my own cot here at the Rock. Hope it doesn't turn out to be cannon fodder.

After we practiced climbing in and out of our trenches about a million times, we marched back and forth toward what will be ground zero. Pretended we were in Korea, chasing down out the invading Chinese. Kind of fun, actually. Amazon Annie goes off, blasts everything nearby, then the Army follows hard on her heels. Shoot at any gooks still left alive. Great sport!

While we were parading, we got to see all the stuff they've laid out for the various tests. Fortifications, bunkers, foxholes of different sizes. Plus a number of trucks, a trailer, and even a locomotive. There's a lot of smaller equipment, too, like machine guns, mortars, howitzers, flamethrowers, and a rocket launcher. Guess they want to see what survives.

I wonder if the animals will survive? That's something I'm not supposed to talk about. We saw a bunch of places where they're going to stake out sheep and dogs and pigs. Some were pretty close to X marks the spot. A couple of days from now, I expect we'll see fried mutton. Glad our trench is a ways back.

The funniest thing we saw was a string of playing cards tacked to some posts. They're supposed to tell us something about the blast effects on different colors—white cards, red hearts and diamonds, black clubs and spades. Only in Nevada!

Here at the Rock we've got a lot of playing cards of our own. Now that he's found a nightly poker game, Ethan's slowed down on the letters to Julie. Glad I'm not a cardsharp. I prefer the slots. Looking forward to spending a night in Las Vegas after all this is over. Captain Jameson promised. Twenty-four hours of free time before we have to catch the train back to Fort Hood. I'm ready, but not before the action's finished here.

HALLELUJAH! We got to see Amazon Annie! She's a big one! Eighty-five tons, 84 feet long, and 10 feet wide! They had a hell of a time getting her from Fort Sill to the Proving Ground. She doesn't turn corners very well. Plus it turns out she has a sister. So they had to bring two cannons by train and then by truck. Nearly caused a wreck along the way. Narrow roads, out here in the West. We didn't see the backup, which is stashed somewhere over in Mercury. If something goes wrong, I guess they'll haul her here. Wonder what her name would be? Sandblast Susie?

Since we're part of the artillery troops, they let us climb onto Annie's loading platform and even let us inspect the big gun's mechanisms. A hoist picks up the atomic projectile and then a fancy hydraulic system inserts it into a tube. Pretty sophisticated, but apparently the mechanism doesn't always work. Sometimes the crew has to seat the projectile manually. The boys just laughed about pounding down an atomic bomb, ramrodding it into place. They made fun of the double recoil system, too. During practice rounds, Annie would lurch two or three feet backward with every shot, so the crew had to jump out of the way. Even those non-nuclear munitions made their ears ring something fierce.

I guess they're going to set the atomic explosion off from a distance. Scared to do it right alongside. It doesn't sound like they're real sure what'll happen. They're just assuming she'll fire dead ahead. Us, too. Glad our trenches are off to the side! I keep saying that, don't I? Glad I'm not on the battery crew either.

After we finished examining Annie, we also got to see the crater made by another one of the tests this spring. It was on Yucca Flat, over the hill from Frenchman. The desert, which is pretty bare anyway, looked absolutely scoured and crinkly, kind of like baked sugar candy. Slippery in some spots, tacky in others.

Then we came back to Frenchman for more practice maneuvers. Like every afternoon in Nevada, the wind came up, and it was hot, too. Dust blowing everywhere. We had to bail out. Couldn't hardly breathe and couldn't see a thing. Jeremy, when he wasn't coughing, and Leo were laughing about the leftover radioactivity from earlier tests. Will our eyes glow in the dark? We all chuckled at that pamphlet they made us study. It says not to worry about impotence. If you get that much radiation, it says, you're dead. Guess that's supposed to make us feel better. Neither option sounds good to me! Dead either way!

Back here at the Rock we're more concerned about the tent than anything else. It keeps trying to blow over. That happened to some boys in the tent on the end of our row. Wind picked up the corner and wham! Their cots and clothes flew all over the place. A real mess. Leo's jerry-rigged a way to keep ours upright. Staked it down and tied it off to the number 10 cans that double as ashtrays. Filled with sand, they're downright heavy. Hope his plan works. Would hate to chase my gear down the block.

One more day, and then we're in business. I feel like a guy going on his first date. Thrilled, but just a tiny bit scared. Mostly excited, though. With apologies to Susie, Amazon Annie's my kind of girl!

ANOTHER POSTPONEMENT! Since Simon in April and Dirty Harry—that's what they're calling the last test—in May, they're being extra careful. Rumor says Harry blew off the charts and sailed over some tiny towns in Utah. Sounds like the residents, mostly Mormons, weren't very happy. Captain Jameson says it's all part of being patriots. We're here at the Rock, helping make America safe, and those Utah people ought to be proud of their contribution too. Can't let the Reds get ahead of us.

The delay meant nothing much happened all day long, not even practice trench warfare. The highlight was sweeping off the tent floor. Again. Wrote postcards to Susie and the folks. Couldn't say much, just that I'm having a swell time. Even sent a card to Father Joseph and the nuns back at school. Told 'em I was being good.

Tried to stay out of the sun. My nose is red and my ears are peeling and my lips are all chapped. Hard to believe we can get so sunburnt in a place that's so damned cold at night.

Could hear lots of traffic going up the hill out of Mercury, but we were stuck at the Rock. Spent some time stacking our gear. Since we have to get up so early tomorrow morning, we had to gather everything in advance. Ordinary combat boots, fatigue shirts and pants, fatigue jacket, and metal helmets. I thought maybe they'd hand out protective clothes of some sort, and maybe some extra equipment. Wrong. They want us outfitted just like always, as if the Commies arrived unannounced and started dropping bombs. No time for anything special. Like any old day at the office, or in the trenches.

Only one oddity, the sarge has a thing about the carbines. They have to be all shiny and polished. Some of the boys got to leave their rifles near ground zero, to see what happens. We have to haul ours into the trenches, to see what happens. Gotta be ready to shoot those imaginary gooks. It's kind of funny to think that my carbine has already been through several atomic tests. A hand-me-down weapon. I wonder if it has its own badge?

Steak for dinner tonight. Guess they're fattening us up for slaughter!

ANOTHER POSTPONEMENT. Another boring day. Hard to complain, though—more steak for dinner.

WOW! It'll take pages and pages to describe all that happened.

First the preliminaries. Woke up at 3 A.M. Needed coffee badly. A couple of hours later we were back in the trucks, headed for Frenchman again. The boys were kind of quiet, until one little squirt with a New York accent started mouthing off. A real Nervous Nellie. Something about losing his hair and shrinking his balls and turning into a freak. I think he's already a freak. If he's so afraid, why the hell did he volunteer in the first place? Ethan slapped him a couple of times, until he finally shut up. Glad he wasn't assigned to our trench.

Finally got to unload and separate into our own combat teams. Stood around and watched the sun come up. Colder than blazes. Jeremy pulled some twigs and brush together and built a little fire so we could warm our hands. That wasn't okay. The loudspeaker boomed at us to put it out. Said we'd have enough fireball heat coming in a couple of hours. Turned out the announcer, a guy that calls himself the Desert Rock Master of Ceremonies, was right.

Stamped our feet and rubbed our hands and walked around in circles. I even smoked a cigarette, only the third or fourth one in my whole life. Tasted terrible. The loudspeaker kept blaring instructions. Don't do this. Don't do that. Then they set off two big blasts of TNT. Just for fun. Wanted us to be able to compare the force of TNT with the force of an atomic shell. Said we'd see an enormous difference, twenty times over.

About half an hour before the final countdown, they told us to get in our trenches. Crouching for thirty minutes turned out to be damned uncomfortable. We were supposed to kneel against the trench's forward side. I'm a good Catholic, but my knees aren't made for kneeling. I remembered the News Nob viewers have bleachers, and even some nice seats. Nothing like that for us grunts.

The loudspeaker shouted more instructions, and then Captain Jameson repeated them. "Stay down until you hear the projectile's blast sound. Then you can stand up and watch the fireball form." I kind of wished we had some of those smoky glasses, but apparently the brass didn't think they were necessary.

While we waited, my hands got clammy and I felt a little sweaty. Maybe I should've gone to confession last week after all. I'll keep that thought all to myself. Sure don't want the other boys thinking I'm like that pansy from New York.

At long last, the loudspeaker voice began counting. "Ten, nine" and on down to "three, two, one." Clutching my carbine, I tucked my head as low as possible and sheltered my face with one hand. The wait was interminable.

Once, when I was a kid, my brother and I got caught in a bad Wisconsin thunderstorm. We huddled together and tried to act small. While we were shivering, one big old bolt slammed into the elm tree right beside us. The sound crackled, louder than anything I'd ever heard before, and an acrid burning smell made the moment feel like hell. Scared Bob to tears and I thought we were dead. I also thought I'd never experience such a moment again. Wrong.

First there was total silence. Then the white flash we expected, so bright I could see the bones in my hands, even with my eyes closed! Like I got X-rayed on the spot. Or like my eyes were glowing in the dark. I confess—I crossed myself.

Then came the noise.

Amazon Annie must have been ten times louder than that Wisconsin crack of thunder, maybe more. Absolutely deafening! The roar not only ricocheted from one side of the playa to the other but it echoed inside my head so that I couldn't hear myself think. Despite the hurricane-force winds, some instinct drove me to my feet. I had to see and touch and taste and smell the monster.

Jeremy and Leo and Ethan and I all stood up at once. We watched a stupendous fireball shoot skyward, brighter than anything I've ever imagined. The brilliance hurt our eyes, but we couldn't look away. Like I was hypnotized, I stared until I started seeing spots and flashes and blurs. I blinked, and in that instant the shock wave bounced us backward against the trench's wall. At the same time, stuff started flying. Dirt and debris from the desert floor got sucked up into a vacuum and then spit out. Everything spun like one of those new washing machines. I hung on to my carbine, but just barely, as the trench started crumbling around us.

By the time the earth stopped heaving, we were halfway buried. Turns out tarpaper and chicken wire aren't so strong after all. We kicked our way free, stood up, and got knocked down again. The shock wave was backfiring, slamming back across the desert from the opposite direction. Not as strong as the first one, but powerful enough to jolt me off my feet. I looked over at the other boys, and we just shook our heads.

The heat blasted us, too. The loudspeaker guy was right about the temperature. It must have shot up fifty, sixty degrees. Much more, out there at ground zero, where it must be about a million degrees Celsius. I wondered if this was what the Bible meant by Armageddon. But it wasn't the end of the world, because things just kept happening. Now the fireball was changing colors quickly. Deep magenta was shading into pink, while the orange fiery core pulsed and glowed. The thing seemed almost alive, splitting into two distinct orbs, as if one monstrous blob was escaping another. It sucked up more and more dust, mixed it with ash, blew higher and wider, and gradually turned from orange to brown. Beautiful and ugly all at the same time, its top fringed with what looked like whipped cream, the infernal cloud towered above us, then began to slide away.

Before we could catch our breaths, Captain Jameson urged us out of the trench and onto the desert floor. Jeremy rubbed his eyes, Ethan took off his helmet and ran his fingers through his hair, Leo just stood there, saying nothing. I didn't say much either, but I knew I was ready to charge ahead. That fireball was calling to me just like a siren in some old Greek myth the nuns at St. Andrews drilled into our heads.

The captain rounded us up, but made us wait until the cloud moved farther to the northeast. Its colors already were starting to fade, but it still was brighter than the sun. Finally we got our orders. Dead ahead, right toward ground zero, past the blast area and out the other side. Off we went, just as if we were chasing the enemy, if there were any vaporized enemy left to pursue.

I imagined shooting an injured gook here and there, but saw only rabbits and pigs and sheep. And they weren't running anywhere. The sheep were the most pathetic. Some seemed just fine, though a little shell-shocked. Others, closer to ground zero and with lesions around their heads and blood seeping from their noses and mouths, smelled of charred wool. Closer yet, and the sheep were deader than doornails. Fried mutton, just as I'd predicted. I tried not to let 'em bother me, but I kept thinking about Wisconsin dairy cattle. Experiments on live animals? Cruel, and kind of nasty.

The rabbits were just as tortured and just as dazed. They were locked in tiny cages pointed straight toward ground zero. They couldn't look away. The experiment was supposed to check for retinal burns. To keep the rabbits awake with their eyes open, someone had set up a series of alarm clocks nearby. As jerry-rigged as Leo's makeshift double-weight tent stakes. I remembered those flashing spots and wavy lines I saw when I looked right into the fireball. Poor rabbits.

Eyeballing the pigs was easier. They'd been anesthetized before the blast, so they hadn't really suffered. In fact, they looked sort of silly, all dressed up in their regulation uniforms. Army fatigues, Navy blues, Air Force leather jackets, all pretty well seared and burned. If we'd been that close to the explosion we'd have been pretty well seared and burned, too. But at least they hadn't felt a thing.

Worst of all were the birds. I don't even know what kind. Not experimental birds, like in cages, but ones that flew in accidentally and got caught in the ball of fire. Flopping hideously around us, both in the air and on the ground. No tails, in some cases; missing a wing, in others. Some were blind, too, like the rabbits. Twittering. Those birds, they bothered me most of all. Innocent bystanders, in a funny sort of way.

Before long, we came to the playing cards. The captain pointed out the obvious. The white cards were intact, but the red numbers were pretty charred and the black ones had vanished, burned away by the heat. The King of Spades, the Queen of Hearts. Turned to ashes on the spot. While we stood there, I looked down at my feet and saw an empty cigarette pack. The cellophane had melted and the LS/MFT logo was burned into the foil. I remembered the warning we'd been given about not touching metal. So I left the pack alone.

The closer we got to ground zero, the more dust in the air. Jeremy was coughing uncontrollably every time he inhaled. I tried to pull my shirt collar up over my nose, but didn't have much luck. Instead of blowing away from us, it almost seemed as if the radiation cloud was coming back. Creating its own mini-sandstorm and raining dirt down on our heads. Ethan looked over at me and raised his eyebrows. But I figured they wouldn't send us out here if it wasn't safe. One guy—I don't know his name—started retching. Guess the dust got caught in his throat.

Before long, we couldn't see much of anything at all. I wondered if we were lost, wandering around in circles, but the captain seemed to have a plan. He led us past the locomotive, then threaded his way between two overturned trucks. A deuce and a half, bounced a hundred yards as if it was a football tossed on its side. A couple of Jeeps, one totally upside down. Machine guns all melted. Another howitzer, useless, too. Or so I thought from what I could see. My eyes were watering badly, and I was tired of breathing in so much junk. But I was fascinated by all that power. A single explosion that could move everything in its range. Or destroy it completely. Made that TNT blast seem minuscule by comparison.

Underfoot the ground looked more and more like the burnt candy sand we saw over on Yucca Flat. The dirt here resembled brown glass, as if the sand had melted into a glaze. Just like I didn't touch anything metal, I didn't touch the ground either.

Suddenly we heard a shout from our right. "What the hell are you doing out here?"

"Just following orders," our captain replied.

"No way! You're in the wrong place!" A major pulled rank, and aimed us off to one side. "Now get the hell out of here," he snarled. "Fast!"

Someone asked the captain what was going on. He shrugged and steered us off to the right. Never did find out what the major's problem was. Sure sounded cranky, though.

Another couple of klicks, and we walked out of the cloud. Looked like we'd been crawling in the dirt instead of just walking through it. The stuff was caked all over our helmets and uniforms. Our faces didn't look real. I laughed at the snot running down Jeremy's face, like wet little rivers in the sand. He laughed back. I guess I looked just as bad, a human dust dervish in Army fatigues. We joined another company and all trudged back to the trucks together. They didn't look as filthy, and were they ever jealous. We'd gotten to see way more stuff. They'd just been walking around the perimeter, wishing they could get closer to the action.

It didn't take long to truck back to the Rock, but it was long enough for me. I could tolerate Jeremy's coughing, but the throwing up was another story. Not Jeremy, but a couple of other boys from our company got really sick. We hung 'em out the back of the truck and hoped to hell the driver would make good time.

Once we got to camp, we sent the two off with a medic, who wanted to know if the rest of us were all okay. Absolutely. After a day like today, seeing what we saw, I felt like a million dollars. Can't believe how lucky we were to get to see Amazon Annie in all her glory.

Once we got rid of the sick guys, we had to stand in a long line that was filing past a long table. Someone checked our names off a list, and we tossed our dirty badges into a big box. Looked to see if mine had changed colors, but couldn't see anything different. Maybe a little tinge of red, but not much. Odd to see all the dosimeters piled together. Some of us had gone a lot closer to ground zero than others. Got grubbier, too. Hard to figure out the differences in dosages with the badges all jumbled up. No one seemed to be trying to keep 'em separate.

After we got out of line, we were handed brooms so we could sweep each other off. I don't think I've ever been so dirty. Some of the boys got showers right away, but our company had to wait a while. A debriefing about where we'd marched after the shot and what we'd seen took an hour or so. The brass wanted to know exactly where we'd been, but then they didn't want us to talk about it to anybody else. Told us to say we'd just been on the perimeter, like the boys in the adjacent company. After we got chewed out some more, a colonel came by and said we were brave soldiers. Keeping the country safe. Front line of defense. Patriotic Americans. Then he snarled at Captain Jameson for not hearing the recall orders, for leading us too close to ground zero. Kind of mixed signals, I'd say.

No showers until just before dinner. We were almost the last group to get cleaned up. Brushed off most of the dirt in the afternoon, but still felt grimy. Being clean sure feels good. Washed my hair three times. Could have stood there under the spray for hours, but the Rock doesn't have much water to waste. After we were done, we piled our fatigues outside the showers. Guess we won't see those uniforms again. Now I'm running out of steam. Been awake since 3 A.M. and I'm beat. All the boys are just as exhausted. Ethan's writing his girl again, Leo's trying to read, Jeremy just keeps coughing. Think I'll cut this short and get some sleep.

MORE DEBRIEFING TODAY, plus more classes. Learned some trivia about yesterday's experiments. Seems that white deflects radiation while black attracts it. That's why the cards were only semi-vaporized. Ought to make our uniforms white in the future instead of khaki. Match the snow in Korea, keep the Army safe from atomic action. All at the same time. Didn't hear about the pigs. From what we saw, no matter what they were wearing, their uniforms pretty much melted. Shouldn't get too close to zero.

Told us more about the maneuvers, too. We're not only guinea pig soldiers but we're also political pawns. That's part of what Grable—that's our cannon's official name—was all about. Ike wants to scare the gooks, make 'em think we can shoot atomic artillery over the 38th parallel. What a joke! According to Annie's crew, that gun couldn't be moved anywhere in Korea. With its weight, it'd bog down in the snow and mud. As long as the gooks don't know that, we'll play the game. So all the headlines today are boasting about Amazon Annie. She sure was some humdinger.

The Army also wants to be sure its soldiers know what to do if the Reds ever drop an atomic bomb on us. Like that *Duck and Cover* movie with the silly turtle showing civilians how to react, we're supposed to know how to respond, too. Johnnys-on-the-spot, ready to help everyone survive. Can't quite see the Reds targeting Oshkosh, Wisconsin. They say the coasts are more vulnerable, and I hope that after this I'll never have to live outside the Midwest again. So I'll probably never use my newfound knowledge. But maybe Susie and I can practice some duck-and-cover stuff.

Now that Grable's over, I'm really ready to head home. Sounds like they'll let us start leaving tomorrow. Hope Wisconsin isn't last, like we were with the showers.

SURE ENOUGH, we're in Las Vegas. At some rinky-dink motel just off Fremont Street, but close enough to walk to four or five casinos. When we climbed on the buses to leave the Rock, the captain shook our hands and gave each of us a certificate and five bucks. Wished us well. The certificate's a hoot. Signed by our captain, the "Pack Rat," and the "Field Rat," our gunny sergeant, it signifies our official induction into the Royal Order of Radiated Desert Rats.

Like the other boys, I've seen a Big Boom and thus been beknighted! You can bet we'll save those pieces of paper to show our kids. Not so the five bucks. That's gone already, plus a little more. Better not tell Susie, since I'm supposed to be saving for the future.

Turns out my immediate future is going to be California instead of Texas and Fort Hood. Somebody changed our orders, so tomorrow we ship off to Fort Cronkhite. It's just outside of San Francisco. Wish Susie could join me there. I've never seen the Pacific Ocean and neither has she. But I sure hope this doesn't keep me in the service any longer than we'd planned. Don't know why we have to go west instead of east. Typical Army, steering us in the wrong direction.

Happy we got steered free of the Rock, though. Can't see why anyone would want to live in Nevada—too hot and too cold, all on the same day. Not sure I want to see another atomic explosion, either. Like heaven and hell, or good and evil, all jumbled together. Good that America can protect herself but evil that she has to build weapons to fight against other nations. Awesome and awful, all at the same time. Would drive the nuns crazy to see something like that old atomic cannon. The world turned upside down. Still, I wouldn't have missed Annie for anything. I've got the certificate to prove it.

```
Royal Order of Radiated Desert Rats
Know ye by These Presents that:
```

Matthew T. Gray
```
Matthew T. Grayson
```

```
   has been stuck in the finger; has breathed and bitten
the dust; has broiled in the day; has frozen at night; and
has dined at ~ ~ Desert Rock ~ ~ ~ ~ Forsaking all else,
wife, PX, civilization, etc., he has seen a Big Boom, and
has suffered Busted eardrums and Jangled nerves, show-
ing the true valor of a RORDR, and is Knighted in Rodents.
   Anno Domini 1953
```

Carl Jameson   *J. B. Crawley*
```
Pack Rat                 Field Rat
```

Climax

A headline in the *Las Vegas Review-Journal* reports that Climax "Hit the Nuclear Jackpot." Scheduled almost as a climactic afterthought and then postponed twice due to unfavorable weather and winds, Climax is worth waiting for. The characteristic white flash lasts for five seconds, the churning fireball for half a minute. Observers say that's twice as long as any previous Nevada detonation. The flames then boil on for two more minutes, before fading into apricot and lavender radioactive clouds. Atmospherically freakish, Climax is silent, as if all the energy went into flames instead of sound. At the same time, Climax propels a violent jolt that sends all those scientists in Command Central scurrying. The building feels as if it's shaking off its foundations. Ten miles away, a wooden test shack disintegrates completely. Joshua trees, sagebrush, and cactus within range all burn instantaneously. Climax is enormous, and an enormous success. Nearly 61 kilotons of success, more productive and perhaps more seductive than any other device of Upshot-Knothole.

Alan

"A toast to Upshot-Knothole!" Tom waves his coffee mug in the air.

Glen hoists his, too, clanging the white porcelain against Tom's half-empty cup. David, Henry, and Alan join in quickly, thumping mugs together as if they hold champagne.

"Too tame!" Tom's adamant. "We need to celebrate with something stronger than coffee."

From across the cafeteria they hear the sounds of another ritual. "Atta girl, Ruthie," someone shouts from the nightly bridge game.

"Thank God! After tonight we don't have to sit here and listen to them ever again!"

Finishing dinner two days past shot Climax, the five colleagues can't wait for tomorrow, when the long spring sequence of Upshot-Knothole finally ends. Glen, on his way home to Livermore, catching an early Air Force flight at dawn. David, Tom, and Henry, bound for Los Alamos shortly before noon. And Alan, who's been away from his wife and children the longest. He has to fly commercial. Hitching a ride to the tiny Las Vegas airport right after breakfast, and then catching a United Airlines puddle jumper. What a pain! Everyone has some packing to finish up, but tonight the fellows are euphoric and free.

"I stopped off in Cactus Springs yesterday afternoon, in anticipation." Tom, the optimist of the crowd, bought a case of Coors.

"Well, I've got an unopened fifth of Jim Beam," Alan admits. "I meant to take a present home to Nan, but I can pick up another bottle in Las Vegas. No point in letting this one go to waste."

"Vodka, anybody?"

"Jeez, Glen. Our heads will be like pumpkins in the morning."

"So what? It's our last night."

"Tomorrow, our wives. Tonight, we party."

Pushing back from their cafeteria table, the five friends head outside. The June Nevada evening is overly warm, with a hint of a thunderstorm in the air. As the men stroll down Trinity Avenue toward their blockish dormitory, a thick sheet of heat lightning snaps across the eastern sky. When no thunder echoes in response, the partiers decide to watch the pyrotechnics. They set up a makeshift bar on a nearby patch of desert dirt, and the celebration begins.

Tom and Henry hunker on the curb while the others lounge in three tacky, uncomfortable chairs they've dragged outside. As soon as everyone else is settled, Tom jumps to his feet. "A toast to Upshot-Knothole!" Brushing a shock of hair back from his forehead, he hoists an icy bottle and repeats his coffee mug words. "A toast to Upshot-Knothole!" Tom and Henry brandish their Coors; David and Alan, plastic glasses half filled with Jim Beam and what they sarcastically call Mercury branch water; Glen, a metal cup of vodka cut with tomato juice pilfered from the cafeteria.

At first, the conversation sounds almost frivolous. The men joke about flying home to their wives in the morning, maybe taking their kids to a movie that evening. Glen's family drove from California to Las Vegas for spring vacation, so he saw them in early April. David's and Henry's wives caught a flight from Kirtland Air Force Base in early May, but their husbands had been almost too busy to enjoy the brief visit. Because the chaotic days between shots Simon and Harry had taken all their concentration, one night in Las Vegas was all they could spare. Now, isolated Los Alamos sounds utterly appealing—gourmet dinners at Fuller Lodge, Little League baseball alongside Ashley Pond, even their boxy Bathtub Row houses. David and Henry can hardly wait.

Long since divorced from his wife, Tom is less nostalgic, although he looks forward to seeing Albuquerque Angie, the most recent in an endless string of girls. Alan is the loneliest. Since Illinois is too many miles away for a casual visit, he hasn't seen his family since February. He scratches his balding head and hopes his wife won't notice. No matter, he can't wait to abandon the desert.

Talk soon drifts away from families and travel plans. When Henry flips the cap off another bottle of Coors, he remembers the question he'd meant to ask earlier. "Tom, when you stopped at Cactus Springs, did you hear more about that spy story?"

"Not a peep."

"Who was tending bar?"

"That cute girl, Sally."

"And the biggest flirt in Nevada didn't quiz her?"

"I started to, but she cut me off. Actually turned her back and walked toward the icebox. Definitely not good for my ego!"

Glen, listening intently, contributes additional information. "I bought vodka over the weekend, Saturday night. Hal was pouring drinks and Sally was waiting tables. Neither had much to say, but the photographers sure were gossiping."

"Those guys are there almost every night, aren't they?"

"Seems that way."

David grows impatient. "So what were they saying? Anything new?"

"Not really. Just that a fake prospector had been hanging around the bar, trying to ingratiate himself with anyone who worked at Mercury. Somebody got suspicious, and called the Feds."

"Who?"

"Nobody's quite sure, though a couple of the cameramen had warned their Lookout Mountain bosses that the guy was asking too many questions."

"A Russian disguised as a prospector? That's a stretch!"

"I dunno if he was a Russian or not. Probably eastern European of some kind, though. Apparently no accent."

"Shades of Los Alamos in the forties. Remember that big scandal at the Cantina in Santa Fe?"

"Of course. The FBI caught two scientists actually selling secrets. Classified data, and some precious drawings!" After studying physics at Harvard, Henry had gone straight to Los Alamos, so he was familiar with all the local rumors around the Hill.

"I don't think the Cactus Springs plot ever got that far off the ground. They nabbed the guy in time."

"Really odd, I'd say. How'd he expect to learn anything worthwhile in a two-bit bar?"

"Maybe make friends with somebody, lots of one-on-one, then offer him a chunk of change."

"That's sounds dumb to me."

"What if somebody dangled half a million dollars in front of your nose? Would you sell out for that?"

"Never!" Pounding his fist on his thigh, Tom jumps back into the discussion. "I wouldn't betray my country for ten times that amount. Or more."

"Moot point, Tommy my boy," Henry laughs. "Nobody'd pay anything for your expertise. Crafting a better tower is just a little cog in the grand scheme of things."

"Whoa," Tom argues back. "Without my tower your dumb devices wouldn't fall straight and true. Think about the new design. Totally wind resistant. Slimmer and trimmer. Perfect!"

"Tommy, the Russians already know how to build towers. There's no big civil engineering secret there. Not like nuclear physics, anyway."

"No fighting, lads." David, always uptight and a little uncomfortable, wants to change the subject. When he's upset, his British accent sounds like he's just flown across the ocean.

A theoretical physicist, Henry thinks his work is more significant than anyone else's; Tom, the happy-go-lucky engineer, counters that without his designs nothing practical could ever take place. Both are partially correct, but the squabble is headed nowhere. No one much cares about their differences, and in truth no one has new information about the so-called Cactus Springs spy. Although they may learn more details sometime in the future, the current rumor mill has hit a dead end. Likewise, Henry's impasse with Tom.

When David stands up and stretches his arms over his head, Glen rises from his chair, too. Tired of the dispute, both need to pack. As they amble away, one going inside to his room and the other heading down the street toward his office, Tom and Henry shrug. Henry downs his Coors, and hoists himself off the curb. "Me, too. Better get stuff organized. Can't be late tomorrow, that's for sure. The wife'd never forgive me if I miss the plane."

"I'm kinda looking forward to Angie, too." Tom wags his fingers in a V for victory.

"Are you serious about that girl?"

"Not really. But she's a hell of a lot of fun."

Alan ignores the banter. Frowning, he lights a cigarette and pours himself some more Jim Beam. The furrow in his high forehead deepens as he tilts his chair back on two legs. He wishes everyone would be more organized. Why on earth aren't they packed already? He's been set to go since yesterday, needs only to add his pajamas in the morning. Tacitly judgmental in the long Nevada twilight, Alan swirls his whiskey and holds his glass up to the alpenglow settling on treeless hills to the east. More lightning, on beyond. Last time he'll see this view. He hopes.

He thinks about Climax, the last device exploded. Sixty-one kilotons of pure atomic power, set off by a newly designed tamper that Glen himself devised. A welcome success story in a series sometimes thwarted by unexpected complications. Glen, frustrated by Nancy's meager output in late March, worked nonstop with his fellow electrical engineers to successfully redesign the mechanism that clunked Nancy's 0.2 kilotons into the desert

dirt. Simon's bellicose 43 kilotons less than a month later proved the effi-
ciency of their new prototype. But Simon blew so frenetically high and so
unexpectedly powerful that the brass got furious. Unwelcome problems
ensued, with downwind residents and fallout and cattle and sheep. The dif-
ficulties compounded when Hamlet, well, Harry, really, blew badly off course.
Not good. Not good at all.

What if the United States, the politicians, decided to use such profligate
weaponry? Against another country? Again?

Tom, uncomfortable with Alan's fretful silence, breaks into his reverie and
changes the subject. Unfortunately, he picks a morose one. "More gossip. Did
you hear about the Grable soldiers in the trenches, the ones near the cannon
and close to the flash?"

"Didn't some of them wander too close to the fallout? Afterwards?" Alan
recalls.

"For sure," Tom continues. "But no one's saying much about their R/h
counts. I heard that the boys from the 9778th Rad Safety Unit gathered up
the badges ASAP."

"Not supposed to get more than 6.0 roentgens at a time," Alan adds.
"Rumor says they got 20, maybe 25."

Tom chuckles. "What they don't know won't hurt 'em, though. Most of
'em shipped out of here the day after the shot. They're long gone."

"I wonder if the Army'll try and track 'em down, do any follow-up?"

"Not much use, not if the Rad Unit dumped all the dosimeters in a single
box."

"Covers their ass, to do it that way."

"Absolutely."

"Sure not fair to the troops, though." Alan is stewing.

"I repeat. What they don't know won't hurt 'em."

"Poor bastards."

"Did you hear about that one rad specialist who really caught it after
Annie?"

"Yeah. He got sent home to Las Vegas. Sent home last year, too. Might not
get hired back in '54."

"More gossip. Seems like Mercury's worse than a college dormitory full of
giggling girls. Worse even than Los Alamos. And that's saying something! A
story gets started, pretty soon it's got twenty variations on a theme."

"What the hell else have we got to do out here in the middle of nowhere?" Alan answers his own question by pouring more Jim Beam. "Drink. That's what." Reaching for his canteen, he changes his mind about bitter local water. Tom's casual dismissal of the soldiers' plight and of the rad specialist's carelessness bothers him somehow. He wonders, as he does so often, about effects of radiation they might not understand. Alan swallows another sip of whiskey and begins musing aloud. "Why are we laughing about those boys in the trenches? Why aren't we wondering why our government is so crass about human suffering?"

"Alan," Tom sighs. "Are you still beating that dead horse?"

"I don't think it's quite dead yet," Alan complains. "Sometimes there's a real disconnect between what we're developing here and how it might be used."

"Won't ever get used again." Tom, already into his third beer, is adamant. "Once we all saw what happened in Hiroshima and Nagasaki, and once the world saw. Well, that's the capper."

"Tell that to the Russians. And to us." Alan is insistent. "Isn't that what we're doing out here? Testing ways to blow everybody up?"

Alan worries more about the aftereffects of atomic testing than he generally lets on to his colleagues and friends. At heart, he agrees with his University of Chicago mentors, who voiced serious misgivings about dropping atomic bombs on Hiroshima and Nagasaki. Several had signed on to the Franck Report, urging President Truman to forgo bombing Japan directly but to instead detonate a demonstration explosion on an uninhabited island somewhere in the South Pacific, to show the entire world community the earth-shattering powers of the Los Alamos creation without actually killing any human beings. Science, in those physicists' view, must be yoked with reasoned ethics. Technology should never be allowed to trump morality.

Truman ignored their words. Choosing a more pragmatic path, he immediately ordered the direct bombing of not one but two Japanese cities. Alan abhors the consequences of Truman's decision. In his opinion, the United Nations should be addressing the issue of arms control, and the United States should be leading that discussion, rather than plunging forward in a frenetic race to build bigger and costlier bombs.

One of Alan's graduate school professors characterized it all as a defect of American leadership. He was convinced that Truman saw the bomb as a way to close a door. To end the war. Period. But that was naive. Instead, Truman had opened a door, a door to a future that no one could define. Or control. Or even comprehend.

Alan tosses his head back, frowning even more deeply and taking a gulp of Jim Beam that starts him coughing. Across the open desert, another sheet of heat lightning flashes, while a low rumble of thunder matches Alan's hacking sounds.

"Too much desert dust?" Standing in the dormitory door, Henry rejoins the conversation.

"Too much booze," Alan sputters. "And cigarettes, I suppose. And too much thinking."

"About what?" Henry innocently asks.

"What we're doing here. Why we're doing it."

"We've got to protect ourselves," Henry insists with certainty. "That's the whole point of Upshot-Knothole. More effective weaponry and a keener understanding of how to take care of Americans if the Russians do something crazy."

"Don't you ever feel guilty?"

"Guilty? Hell, no!" Alongside Henry in the doorway, Glen's baritone carries definitively. He's a man who rarely has second thoughts about much of anything, except how to solve a technical conundrum. "We came here to do a job. And that job is to build atomic devices. Nothing less."

"I agree, mates, in a way, but I also disagree." David, who often straddles both sides of an issue but who ultimately comes down on the side of pure science, wanders back up the street in time to commandeer a rickety chair and join the conversation. "We're here to extend our knowledge. Our understanding of atomic physics. If we could do that without building bombs, that'd be great. But we can't. It's like a treadmill. We can't get off. And we shouldn't."

"Sure we can," Alan dissents. "If the United States hadn't been at war, the Manhattan Project might well have set its sights on peacetime atomic uses."

"But if the United States hadn't been at war, there might never have been a Manhattan Project."

"That's all water under the bridge. Nobody can go back and rewrite history. What's done is done. Now it's 1953. We're in the midst of a Cold War with Russia, and we've got to win. From New York to Los Angeles, Americans are depending on us. We've got to protect them," Henry maintains. "That's the whole point of Upshot-Knothole. More effective weaponry is a means to that end."

Henry's speechifying takes over. As far as he's concerned, the Proving Ground work is imperative. He can argue for hours that the United States has no choice but to charge ahead with bomb making. The government simply must investigate every possible way to protect Americans against communism. In fact, he's eager for one specific rumor to prove true. He's recently heard that the senator from Wisconsin, a man named McCarthy, is planning some congressional hearings about communist infiltration. Like at the Cantina in New Mexico, and maybe the supposed spy plot in Cactus Springs. Only McCarthy's aiming higher, looking at the loyalty of everyone in government, Hollywood, too, men and women who've spoken out against their country in any way whatsoever. He'll get those Commies, for sure. Right now, Henry wishes Alan would be more careful. Voicing negative sentiments, calling the gadgets evil, questioning nuclear morality? Probably okay, here among friends. They've downed a few drinks tonight, after all, and everyone feels relaxed after the pressures of the past several months. But what if someone overheard their conversation? And reported the slender idealist from Chicago? "The world's depending on us," Henry repeats, muttering a little.

"That's not the point."

"Sure it is."

"No, you're thinking about politics. I'm thinking about morality. Are you implying that you have no scruples at all?" Alan returns to David's earlier logic. "That it doesn't matter if we're generating hell on earth?"

"Not really," David responds. "Not my cup of tea. I'm a problem solver. I just think about the mathematical calculations themselves, not any sort of public consequences."

"I don't know how you can do that. The science and the ethics, they're inextricably tied."

Glen picks up one thread of the conversation. "I don't think scientists should be involved in public policy at all. It's not our business."

"How can you say that?" Alan is incensed. "Doesn't that sentiment fly in the face of the FAS?"

"Hans Bethe's outfit, the Federation of American Scientists?"

"Yeah."

"Wasn't the FAS formed right after Truman dropped the bombs?" Tom wonders out loud.

"In 1945. A group of physicists from the Manhattan Project were horrified when they saw the Hiroshima and Nagasaki pictures. Thought it was their scientific responsibility to warn public policy decision makers about where technological advances might lead."

"Alan, if you're so all-fired conflicted, what the hell are you doing at Mercury?" Trigger-happy Tom is losing patience.

Pouring a little more Jim Beam, Alan tries to respond. "I've asked myself that hundreds of times. Never have come up with a good answer. I guess I'm here 'cause I want to be on the cutting edge of science. I like my liaison job between the Chicago lab and the Proving Ground. I like knowing exactly, and I mean exactly, what's going on." He shrugs. "I like putting food on the table for Nan and the boys, too."

"Just seems odd to me. Every so often, you jabber on about what we're doing. But you just keep on doing it, working on gadgets—on bombs—like the rest of us."

Tom's observation isn't unusual. The two physicists, the mathematician, and the unlikely pair of engineers, whenever they get together and especially after they've had a few drinks, often disagree about their roles and responsibilities while developing devices powerful enough to obliterate civilization. Their debates echo similar ones from the previous decade. After seeing horrific pictures from the *Enola Gay*'s flight over Japan, some Los Alamos scientists immediately quit their jobs. Other nuclear physicists stayed put, pushing the searing images out of their minds. In the six years Tom's been in New Mexico, he's heard a lot of hotheaded arguments. Lately, though, the disputes have largely faded away. Most of the true idealists abandoned the program in the late 1940s, leaving few behind to articulate any hints of pacifism. Alan is actually anachronistic, a throwback to Trinity times. If he'd been on the Hill in the forties, he'd probably have quit, too.

Alan shakes his head, knowing he's already had too much to drink and surmising he'll keep on until the bottle is empty. "Maybe I just want to contribute to history."

"But at what cost?"

"Let's think about it another way, in terms of absolute good versus relative good," Henry suggests.

"I like that notion," Glen adds. "We haven't even talked about what other uses might be made of atomic energy."

"Medicine? Fuel? Maybe something no one's thought of yet."

"If that's true, then why are we making bombs? Why not agree on no more weapons at all?"

"Because we're still learning." Glen's clipped words counter Alan's question. "The H-bomb, for example. From fission to fusion. That's a big step being made."

"But to what end? If you can rub out half a city's population in a matter of seconds, why go on to create something that can rub out ten times that many people? In half the time? It doesn't make sense."

"Relax, Alan." Glen reaches out and taps his friend on the forearm. "It's the American way. The quintessential American builds a better mousetrap. Always."

"But what about the costs?"

"What sort of costs?"

Alan has thought about this dilemma at great length, so he takes his time finding exactly the right words. "First of all, there's the dollar costs. Atomic testing is damned expensive. Playing in the desert takes money away from other things."

"Like what?" To Henry, the knowledge gleaned from atomic testing and the attendant understanding of civil defense and human safety will always be worth any price. So what Alan says doesn't compute. Military might, Henry believes, must always take precedence over any other government activity. As with Alan, though, Jim Beam is blurring Henry's thinking, making it hard for him to argue the obvious. The West absolutely must win the Cold War, and that means growing mushrooms in the desert.

Unlike Henry, Alan doesn't lose his train of thought. "And then there are the human costs," he says. "Like the soldiers in the trenches who got too much radiation. And haven't been told."

Glen nods. "I see what you mean, but I don't see that's any of our business. Besides, they volunteered."

"No one told 'em about the radiation, though."

"Sure they did."

"Not so's they'd really understand the danger."

"Hell, we don't even understand the danger."

"I s'pose that's true to a degree, but at least we're more aware of possible problems."

"We haven't figured out how to solve 'em, though."

Glen is puzzled. Ever meticulous, he takes extra care when working at either Frenchman or Yucca Flat. Anytime he comes in contact with possible radiation, he follows the precautions described in the field manual. Sweeping his dusty clothes off with a broom. Hosing down his Jeep. Taking a shower before dinner. Checking his dosimeter. Of course he's never in any real danger because the bulk of his work occurs pre- rather than post-shot. By the time one hot spot develops, Glen is already working on a gadget in another section of the desert. Not like those boys in the trenches.

Alan persists. "I don't think we really have the full picture about radiation. How it spreads. How it stays on the ground and in the air. How it affects people in the long term."

David thinks Alan is onto something. He recently read an article about the Japanese. Almost a decade after the bombings, people are still getting sick. And sicker. Burns aren't healing, mysterious cancers are developing, strange symptoms that no one can explain. And then there are the stories out of Utah. First the sheep. Now the Mormons. "What do you know about what's happening east of here?" he asks in a tentative tone.

"Mostly rumors, just like Cactus Springs," Tom quickly replies. "But I know there's been a government investigation of the sheep complaints. Turned up nothing."

"You mean those sheep just got sunburned through their wool?" Alan sounds incredulous.

"Not likely," Henry observes. "But there's no proof the fallout did any real damage."

"What about all those malformed lambs?"

"I'm pretty sure the tests came up negative. Didn't support the sheep-herders' complaints at all. I think there's a new government report stating that the problems most likely stemmed from poor forage. It's been pretty dry out there the last four or five years."

"So the Public Health people took no responsibility?"

"Alan, don't be naive." Sometimes Henry can't believe how either Alan or David can function, with their heads in the clouds. "The government can't possibly acknowledge any responsibility at all. Otherwise there'd be unfounded lawsuits from all sorts of lunatics."

"How can you say unfounded? And it doesn't sound to me as if those sheepmen were lunatics."

"Yeah, but there'd be others waiting in line. Better to harm a few dumb creatures, and that's assuming blame when no one knows for sure, in order to save millions of American lives in the future. That's the trade-off. A little damage now, a lot of subsequent good in the years ahead."

Alan doesn't buy Henry's logic. At the same time David was reading that article about Hiroshima and Nagasaki, Alan had been following newspaper stories about the St. George residents who had Upshot-Knothole fallout trailing directly over their friendly community. They were complaining about all sorts of unusual symptoms, like headaches and nausea, fevers and thirst, diarrhea and loss of appetite. Even discolored fingernails, a dead giveaway that they'd had too much radiation. No official acknowledged this, of course, but any atomic scientist working with uranium knows he should pay attention to his fingernails. "You say a few dumb creatures," Alan complains, "but people downwind from here have been affected, too."

"Not many, though."

"How many is too many?" Alan sounds stubborn. "Ten? A hundred? A thousand human beings?"

"Better a handful from St. George than a million from New York City."

Even David thinks Glen is being crass. Too much vodka, perhaps. Glen has a point, of course, that a few might serve as guinea pigs to save the many, but those folks aren't lab animals like the suffering rabbits and baying beagles that Proving Ground biologists staked near ground zero. Alan's right. It's indecent to harm fellow human beings. Actually, David knows even more about St. George than any of the others. He attended a recent briefing, where the military wanted him to analyze some numbers, and he'd learned a Pandora's box full of facts. Dredging up the statistics isn't easy after nearly half a fifth of Jim Beam, but he tries.

"I can tell you the estimates," David says, "but don't quote me. This info is really hush-hush, and they'd ship me back to London, or maybe worse, if it got out. A colonel from the Army Rad Unit reported that the airborne radio-iodine reached 120 to 440 rads. In effect that gave every St. George resident direct contact with the toxins and contaminated some with as much as four hundred times the radiation allowable dose."

"Unbelievable!"

"More than any of us will get in a lifetime. And we work around this stuff every day."

"More dangerous for kids than adults, too. Especially iodine 131. Gets into their thyroids plenty fast."

"A doctor in Salt Lake City estimated that some St. George infants may have gotten as much as five hundred times the allowable dosage."

"They're dead. Not right away, maybe, but in a few years."

"Well, you won't hear the AEC say that! Instead, they made a show of good faith and analyzed the milk. Found nothing, though the milk scare made the news pop for a few days. The local station in Cedar City had a field day." David rubs his forehead. "I can tell you lads another secret, but again, it's classified. Except among friends."

"What's that?"

"When they took the samples to be analyzed, they used bottled milk from the stores, bottled milk shipped in from someplace else. Didn't check the raw dairy milk, the unpasteurized kind that rural kids drink. Didn't check any homegrown St. George milk at all."

"So the sample's flawed?"

"You said it, not me." Then David grimaces. "There's bloody more. The colonel said they did that for a reason, because they didn't want to alarm the community any more than folks already were stirred up."

Alan blinks. "I read a story about that just yesterday. The AEC said precautions were being taken, and that St. George residents need not worry. One dairyman, a fellow named Donaldson, upended his milk anyway. Better for his business in the long run, 'cause it looked like he was being careful, though he had to lay off some of his workers."

"I don't get it."

"That's 'cause you're a London boy, David. Grazing cows digest radioactive grass right into their systems. Next step in the production line, they make milk. Voilà! Radioactive milk for the St. George kids to drink."

"But the kids are already affected. You can't reverse the consequences, once contact and contamination occurs."

"Right. And simply dumping milk doesn't solve the problem of the people who were outside or who already served contaminated milk to their kids. Dirty Harry was a big one, more powerful than the AEC likes to admit out loud, with a super big hot spot and a huge long radiation trail. No way to escape the fallout plume. Even indoors there was noxious dust seeping through cracks and alongside windows."

"And what we've heard so far is only the tip of the iceberg. What'll happen to those people years from now?"

"Like I said, they're dead."

"Maybe. Maybe not. I don't think anyone has the foggiest notion."

"Isn't that the point?" Alan, incensed by what he's hearing, rocks his chair front legs to back. "Those Public Health people don't really know what to do."

"Nor do we. It's all a big unknown. How far the radiation carries; how long it stays around."

"But we're studying all that," Henry argues. "Without our tests out here, we wouldn't have any data at all. Now we're collecting the information we need."

"At the expense of all those people in southwestern Utah?"

"All? All those people? How many? Greatest good for the greatest number, that's what the government's counting on, though they'll never admit it."

Alan pushes back his chair, knocking it over and stumbling slightly. "Anybody got any more booze?"

"I don't think vodka mixes well with whiskey," Glen observes. "You'll be sicker than a dog."

"Here, take the last beer," Tom volunteers.

Alan shakes his head. "I need something, though."

Henry sighs. "Okay, I wasn't going to tell you boys, but I've got some Jack Daniel's. Just a few drops left." He kicks back the chair he grabbed from Glen and high-steps carefully, very carefully, toward the dormitory. While he's gone, the conversation pauses. His friends stare out into the midnight darkness and ponder what they've all been saying. Waiting for Henry to return, Tom lights a cigar he's been saving. The sweet tobacco smell pools with the dry desert air, a fragrant disconnect as out of sorts as radiation and summer rain. Or so Alan's befuddled brain believes, as he lights another Lucky Strike and flips a match into the dirt. While Tom and Alan smoke quietly, David begins an ambitious monologue.

"Lads, I think you're missing the point."

"How can you say that?" Alan spears a smoke ring with his finger.

"I don't know how to put this exactly," David stutters, "and I'm maybe too bladdered to talk straight. For me, it's the beauty of nuclear power. The flash. Knowing that we, you and I, human beings, made that flash happen. The power. Like seeing God, right before our eyes. When Climax exploded, I could feel the energy deep inside, pounding down into the desert and up into the sky and right into my guts, simultaneously. Just so immensely beautiful. The colors, a whole spectroscopy of reds. The yellows, the umbers, and even the browns. More gorgeous, more spectacular than anything I've ever seen. Like heaven, if I can imagine a place where science and beauty converge."

The others remain silent. The restive Brit rarely opens up about his feelings, so such a dissertation is most unusual. Alan clears his throat, but before he can say anything David continues. "It's like an epiphany, I guess. Watching the incredible sequences of colors and omnipotent might. It's like seeing God," he repeats.

"Maybe like being God," Glen adds. "That's what Teller thought. Oppenheimer, too."

"I don't mean to be sacrilegious, though, not at all," David goes on. "But what we're doing, it's larger than ourselves. It's like turning loose the entire universe. And doing it here on earth." He pauses, leaving time for Alan to jump in.

"And you're saying this is good?"

"Roger that. I guess I'm remembering my old philosophy course at Cambridge. Plato. Good. True. Beautiful. Especially true and beautiful."

Tom, puffing on his cigar and vaguely missing the point, nods his approval. "Damn right," he concurs. Another rumble of thunder—closer this time—underscores his words.

Henry, returning with a partially filled fifth of Jack Daniel's, breaks into David's soliloquy. Alan kicks the empty bottle of Jim Beam under his chair, while David holds out his glass and stifles a burp. "I'm already knackered; better Jack than Jim." Then he keeps talking, going off on a tangent about Grable, the atomic cannon, and trying to connect it with the tower detonations. Particularly intriguing to David is the double fireball that split the mushroom cloud into two distinct whorls of flame. He speculates that the trajectory of the device caused this unusual phenomenon and wishes he could figure a mathematical formula to explain the link.

Glen, on the other hand, is equally intrigued by Grable's trigger mechanism. Firing an atomic device from a howitzer took some precise technical savvy and some unbelievable imagination. The two men jabber back and forth, not really talking directly with each other but each pursuing a singular line of reasoning. In so doing, they break the gravity of the evening's discussion.

Tom snatches up the last bottle of Coors, while Henry, determining that he definitely shouldn't have any more to drink, borrows a cigarette from Alan. It seems like everyone suddenly is talking at once. Except for Alan, the only one of the five intrinsically dismayed by the government's decisions. The others take refuge in their abstractions. David, the purist; Henry, the patriot; Glen, the craftsman; Tom, the joker. Meanwhile, Alan can't get his mind off Hiroshima and Nagasaki. And St. George. Just as the Japanese citizens became unwilling surrogates for their country's leaders, so the people living downwind from the Proving Ground are innocent sacrificial pawns. Such thoughts infuriate him, especially late at night, particularly when he's working on his sixth or seventh whiskey. "Might as well tie one on," he mutters sarcastically to no one in particular. "That way we don't have to think about what we're doing." His hand shaking, he lights another Lucky Strike and lifts his Jack Daniel's in a make-believe toast as another sheet of white lightning stretches across the sky.

NO DIRECT FLIGHT flies nonstop from Las Vegas to Chicago, so Alan changes planes in Denver. Winds gust fiercely across the Rocky Mountains that day, jolting Alan severely and making several of his fellow passengers ill. The elevator updrafts and down-shafts don't help his hangover at all. On the ground at Stapleton Airfield, he plans to grab a quick beer to stave off his pounding head, but his Las Vegas flight arrives late and his connection to Chicago departs on time, so he has only a few minutes to dash from one plane to the other. In-flight coffee has to suffice. He can't complain, though, as he'll soon be home with Nan and the boys.

Not soon enough. The DC-4 has to skirt potential tornadoes over Kansas and rain squalls pummeling Nebraska and Iowa. By the time the tired passengers reach Midway Airfield, the flight is more than half an hour late. Alan's family is there, though, waiting on the tarmac for his plane to land. When he descends the stairs, Nan and the boys are all smiles. Hugging everyone fiercely and breathing the sultry air of an Illinois evening in June, Alan smiles and sighs. His head no longer aches at all.

Home they go, to their bungalow on Chicago's South Side, where they can sit on the stoop and sip iced tea until long twilight turns to darkness. The boys, staying up past their normal bedtimes, play marbles on the sidewalk, while Alan and Nan talk softly together. Alan speaks about the weather, about his friends, about the makeshift Mercury accommodations. He doesn't say much about the atomic explosions themselves. When asked, he mentions the mushroom colors and the dust, and then quickly changes the subject back to family affairs. How are the boys doing in school? What are their plans for the summer?

Actually, his knowledge of his children's day-to-day activities is totally up to date. Ever since Alan left for the isolated western desert, Nan's been writing letters three or four times a week. Alan has responded when he could, which wasn't nearly often enough, as she indicated more than once. Now at home again, he continues holding his thoughts inside. When pressed, he turns the conversation away from Mercury and back to family, getting everyone engaged in an enthusiastic discussion about vacation plans. Right after the boys' school semester ends. Before Alan gets too busy back in his University of Chicago lab. Northern Wisconsin? Northern Michigan? Somewhere very green, Alan hopes, with lots of water. Lots of water. No wind and no dust.

Everyone agrees that canoeing ought to top their list of vacation activities, so they happily settle on northern Minnesota's lake country. Finally, the boys succumb to the definitive announcement of "bedtime." Nan's voice is firm. After tucking his two sons into their bunks, Alan reads to them for a while, a Tom Swift story they've always loved. Nan hovers outside the bedroom door, glad to see the tableau, eager for some time with her husband alone. The evening feels idyllic to them all.

Later that night, with one arm around his wife and her cheek resting on his shoulder, Alan listens to Nan's steady breathing and relives his months away. The narrow cot alone, with a lumpy pillow and skimpy blankets. The overcooked eggs and the tasteless dried-out roast beef. The wind, day after day. The pure physics, and the euphoric joy when an equation worked out well. The despair when a calculation failed. The endless conversations with his buddies. The arguments, and the camaraderie. He will miss the latter, and the scientific puzzles and their intricate solutions, but not much of anything else.

After staring at the ceiling for almost an hour and wishing desperately for a cigarette, he finally closes his eyes. There, in his bone-tired imagination, mushroom clouds begin to grow. Malevolent shapes, polar opposites of David's beauteous forms, evil designs domed at first in shades of gray and black, and then floating free in prisms of copper, scarlet, and claret. The images expand, filling the warm night air until he no longer can remember exactly where he is. Yucca Flat, Frenchman Flat, Los Alamos, south Chicago. His head throbs, not from too much booze but from the incessant internal hammering of atomic detonations. Over and over again. Annie! Nancy! Ruth! Dixie! Ray! Badger! Simon! Encore! Harry! Grable! Climax! Climax, over and over again. Mega-kiloton waves of unmitigated power, raw and uncontrolled, oscillating and undulating cacophonously in his mind.

Alan shakes his head a little, side to side, trying not to wake Nan. The movement doesn't mitigate his dreams, though the scenes change radically. Images of Hiroshima and Nagasaki children, their flesh seared as if hot irons had been pressed to their skin, stumble interchangeably with those of Doom Town dummies, plastic limbs torn away from torsos, heads shriveled by incomparable heat. Then sheep begin parading across the wizened atomic desert, one by one, two by two. Muzzles whitened in the dust, radiation burns braiding down their backs. Malformed lambs, hearts wickedly beating, limbs bloodstained and shorn, trail after the ewes until they fall to the earth, unable to sustain the pace.

More injured children, illuminated by a bloodshot mushroom cloud that bloats and swells, deflates and comes to life again in a nightmare universe that has no end. Alan lies there, trapped by his imagination. And his guilt. What should have been a glorious scientific achievement, splitting the atom for the good of humankind, is torturing him instead. David may have been right, that the scientific enterprise takes precedence over any qualms, that a search for truth is always of the highest priority. Pure science, pure beauty, all that matters. Absolute truth. Nothing more. Glen, too, insisting that just making things work is enough. Nothing but good can follow from that. For him, atomic testing is almost an addiction. To build a better gadget, and a better one after that.

Henry has a point as well. The Red Menace, whether Russian or Chinese, threatens America's future. To ensure its long-range survival, to guarantee its freedom, the United States must prevail. No questions. No reservations. Patriotism trumps all else. Even Tom's attitude, devil-may-care Tom, has its merits—trusting in God, the American entrepreneurial spirit, and his own optimism. Besides, he so often argues, the genie can't go back in the bottle. Atomic fission, atomic fusion, nuclear omnipotence, they're now all facts. What's past is past. Let the future take care of itself.

Alan is not so sanguine. Intellectually, he understands and even appreciates his friends' points of view, but he cannot, simply cannot, get past the specters of his dreams. Even now, comforted by Nan's warmth and her love, his qualms surface and resurface. Wild phantoms overtake his mind. The horrific cloud of his imagination shimmers and loops in the air, tendrils like the fires of hell drip from its sides, while offshoots of yellow and gold warn of yet unspoken dangers dropping from the sky. Terrible in its catastrophic colors, at the same time beautiful to behold. What had Robert Oppenheimer, the so-called father of the atomic bomb, said about Trinity? "The radiance of a thousand suns." And atomic physicists hold that luminescence in their hands.

Better to be a part of that power than to not have a say in its development or use. That's what Alan tells himself, in the dark of the night when dreadful demons ride the sky. Better to harness atomic energy for good—that's his rationalization, to participate rather than stand to one side. The irony of building bombs for the good of humankind, however, that conundrum haunts him. Always. As do the tainted children. The animals. Their stories.

And so the hallucinations continue, while monstrous ebony chimeras plague his dreams. Appearing in Technicolor one time, black-and-white the next. Three-dimensional. Flat. Static. Dynamic. Almost alive. Explosions. Aftershocks. Sounds of obliteration. Landscape tossed in the air. Irreparable radiation. A literal rain of terror spreading unchecked. The fallout—fatal, not friendly. Poisoning, desiccating, destroying families like his own.

What else did Oppenheimer say? Alan tries to remember. Also from the *Bhagavad Gita*? "Now I am become Death, the destroyer of worlds." Yes, those are Robert Oppenheimer's words. In the night of disquieting mushroom clouds, in his devilish nightmare without end, Alan hears the dissonant mantra over and over again.

Now I am become Death, the destroyer of worlds.

ALAMO, NEVADA · 30 JUNE 1953

Crystal Springs effervesces underneath a series of shaded pools. Late spring and early summer find the waters alive with creatures and vegetation. Waterlogged frogs croak sounds of love and despair, while zebra fish swim in circles. Where dragonflies dart in the warm noontime air, Bullock's orioles and summer tanagers and yellow warblers flit from tree to tree. The warblers' refrain, a rapid variable, repeats itself—"Sweet, sweet, I'm so sweet." Cottonwoods block the sunlight, their leaves casting shadowed patterns on the ground. White flocked flowers, called yerba mansa, cluster everywhere. A gentle wind ripples the thick grasses, the sweet smells permeating every breath taken by those picnicking nearby. An American family—father, mother, son, daughter—feast on fried chicken, potato salad, and fruit Jell-O. After lunch, Mom and young Edward splash in the water, catching frogs. Dad carries baby Ann on his shoulders. She grabs willow leaves and laughs. No one notices the dust in the air, the radioactivity having long since dispersed. Or so they suppose, and trust.

Author's Notes

To begin unraveling the entanglements generated by miscalculations of "friendly fallout," I read general histories about atomic testing before delving into the specific events of 1953. Barton Hacker's *Elements of Controversy: The Atomic Energy Commission and Radiation Safety in Nuclear Weapons Testing, 1947–1974* set the context. Richard L. Miller's *Under the Cloud: The Decades of Nuclear Testing* provided more overall information. The Center for Land Use Interpretations offered a more focused overview in *The Nevada Test Site: A Guide to America's Nuclear Proving Ground.* Several government publications added further knowledge of the locale: *Anatomy of the Nevada Test Site, Origins of the Nevada Test Site,* and *Nevada Test Site Guide.* A recent Department of Energy volume, *Atmospheric Nuclear Weapons Testing 1951–1963,* was invaluable. DVDs gave me graphic images of atomic testing: *Atomic Filmmakers: Hollywood's Secret Film Studio, Trinity and Beyond: The Atomic Bomb Movie,* and *America's Atomic Bomb Tests at Ground Zero.*

I gleaned more crucial information at the Atomic Testing Museum in Las Vegas. It is the single most intriguing technical museum I've ever visited, with hands-on displays, countless videos, and wondrous exhibits. My favorite room replicates an aboveground atomic explosion, complete with countdown, white flash, colors, and clouds, even a shock wave that rocks the bleacher seats. I sat through the sequence two dozen times or more, trying to glean some understanding of the physical, psychological, and emotional impacts that might occur when one watches an aboveground test in person. My experiences in that room inspired the interludes of *Friendly Fallout 1953.* The factual detonation statistics came from the Department of Energy archives; the different descriptions, from eyewitness accounts of the various colors, shapes, and sizes. No two events turned out to be exactly alike. An overview can be found at www.nuclearweaponarchive.org. My characterizations of the individual "devices" stick as closely to the facts as possible.

At the Atomic Testing Museum I met several people whose help was invaluable. Jeff Gordon, who supervised the reading room while I was there, patiently helped me negotiate unfamiliar Web sites and crucial archival material. Then he sent me upstairs to the Atomic Archives, maintained by the Department of Energy. There Martha DeMurre gave me access to a treasure trove of documents, photos, and articles that spelled out more details of what was happening in the Nevada desert in the 1950s. After answering all my naive questions, she introduced me to Vanya Scott, who oversees donations made to the Nevada Test Site Historical Foundation by people connected in one way or another to the atomic past. Vanya, in turn, suggested particular men and women I might contact in order to learn further details. Such practical guidance helped keep my imagination somewhat on track.

However, I want to stress that no one directly tied to the early days of aboveground atomic testing or to the twenty-first-century Department of Energy or to the Atomic Testing Museum in Las Vegas will unreservedly endorse the complex array of points of view I finally chose. Even my title, *Friendly Fallout 1953*, is an oxymoron reflecting the multiplicity of mind-sets about that fateful year. Facts about the 1950s experiments are still elusive, so I simply braided together what I could glean objectively with what I could imagine subjectively.

For example, Jack, the newspaper reporter, sees exactly what News Nob viewers saw and does exactly what all the civilian invitees did in the three days leading up to the Annie tower drop. Almost every detail in his chapter is true, except for the created characters. Thanks to materials available at the Atomic Testing Museum, I not only was able to find step-by-step information about Doom Town and Annie, but I could read countless 1953 newspaper headlines, stories, articles, and descriptions from across the country. I found even more firsthand accounts at the Nevada Historical Society Museums in Reno and Las Vegas, plus many of Jack's headlines. For the ambiance of the 1950s, I regularly consulted the Prelinger Archives at www.archive .org/details/prelinger.

Dennis's activities are accurate, too, although a real Dennis would have taken more care when taping his protective garb together. It is true, however, that many radiation specialists had to go home each year because their dosimeters exceeded the allowable gamma ray dosage. It is true, too, that because the available data were unreliable, the government set an arbitrary limit. Much of what I learned came from the research archives at the Atomic Testing Museum, where I found a number of photos taken almost immediately following Annie's detonation, some even posing white-suited men near the radiated vehicles. They often had their helmets off. The most innovative part of this chapter, aside from Dennis's carelessness, is the fact that most such forays into the hot zones were made by teams of three instead of two. I chose not to complicate the conversations. Such minutiae as the high school driver's education students squiring the manikins out to the Proving Ground, the manikins' individual attire and their unfortunate fates, and even the lizard's remarkable appearance are completely factual.

Ruthie's story is accurate as well, except for the direct allusions to Dennis. Even so, the typed report of "someone's" radiation is taken verbatim from the record. So are the other excerpted memos that Ruthie types and the pamphlet "You and Atomic Warfare" that she reads. All of this information, and more, can be found at two government Web sites: www.nv.doe.gov and www.osti.gov/opennet. The former offers more general access; the latter, a treasure trove of now declassified detail. Some of the Office of Scientific and Technical Information (OSTI) pages are heavily redacted, while others are quite forthcoming. Mary Palevsky, who led the University of Nevada, Las Vegas, atomic testing oral history project, shared in-depth interviews with two AEC secretaries—Norma Cox and Dorothy Grier. Both women refer to the teletype machine, which they loved, and each talks about a day when she got to fly over Mercury, one in a small Piper Cub, the other in a helicopter. Information about these interviews and many more can be accessed at www .digital.library.unlv.edu.

Hal's story is not based on facts, although Cactus Springs was indeed a favorite wide spot in the road between the Indian Springs Air Force Base and Mercury. There are several incidences of FBI agents working undercover in Los Alamos and Santa Fe, but I never found any indication of such activity around Mercury, probably because most of the more theoretical work was being done elsewhere. The conversations between the photographers and the pilots, however, replicate declassified information taken from the Web sites listed above. Peter Kuran's *How to Photograph an Atomic Bomb* describes the cameramen's challenges in thorough detail. It also includes a number of diagrams and drawings like the two that Mike sketches on napkins.

Archie's night at The Farm is mostly fictional, too, because there are very few declassified details about the animal testing. Apparently each experiment was designed and conducted quite separately from the others, so no one would have been overseeing all the animals. In the late 1950s, however, there was a place called The Farm on Yucca Flat, so I decided to merge what documented information I could find. I know that in 1953 scientists were examining atomic aftereffects on beagle circulatory systems and rabbit optics, but the available details are sketchy. Monkeys and rats did indeed ride in drone aircraft, and occasionally the monkeys did run wild in the aisles. The story of the pigs and the subsequent luaus is absolutely true, as General Edward Bonfoy Giller explains in a UNLV Nevada Test Site oral history. Archie himself could easily have been a Will James look-alike during Reno's heyday as the divorce capital of the world. His lullaby can be found in *Cowboy Songs and Other Frontier Ballads: Revised and Enlarged,* collected by John A. Lomax and Alan Lomax.

Many Las Vegas showgirls danced at Camp Desert Rock, and the boys loved the days when they came to entertain. Nancy Williams, who performed at the Tropicana fifty years ago, gave me an animated recollection of her visits there. Now in her late seventies, she still exhibited a joie de vivre as she described the fun. "Oh, honey," she repeated several times when we talked, "we had a hell of a good time." She remembers Camp Desert Rock as bitterly cold, but says the boys whooped and hollered and made the chilly air feel hot. A single ballet dancer, rather than two showgirls, did dance by the light of an atomic cloud, a sequence resulting in a stark photograph widely circulated at the time. For more information about Las Vegas in the 1950s, I recommend Eugene P. Moehring's *Resort City in the Sunbelt: Las Vegas 1930–1970.* A. Costandina Titus's *Bombs in the Backyard: Atomic Testing and American Politics* focuses more acutely on the city's atomic history. Both are now available in updated second editions.

Every detail from the sheep irradiation story is well documented and true, but I created the voice and character of Liz in order to give a slightly different perspective. What she sees is totally accurate, as is what she hears, filtered through the mind of a girl who would have been my age in 1953. A government official did actually call one of the sheepmen a "dumb farmer." The man in question grew so angry that he suffered a heart attack and died later that evening, an event so astonishing that I thought today's readers would never believe it. However the real-life county extension agent, Steve Brower, was "a good guy," as one informant told me, who was extraordinarily helpful to the Cedar City ranchers. Stewart Udall's *The Myths of August: A Personal Exploration of Our Tragic Cold War Affair with the Atom* emphasizes Brower's positive support, too, but I thought this particular vignette worked better if I created the hopelessly naive Merrill to play the role. Meanwhile, no official responsibility was ever acknowledged and no restitution was ever made for the sheepmen's losses.

Roadblocks occurred in several isolated spots throughout the late spring of 1953. For Daniel's story, I combined a number of roadblock anecdotes into a single day at a single location. So the vehicular details and the drivers' responses are accurately described, although the actual people are fabricated. The Paiute family comes from my imagination, too. Because two reservations sit precisely in the middle of the worst 1953 fallout, I wanted to write a chapter about downwind Native Americans. But I discovered that almost no one from that midcentury generation survived to middle or old age. While I talked at some length with tribal administrators and leaders in Cedar City, Utah, and on the Moapa Reservation, there was no one left for me to consult directly, and no written record of what happened there. Thus, I wrote a vignette about the government's indifference to the Paiutes' plight.

An AEC pamphlet, "Continental Weapons Tests . . . Public Safety," explains the governmental policy regarding downwind assurances. Reading it, I began to understand the complicated 1953 psychological climate surrounding atomic testing and its possible dangers. There was always a great deal of tension at the control point as each countdown progressed, tension that increased not only as the tests grew larger and larger but also with each ensuing delay. One of my informants, who chose to remain nameless, was quite incensed when he read a Roger draft, insisting that control point participants wouldn't be so ambivalent about public safety. But I found OSTI documentation directly citing the cavalier way the officials discussed the incoming weather and dismissed potential radiation in tiny towns to the east of the Proving Ground. So the details of the postponements in this story are correct, as are the meteorological and subsequent fallout data, and as are the comments like "nuisance value" and "calculated risk."

Many books have been written about the horrific Dirty Harry aftereffects suffered by St. George residents. The most detailed are John G. Fuller's *The Day We Bombed Utah* and Philip Fradkin's *Fallout: An American Nuclear Tragedy*. Both offer crucial personal details about how the Utah Mormons were conflicted by 1953 events. Loyal patriotic Americans, they found themselves in dire physical distress from the radiation and in difficult psychological distress from the apparent government lies. Carole Gallagher's *Nuclear Towns: Radiation Victims of the American Southwest* pictorially represents what happened in the cancerous aftermath. I also recommend the work of Janet Burton Seegmiller, from the Southern Utah University, who has conducted numerous oral histories and whose book *A History of Iron County: Commu-*

nity Above Self was invaluable. One novel, *Downwinders: An Atomic Tale,* by Curtis Oberhansly and Dianne Nelson Oberhansly, fictionalizes the Utahans' plight, as I have done here. Two Reno colleagues, Steven Hall and Mark Farnsworth, helped me with *The Book of Mormon* allusions and citations.

Stories of atomic soldiers abound. The Web site www.aracnet.com has posted many such first-person accounts. Howard L. Rosenberg's *Atomic Soldiers: American Victims of Nuclear Experiments* collects other observations and experiences. Carole Gallagher and Keith Schneider's *American Ground Zero: The Secret Nuclear War* also contains eyewitness accounts. Matthew's story is real, in that everything described by him did occur to someone sometime, but as in the roadblock story, I conflated several events into a single day. I received on-the-spot advice from Robert Clough, an atomic soldier who personally witnessed one of the detonations that preceded Grable. He was very helpful as he described the living conditions at Camp Desert Rock and the nature of the soldiers' moments in the trenches. A month or so after Robert read a draft of Matt's vignette, he sent an urgent e-mail. He had awakened in the middle of the night and remembered, for the first time in more than fifty years, the crippled birds. And he wanted to be sure that I let Matthew see them, too. Robert also emphasized his innocence in 1953. He was one of the lucky ones whose future health was untarnished by radiation. As I did the research for Matt's narrative, I learned that there seems to be no logical explanation for that. Some men were profoundly affected by the fallout, others not at all. In fact, the men closest to ground zero were often touched the least, whereas those farther away received the heaviest dusting. The Royal Order of Radiated Desert Rats certification is real, although this particular wording dates from 1951.

The scientists in Alan's chapter represent a range of viewpoints in the scientific community. Two books spell out the dilemmas that conflicted the Manhattan Project physicists and the participants in atomic testing: *All in Our Time: The Reminiscences of Twelve Nuclear Pioneers,* edited by Jane Wilson, and Mary Palevsky's *Atomic Fragments: A Daughter's Questions.* The Alan debate could not exist without their guidance. Some scientists were so disturbed by Hiroshima and Nagasaki that they quit nuclear research completely, while others were caught up by patriotic zeal, by the pursuit of pure science, or by the desire to build a better mousetrap. This chapter replicates the widespread differences, although the scientists themselves are pure conjecture. John Hunner's *Inventing Los Alamos: The Growth of an Atomic Community* contextualized the physicists' private lives for me, while Ron Phaneuf, a physicist from Oak Ridge and now the University of Nevada, Reno, double-checked the chapter's accuracy. I'm grateful to Mary Palevsky, too, for pointing the way toward Robert Oppenheimer's reading of the *Bhagavad Gita.* Just as certain phrases provide a backbone for *Atomic Fragments,* so they're vital to Alan as well.

Finally, I want to thank Scott Casper, Valerie Cohen, Muriel Davis, Cheryll Glotfelty, and Lois Snedden. They read different drafts, applauded when appropriate and urged serious emendations when necessary. I'd also like to thank Margaret Dalrymple, who helped me articulate just exactly what a fact/fiction hybrid might mean to editors and audiences. Ultimately, the cross-genre format allowed me to turn many disparate snapshots of history into the imagined and imaginary stories of *Friendly Fallout 1953.*